WICKED COOL JAVA

WICKED COOL JAVA

Code Bits, Open-Source Libraries, and Project Ideas

by Brian D. Eubanks

**NO STARCH
PRESS**

San Francisco

1 2 3 4 5 6 7 8 9 10 – 08 07 06 05

No Starch Press and the No Starch Press logo are registered trademarks of No Starch Press, Inc. Other product and company names mentioned herein may be the trademarks of their respective owners. Rather than use a trademark symbol with every occurrence of a trademarked name, we are using the names only in an editorial fashion and to the benefit of the trademark owner, with no intention of infringement of the trademark.

Publisher: William Pollock
Managing Editors: Susan Berge, Elizabeth Campbell
Cover and Interior Design: Octopod Studios
Copyeditor: Linda Recktenwald
Compositor: Riley Hoffman
Proofreader: Stephanie Provines
Indexer: Ted Laux

For information on book distributors or translations, please contact No Starch Press, Inc. directly:

No Starch Press, Inc.
555 De Haro Street, Suite 250, San Francisco, CA 94107
phone: 415.863.9900; fax: 415.863.9950; info@nostarch.com; www.nostarch.com

The information in this book is distributed on an "As Is" basis, without warranty. While every precaution has been taken in the preparation of this work, neither the author nor No Starch Press, Inc. shall have any liability to any person or entity with respect to any loss or damage caused or alleged to be caused directly or indirectly by the information contained in it.

Library of Congress Cataloging-in-Publication Data

```
Eubanks, Brian D.
  Wicked cool Java : code bits, open-source libraries, and project ideas / Brian D. Eubanks.-- 1st ed.
      p. cm.
  Includes index.
  ISBN 1-59327-061-5
  1.  Java (Computer program language) 2.  Object-oriented programming (Computer science)  I. Title.
  QA76.73.J38E92 2005
  005.13'3--dc22
                                                         2005024341
```

This book is dedicated to my son Kai—his inquisitive mind continually inspires me and reminds me that there is wonder in everyday things.

BRIEF CONTENTS

CONTENTS IN DETAIL

3
PROCESSING XML AND HTML   43

4
CRAWLING THE SEMANTIC WEB   79

5
SCIENTIFIC AND MATHEMATICAL APPLICATIONS   101

6
GRAPHICS AND DATA VISUALIZATION 133

7
MULTIMEDIA AND SYNCHRONIZATION 153

8
FUN, INTEGRATION, AND PROJECT IDEAS 171

ACKNOWLEDGEMENTS

A thousand thanks to my family for understanding when I was invisible and unresponsive for long periods of time. I also appreciate the many friends who kept things positive with their constant encouragement and support. I am grateful to the QA team for their help: Curtis Eubanks, Mat Keller, and Vinnie Luther. Thanks to the many colleagues who suggested projects, looked at drafts, analyzed code, and pointed out when I was on target as well as when I was "full of it." Charles E. Brown deserves a special mention for introducing me to the world of publishing, and for connecting me with a great agent. Jawahara Saidullah helped with the "nuts and bolts" of contracts, and my agent Margot Hutchison did a great job of keeping things running smoothly. Finally, an enormous thanks to all the great folks at No Starch.

INTRODUCTION

This book is about the Java programming language created by Sun Microsystems. The book is targeted toward Java developers at any level of expertise who are looking for interesting and useful APIs or for project ideas. Java has come a long way since it was first released. When I discovered Java in 1996, the version was 1.0 and only a small group of people even knew what it was. Java had no experienced developers, very few code libraries, and no enterprise servers—it was just an immature language with big dreams. But looks were deceiving; the power of the JVM's platform independence was the key to Java's growth. Today, Java is an ubiquitous, mature technology over 10 years old. The core API itself contains over 3,000 classes in a number of subject areas. Fortune 500 companies now build their entire corporate computing strategies around Java, and millions of websites are running servlets or client-side applets.

I'm amazed at how often developers will look at the core API and think that it's all you can do with the language. Besides what is in the core, there is a great wealth of free, open-source libraries for Java. It is because of these libraries that *Wicked Cool Java* was born; I wanted to give you a taste of some of the interesting and useful things that Java can do. What I didn't want was to write another "how-to-program-in-Java" book—there are plenty of good books for getting people started in writing Java code. Instead, what I wanted was a book just for the joy of discovering interesting things to do in Java without reinventing the wheel. This book is intended for the programmer who has knowledge of Java from a basic to an intermediate level and is looking for ways to enhance his or her code.

The book has a lot of sample code and "Hello World" programs for various APIs. Some are introductory-level examples, and others are more advanced. Occasionally there are code tips, and sometimes there are ideas for new projects that could become successful open-source projects if someone would only write them! If you implement any of these project ideas, I strongly encourage you to go to the book's website and work with other readers to avoid duplicating efforts. One of the greatest things we can do as developers is to work together and to share the fruits of our efforts with others.

Organization of This Book

This book is organized into eight chapters, each covering a particular area of Java. The following gives a short outline of each chapter:

Chapter 1

In the first chapter, we discuss some of the core API features—some that are older but less well known and some that are new to Java 5. We discuss the new for loop, enums, generics, anonymous classes, and assertions.

Chapter 2

Next we discuss String processing techniques. We start with regular expressions, and we also discuss random text, arrays, binary strings, and message formatting. Regex is a very powerful tool for searching, splitting, and substituting text. It has been around since Java 1.4, and many new Java programmers are still not familiar with it. Regular expressions are a good starting point for parsing more complex documents.

Chapter 3

In this chapter, we process XML and HTML documents and other types of structured text. We introduce a parser generator and show some sample code for working with it.

Chapter 4

Chapter 4 explores the Semantic Web, a next-generation web where the links are between concepts rather than documents containing text. We introduce some APIs for working with RDF and RSS.

Chapter 5

This chapter explores scientific and mathematical applications in Java. We link to a number of open-source projects for working with different aspects of science and mathematics.

Chapter 6

Here we talk about APIs for making it easier to develop graphical applications or to add new features.

Chapter 7

This chapter deals with sound and music APIs, with a section on advanced thread synchronization.

Chapter 8

The final chapter of this book looks at miscellaneous open-source projects and discusses ideas for creating your own projects and integrating code from earlier sections.

The Website

Java can be a lot of fun, and we certainly look at some cool projects in this book, but the book also introduces you to some useful tools and techniques that you can use with your own projects. To get the most out of Java, you will need to work with open-source projects at some point. This book has a companion website at http://wickedcooljava.com that has links to projects mentioned in the text, errata, and code samples. The website has a forum for discussing the book with other readers and for organizing new projects. I hope that this will encourage you to look at more than just the Java core APIs and to continue the learning process.

1

JAVA LANGUAGE AND CORE API

This book assumes that you've had some exposure to Java and are familiar with the basics of the Java language and its core *Application Programming Interface (API)*. With the release of Java 5 (also known as Java 1.5, or *Tiger*), there were some major new features added to the language and core API. In this chapter, we will give examples of some of the new features, as well as some other useful classes and methods that are often unknown to Java developers. The Java API is huge, and with over 3,000 classes it can be tough keeping track of everything. There are classes available in the core packages that even experienced Java developers might overlook, simply because they have never seen them before or needed to work with them.

Many programmers think of Java as just another language and syntax to learn. But the most effective Java programmers must think in terms of object hierarchies, behaviors, and relationships, rather than function calls and procedures as in procedural languages. In introductory seminars, I always emphasize the three-part harmony of Java.

The Object-Oriented Language

Working effectively in Java means understanding *object-oriented programming (OOP)*, not just the syntax of Java. If your past experience has been in procedural languages such as C or Pascal, it's important to acclimate yourself to OOP before writing Java code. For this book I make the assumption that you have already worked with Java to some extent. If you are unfamiliar with OOP, a good introduction can be found at http://java.sun.com/docs/books/tutorial/java/concepts. In this chapter, we'll talk about some recent changes to the syntax that are useful to know.

The Java Virtual Machine (JVM)

The Java Virtual Machine was the most groundbreaking aspect of Java when it was released. Instead of recompiling or modifying source code for each target platform, as in other languages, you need to compile the source code only once. The executable code, or *bytecodes*, can then run on any target system that has the JVM installed. Bytecodes work like a cross-platform machine language. Languages other than Java can also be compiled into JVM bytecodes, and we will look at that possibility in a later chapter.

The Core APIs

The sheer size of the Java core libraries is sometimes overwhelming for developers. The core libraries include packages for networking, graphics, sound, multithreading, I/O, security, cryptography, databases, XML, and many others. In later chapters, we'll explore advanced features of some of the core APIs. We'll also look at open-source Java projects that provide useful functionality beyond what is available in the core. For this chapter, we'll work with just a few core classes and some new syntax from Java 5.

There Is No *for* In Java: Using the for Loop Enhancements

 In some programming languages, it's very easy to iterate through a list or an array, automatically repeating through a loop "for each" item in the list and assigning the item to a local variable. I once started to tell a colleague how I thought the for loop in Java was broken, because it didn't have a for-each. What actually came out of my mouth was "There is no **for** in Java." My friend was also an experienced Java developer, and he responded with "Are you crazy? Of course there's a **for** in Java!" For a long time after that he continued to tease me, periodically reminding me that there was a **for** in Java (just in case I had forgotten). But I have some good news for him and for all Java developers: there is now a *real* **for** in Java!

Consider the case where you would like to find the sum of all of the values in a collection (such as `java.util.ArrayList`) of `Integer` objects. You've probably written code like the following:

```
ArrayList theList = new ArrayList();
theList.add(new Integer(2));
theList.add(new Integer(3));
```

```
theList.add(new Integer(5));
theList.add(new Integer(7));
int sum = 0;
// The old way to iterate
for (Iterator iter = theList.iterator(); iter.hasNext(); ) {
    Integer x = (Integer) iter.next();
    sum = sum + x.intValue();
}
System.out.println("The sum is " + sum);
```

This is a bit awkward. Shouldn't the compiler already know that you are iterating? You *are* in a for loop, after all! In Java 5, the enhanced for loop now supports Collection objects. You no longer need to get an Iterator. In the following revamped code, a for loop iterates through the list and prints out each value:

```
ArrayList<Integer> theList = new ArrayList<Integer>();
theList.add(2);
theList.add(3);
theList.add(5);
theList.add(7);
int sum = 0;
// new Java 5 iteration syntax
for (Integer item : theList) {
    sum = sum + item;
}
System.out.println("The sum is " + sum);
```

The for loop defines a local variable, called item, which gets assigned the next value in the list during each iteration. Besides the beautiful for loop syntax, there are two other ways in which this code is different than the old Java code:

Generics

The syntax above, with the funny angle brackets, is new to Java 5. *Generics* let you define classes that work with some specific type of object, but the type is not known until you create an instance of the class. The compiler will enforce the type restriction. In our example, the ArrayList is a special one that accepts only integers for the add method (and returns only integers from the next method of its Iterator). This means that no casting is required when objects are retrieved from the list: they can immediately be treated as Integer instances. Without using generics, you could still use the new for loop syntax, but you would need to cast from Object to Integer. Generics will be treated in more detail in the section "Generally Generic: Writing Methods with Generic Parameters."

Integer/int equivalence

In Java 5, an Integer object can be treated as an int. The compiler will automatically perform the conversion from int to Integer objects (and vice versa). This process is called *autoboxing.* When we retrieve the item out of the loop as an `Integer`, we can add it to an `int` value without doing an explicit conversion.

The new for syntax also works with arrays:

```
int[] theList = new int[] {2,3,5,7};
int sum = 0;
for (int x : theList) {
    sum = sum + x;
}
System.out.println("The sum is " + sum);
```

This new syntax certainly makes the code a lot more readable and compact. Unfortunately, you can't completely throw away your iterators yet, at least for a while, because there are still many developers who have not upgraded their JDK to version 5.

Let Me Count the Ways: Using the enum

JAVA 5+ Most applications need to keep track of a finite set of values—constants that represent a set of choices or states in the application. One common Java programming practice is to use `static int` variables to represent these values. Programs then make decisions by comparing the values of other variables against them. Although the core Java API itself uses this practice, it can lead to serious problems! The following example class returns information about fruits for an imaginary menu-planning system. It shows some of the problems in using `int` variables to represent enumerated data:

```
public class FruitConstants {
    // this is not such a good practice
    public static final int APPLE = 1;
    public static final int ORANGE = 2;
    public static final int GRAPEFRUIT = 3;
    public static final int BANANA = 4;
    public static final int DURIAN = 5;
    public static final int CITRUS = 6;
    public static final int SWEET = 7;
    public static final int SMELLY = 8;
    public static final int UNKNOWN = 9;

    public static int getCategory(int fruit) {
      switch(fruit) {
        case APPLE:   case BANANA:
          return SWEET;
        case ORANGE:  case GRAPEFRUIT:
          return CITRUS;
        case DURIAN:
```

```
        return SMELLY;
    }
    return UNKNOWN;
  }
}
```

The durian fruit, which comes from Southeast Asia, is both smelly *and* sweet, but we will assume in our system that fruits can be only of a single type, that is, all values are assumed to be single values rather than composite ones. The main problem here is that any int value can be passed to the getCategory method, whether it is a valid fruit or not. This can lead to subtle bugs, since the compiler will not care if you call getCategory(SWEET) or even getCategory(42). And if the values of the integer constants ever change, the meaning of getCategory(3) may no longer be obvious or correct!

A different problem is that there is no distinction between the use of int values for fruits and for categories—they are all just plain-old int values. You could partially solve the fruit/category separation problem by simply placing the category constants into a separate class, but they are still just int values and are not typesafe. Nothing restricts the parameter of getCategory to a fixed set of values.

In Java 5, there is an elegant solution: you can create enumerated types, just like in C. This is a new feature, which creates a class that contains a list of all its allowed instances. Other than what is defined within the enum, no other instances are allowed. Take a close look at some enum examples:

```
enum Fruit {APPLE, ORANGE, GRAPEFRUIT, BANANA, DURIAN}
enum FruitCategory {SWEET, CITRUS, SMELLY, UNKNOWN}
enum Dessert {PIE, CAKE, ICECREAM, BROWNIE}
```

Each of these examples defines a separate group of enumerated elements (choices). The beauty of this is that the Fruit values cannot be mixed with or confused with another type. Each enum is treated as if it were a different class. You cannot pass a FruitCategory as a parameter to a method that expects a Dessert. Nor can you pass an int value. Let's expand the Fruit enum to include the functionality of our original FruitConstants class:

```
public enum Fruit {
    APPLE, ORANGE, GRAPEFRUIT, BANANA, DURIAN;

    public static FruitCategory getCategory(Fruit fruit) {
        switch(fruit) {
            case APPLE: case BANANA:
                return FruitCategory.SWEET;
            case ORANGE: case GRAPEFRUIT:
                return FruitCategory.CITRUS;
            case DURIAN:
                return FruitCategory.SMELLY;
```

```
        }
        return FruitCategory.UNKNOWN;
    }
}
```

Notice that an enum can define methods, just like a class. The getCategory method now takes a Fruit as a parameter, and the only allowed values are the ones defined in the enum. This next code snippet would cause compile errors rather than unexpected runtime results that would have occurred in calling the original unprotected getCategory method:

```
Fruit.getCategory(Dessert.PIE);    // compile error
Fruit.getCategory(10);             // compile error
```

It would be better if each fruit managed its own category, so to complete the Fruit class, we'll now remove the fruit parameter of getCategory and make the method return a different value for each enum state. We can do this by creating an abstract getCategory method that applies to all the values and override it differently for each enum. It's very similar to writing a different subclass for each enumerated value and having each of those classes override the abstract method.

```
public enum Fruit {
    APPLE
        { FruitCategory getCategory() {return FruitCategory.SWEET;} },
    ORANGE
        { FruitCategory getCategory() {return FruitCategory.CITRUS;} },
    GRAPEFRUIT
        { FruitCategory getCategory() {return FruitCategory.CITRUS;} },
    BANANA
        { FruitCategory getCategory() {return FruitCategory.SWEET;} },
    DURIAN
        { FruitCategory getCategory() {return FruitCategory.SMELLY;} };

    abstract FruitCategory getCategory();
}
```

Once you create an enum like this, you can treat an APPLE value like you would any other object (using the static Fruit.APPLE reference), and you can call its getCategory method to get the associated category. We can now add a main method to the above class to show how to use the new Fruit enum:

```
public static void main(String[] args) {
    Fruit a = Fruit.APPLE;
    // toString() returns "APPLE"
    System.out.println ("The toString() for a: " + a);
    // getCategory() returns "SWEET"
    System.out.println ("a.getCategory() is: " + a.getCategory());
```

```
    for (Fruit f : Fruit.values()) {
        System.out.println ("Fruit is: " + f);
    }
}
```

As this code illustrates, you can use the values method to iterate through all the values within the enum. The toString method of an enum will return a String with the same name as the value. Using an enum to represent state, instead of an int, can make your code much more readable as well as more error-resistant. It clearly defines all the values for a particular enumerated state and prevents someone from using inappropriate values.

Practice Safe Putting: Using Typesafe Maps

We saw earlier, during the for loop discussion, how using generics can help to make your code simpler and less error-prone. The for loop was able to assume that the ArrayList contained only Integer objects, because we defined the ArrayList as *consisting strictly of Integer objects.* We could then avoid the cast from Object to Integer as we retrieved items from the list.

Java 5 made many changes to the core API that take advantage of generics. Looking at the documentation, you will see that many of the classes are now redefined so that generics can be used. If you wish, you can still construct and use any of these classes the old way, for example, new ArrayList(). This might be done for compatibility reasons, so that your code would still work under older versions of the compiler. Of course, you would then lose the convenience and safety of the type-checking process provided by generics.

One class that has been nicely revamped is java.util.Map (and HashMap). You may recall that maps work like lookup tables, with each value stored under a unique key. In earlier versions of Java, when you place items in the map, they go in as Object entries. As you retrieve an item from the map, it is treated as a standard Object reference, which you must cast to the appropriate subclass in order for it to be recognized as its true type. The same dangers apply here as in a List. The object may not be what you assume, and a Class-CastException is the unfortunate result. How many times have we seen those?

Imagine that we have an Employee class for maintaining employee data. Here is some typical code for working with a HashMap:

```
Employee brian = new Employee();
brian.setName("Brian", "Eubanks");
brian.setSalary(100000.00);
brian.setTitle("Boss");

HashMap employees = new HashMap();
employees.put("Brian", brian);

Employee newHire = (Employee) employees.get("Brian");
newHire.setHireDate(new Date());
```

The biggest danger is during the cast, when the item is retrieved. With Java 5, you can do without a cast, as long as the Map was instantiated with the correct type. You can add a constraint on the types of both the keys and the values. In the example below, only String keys and Employee values are allowed:

```
Employee brian = new Employee();
brian.setName("Brian", "Eubanks");
brian.setSalary(100000.00);
brian.setTitle("Boss");

HashMap<String,Employee> employees = new HashMap<String,Employee>();
employees.put("Brian", brian);

// no cast is necessary here
Employee newHire = employees.get("Brian");
newHire.setHireDate(new Date());
```

By using typesafe maps, you can avoid ClassCastException problems when retrieving items from a map. This makes your code much more stable and less sensitive to the contents of the map. Unfortunately, if your code has to run on earlier versions of Java, you're out of luck and you'll need to keep on casting for a while. In the next section, we create our own generic class.

Generally Generic: Writing Methods with Generic Parameters

JAVA 5+ We saw in earlier sections how generics can simplify Java code and make it resistant to ClassCastException problems. In addition to using generics that are part of the JDK, you can write your own. This is useful when you are working with objects that are all of the same type, but you don't know which type it will be until you instantiate your class. This is ideal for classes that have an associated collection of items or involve a lookup.

Let's write a method that uses generic parameters. Recall how we used the ArrayList class earlier—only when we constructed the ArrayList did we specify which object types it used. We don't know the type when we are defining the class, and we can't use java.lang.Object as the type, because we would end up with the same casting problem as before. When you define a generic, you must use a special syntax to stand in for the type. This is done when you declare the class name. In the following example, <T> represents a type that will be used by our class:

```
public class RandomSelection<T> { }
```

The type indicator brackets look strangely like HTML syntax but actually have nothing to do with HTML, nor do they indicate less than or greater than! The angle brackets are used in cases where a generic's class name is combined with a type, as in the ArrayList<Integer> that we used earlier. Although the real type will not be known until the constructor is called, we can use the substitute type in our method definitions. We are really defining "a class called RandomSelection that works with another class of some type, which we will call T for now." The name of the class is still RandomSelection, however. By the way, you can do this for more than one type at a time, as the definition of java.util.Map does. In these cases, use a comma-separated list of identifiers after the class name:

```
public class MyGeneric<T,U,V> {  }
```

The MyGeneric class defined above works with three classes and we are calling them T, U, and V. Let's expand the RandomSelection class by writing a method that adds an item to an internally managed ArrayList of the generic type T:

```
public class RandomSelection<T> {
   private ArrayList<T> list;

   public RandomSelection() {
      list = new ArrayList<T>();
   }

   public void add(T element) {
      list.add(element);
   }
}
```

Remember that we are not actually dealing with a class called T. Instead, T is a stand-in for whichever class is used when someone creates an instance of RandomSelection. The Java specification allows you to use any identifier that you want, but the standard convention is to use a single uppercase letter to distinguish it from a normal class name. Now that we have defined the add method as taking a type T parameter, it can be called only with the same type used in the construction of the RandomSelection instance. The following code is illegal and generates a compile error:

```
RandomSelection<String> rs = new RandomSelection<String>();
rs.add(new Date());     // illegal for a RandomSelection<String>
```

If you want to return a generic type from a method, you can use it as the return type of the method's signature, as this definition does:

```
import java.util.Random;
public class RandomSelection<T> {
    private java.util.Random random = new Random();
    // ..... earlier methods omitted

    public T getRandomElement() {
       int index = random.nextInt(list.size());
```

```
        return list.get(index);
    }
}
```

The getRandomElement method returns a type T, the same type marker that was defined in the class declaration. We can now use the RandomSelection class that we have just defined, by constructing a typed instance:

```
RandomSelection<Integer> selector = new RandomSelection<Integer>();
selector.add(2);
selector.add(3);
selector.add(5);
selector.add(7);
selector.add(11);
Integer choice = selector.getRandomElement();
System.out.println(choice);
```

The assignment to an Integer variable (choice) is safe; we will always get an Integer from the getRandomElement method of selector. This is true only because we constructed our selector instance using an Integer for the generic type. The definitions for the add and getRandomElement methods have the same type as the constructor's definition, and the compiler will enforce this constraint. Let's try using the RandomSelection class with a different type in the constructor, this time using the Fruit enum class that we defined earlier:

```
RandomSelection<Fruit> fruitSelector = new RandomSelection<Fruit>();
fruitSelector.add(Fruit.APPLE);
fruitSelector.add(Fruit.ORANGE);
fruitSelector.add(Fruit.GRAPEFRUIT);
fruitSelector.add(Fruit.BANANA);
fruitSelector.add(Fruit.DURIAN);
Fruit fruitChoice = fruitSelector.getRandomElement();
System.out.println(fruitChoice);
```

Notice that we were able to directly use the Fruit return value from the getRandomElement method, just as we had done earlier with the Integer. This is because we constructed RandomSelection using the Fruit type. You can define your own generics in cases where you want a class to work with objects of some type (that you don't know until you construct the class) and where you want the compiler to strictly enforce the type restriction. The main advantages in doing this are safety and convenience. See the Generics Tutorial at http://java.sun.com/j2se/1.5.0/docs/guide/language/generics.html and the Java 5 documentation for more information on generics.

Arguments and More Arguments: Writing Vararg Methods

JAVA 5+   Java programmers often need to write methods that accept a parameter containing multiple values. This might take the form of a List or an array, for example.

```
public int add(int[] list) {
    int sum = 0;
    for (int i=0; i < list.length; i++) {
        sum += list[i];
    }
    return sum;
}
```

The same code could also have been written as several overloaded methods, each with a signature that takes a different number of int parameters. This sometimes makes the method easier to use, since the calling code does not need to create an array first.

```
public int add(int a, int b) {
    return a + b;
}

public int add(int a, int b, int c) {
    return a + b + c;
}

public int add(int a, int b, int c, int d) {
    return a + b + c + d;
}
```

This is easier for the calling code, if there are only a few values, since now we can use add(12,14,16) instead of add(new int[] {12,14,16}). However, there are problems with writing methods like this. Of course, we would need to write different versions of the method for each possible combination of parameters. But what if we wanted to allow the most flexibility in how the method is used? Without making a huge class with thousands of methods, there is a rather small limit to the number of parameters that this overloaded method will accept.

In Java 5, you can write a method so that it allows a variable number of parameters and let the compiler do the work of packaging the list into an array. We're still dealing with an array internally, but the details are now hidden by the compiler. The following code rewrites the add method using variable arguments (*varargs*).

```
public int add(int... list) {
    int sum = 0;
    for (int item : list) {
        sum += item;
    }
    return sum;
}
```

Yes, those strange dots are the real syntax for varargs! Since this change requires Java 5, we might as well use the Java 5 enhanced for loop syntax too. Once you write the method this way, you can call it with as many parameters as you want! You can also pass an array (but not a List or Collection object) as the parameter:

```
add(1,3,5,7,9,11,13,15,17,19,21,23,25);
add(new int[] {12,14,16});
```

It's worth noting that you can use this shortcut only once when defining a parameter list, and it has to be the last item. The following would not work, because the variable parameter is not the last item:

```
public void badMethod(int... data, String comment) { } // wrong!
```

Instead, you must write it as:

```
public void goodMethod(String comment, int... data) { }
```

In some cases, using varargs in a method definition can make the method much more usable. This is especially true in cases where a parameter list contains literal (hard-coded) values, such as the int values shown in the example above.

Being Assertive: Using Java Assertions

JAVA 1.4+   The programmer is always right—it's the compiler and interpreter that get it wrong! I'm sure you can identify with that thought process. As programmers, we often make assumptions about the values of variables and write code that relies on these assumptions. As much as we hate to admit that we might be wrong in our design or implementation, variables and parameters sometimes don't have the values that we expect.

Code will work properly only as long as the original assumptions that we made when designing and writing it still hold true. If these assumptions are not explicitly stated somewhere, then anyone reading the code (including you!) will not know what they are. Future changes may violate those assumptions and introduce bugs that are difficult to locate. Many people document their assumptions in comments, so that anyone modifying the code later will avoid making such changes.

Using comments to document assumptions is a good start. But when something violates an assumption, the program keeps on running as if nothing is wrong. In some cases, the result is immediately obvious and the developer can fix the problem. Other times, there is a silent bug that might have a negative impact in another part of the application or, with distributed systems, in another application altogether! Tracing such problems is extremely difficult.

Java 1.4 added the assertion feature to the language to simplify testing and debugging, strengthen documentation, and improve the maintainability of Java-based systems. You make an assertion by using a Boolean expression to test something that you are assuming about the current state of the system. If the assertion fails, the runtime will throw an `AssertionError`. Here is a very simple assertion:

```
String name = "Brian";
assert name != null;
```

We can say with some certainty that after we assign the value "Brian" to the name variable its value will be non-null. If this is not true, then something is seriously wrong! This assertion is a statement of an assumption that we are making about the value of the variable at that point in the program. It would be silly, and wasteful, to do this for such a trivial case. However, consider the situation where multiple methods are affecting the state of an object. We would like to be able to assume that the object is still usable afterwards, according to some requirements of the application. In this following example, we make the assertion that before we can assign any tasks to a new employee, a supervisor has already been assigned.

```
Employee worker =
    new Employee("John", "Smith", 100000, "Developer");
assignOffice(worker);
setUpVoiceMail(worker);
moreAdministrivia(worker);
assert worker.getSupervisor() != null : "Supervisor cannot be null";
assignTasks(worker);
```

You will want to make assertions about an object before performing a critical operation on it. This helps you to make your code more error-resistant, and if something goes wrong in the program, you will have an easier time debugging it. This is a lot better than finding out through a side effect where the program fails somewhere else. The cause of the error is much easier to trace when you know that it failed because the program violated an assumption you made. In this example code, we used the assert option that returns a more useful message. Without it, we get no identifying information about the assertion, other than the line number.

On some versions of the compiler, you will need to use a command option to set the compiler's source compatibility mode when you compile your source code (1.4 or 1.5, depending on your compiler version):

```
javac -source 1.5 MyClass.java
```

Now let's force an assertion to fail and see what happens:

```
public class AssertBad {
    public static void main(String[] args) {
        int total = 20;
        int itemCount = 0;
```

```
        assert itemCount > 0;
        int average = total / itemCount;
    }
}
```

By default, the runtime environment does not enable assertions, and you must start the JRE using the ea (enable assertions) command option. This code would cause the following result:

```
C:\projects\wcj1> java -ea AssertBad
Exception in thread "main" java.lang.AssertionError
        at AssertBad.main(AssertBad.java:12)
```

Remember that assertions are for true "sanity checks" for conditions you believe should never happen. You should not use them in place of your normal error checking.

WARNING   *Do not allow assertion statements to change state/values in your code. When you eventually turn off assertions, your code will act differently than it did when you had assertions enabled. For example, do* not *do the following:*

```
assert (++i > 10);  // BAD: i changes only with assertions enabled!
```

You will want to leave assertions enabled throughout the development phase. Once you thoroughly test the system and move it into a production environment, you will probably want to disable assertions. There will be a slight performance gain in doing so. Don't change the code to do this, and don't remove the assertions. You want the assertions to remain in the code for documentation purposes anyway. That way, when changes are made at a later date, the programmers will be reminded to keep all of the assumptions valid, and this will also be testable.

Living on Nano Time: Using System.nanoTime

JAVA 5+   *Moore's law* is the name of a well-known observation that the number of transistors in a computer and its processing speed increase exponentially over time. Gordon Moore, as director of research and development at Fairchild Semiconductor, made the observation way back in 1965. So far, it still holds true.

With much faster computers now than we had when Java first arrived, millisecond timing is no longer good enough for many applications. Perhaps you have used the java.lang.System class to obtain timing information for a method call or a section of code, using the currentTimeMillis method. We'd often use this to measure how long it takes to perform certain operations. However, the operation might take far less than a millisecond on faster computers, and we'd end up doing the operation hundreds or thousands of times in a for loop and dividing by the loop count to calculate the unit time. Consider the following:

```
long startTime = System.currentTimeMillis();
for (int i=0; i<1000; i++) {
   performOperation();    // something we want to measure
}
long endTime = System.currentTimeMillis();
long totalTimeInMillis = endTime - startTime;
// because the count was 1000, it's easy to get the unit time
long unitTimeInMicros = totalTimeInMillis;
```

This was an easy calculation, since I used a for loop count of 1000. But what about sub-microsecond measurements?

```
for(int i=0; i<1000000; i++) { performOperation(); }
```

If I were to project human feelings onto the code, that poor for loop would get awfully tired from the million-count busy loop! Besides, the for loop method of timing is useful only in cases where there are no side effects from repeating the operation. If the operation were a call to the java.util .Collections.sort method, it would be much more difficult to figure out how long the sorting process took. In Java 5, the System class has a new method, nanoTime, that returns a nanosecond-resolution counter. You can't use it for measuring absolute time, but it works great for measuring time differences.

```
List myList = initializeList();     // initialize the List somehow
long startTime = System.nanoTime();
Collections.sort(myList);           // measuring the sort time
long endTime = System.nanoTime();
long differenceInNanoseconds = endTime - startTime;
```

Unfortunately, we have no guarantee that we will actually get nanosecond measurements when we run this code. But with a faster machine and a good JRE implementation, it's a useful measurement for testing purposes. You can find more information on this method in the JDK 5 documentation. Because of operating system characteristics, machine processing speed, and system load, you may get a wide variation in the values returned by the nanoTime method. This issue should improve over time; Moore's law almost guarantees it.

Resources

For Moore's original paper, see Gordon E. Moore, "Cramming More Components onto Integrated Circuits," *Electronics*, Vol. 38, No. 8 (April 19, 1965). This article is also available online. See this book's website at http:// wickedcooljava.com for the URL.

Taking a Very Short Nap: Sub-Millisecond Sleep for Threads

JAVA 1.1+ As we discussed in the previous section, Java 5 added a nanoTime method to the System class to ensure that time measurements can keep up with faster systems. Even in earlier versions of Java, threads can have sleep times of less than a millisecond. You might recall that Java's threading mechanism has a sleep method that takes an int parameter representing the sleep time in milliseconds. There is also a sleep method that accepts the millisecond parameter, plus an additional time in nanoseconds. If you set the millisecond time to 0, then the thread will sleep for the specified number of nanoseconds (ns).

```
public class MyThread extends Thread {
  public void run() {
   try {
    sleep(10);         // sleep for 10 milliseconds
    sleep(0, 10000);    // sleep for 0.01 milliseconds (10000 ns)
   } catch (InterruptedException e) {
     e.printStackTrace();
   }
  }
}
```

The same thing applies here as in the nanoTime method described earlier. Because of operating system characteristics, machine processing speed, and system load, the actual sleep period could be different than you would expect.

You Shall Remain Nameless: Creating an Anonymous Class

JAVA 1.1+ When you are doing Java development, you sometimes need to implement an interface that only has one or two methods, with only one or two lines of code for each method. This happens quite often in AWT and Swing development, when a display component needs an event callback method (such as a button's ActionListener). If you use normal classes for this, you'll end up with many small classes that are used in only a single location. Many developers may not be aware that Java allows you to define inner classes or that inner classes don't have to be used within a GUI framework.

An *inner class* is a class that is defined within another class. You can define inner classes as members of a class, as in the following example:

```
public class Linker {
  public class LinkedNode {
    LinkedNode prev, next;
    Object contents;
  }

  public Linker() {
    LinkedNode first = new LinkedNode();
    LinkedNode second = new LinkedNode();
    first.next = second;
```

```
    first.contents = "This is the first item";
    second.prev = first;
    second.contents = "This is the second item";
  }
}
```

This is a simple implementation of a *linked list* in Java. The LinkedNode class is an inner class of our Linker class. Although it is contained within the Linker class, it can still be accessed from other classes because we defined it as public. From other classes, you can create an instance of it by using: new Linker.LinkedNode(). One such class from the core API is the Map.Entry class, used by the java.util.Map class when you retrieve the set of key/value entries in a map.

You can also define an inner class that is local to a method. This type of class is visible only within the method where it is defined. You may want to do this if you are implementing an interface and you want to use the local class more than once within the method, as this tongue-in-cheek example shows:

```
public class Happiness {
  interface Smiler { public void smile(); }

  public static void main(String[] args)
  {
    class Happy implements Smiler {
      private String more = "";
      public void smile() {
        System.out.println(":-)" + more);
      }
      public void happier() {
        more += ")";
      }
    }

    Happy h1 = new Happy();
    h1.smile();
    Happy h2 = new Happy();
    h2.happier();
    h2.smile();
  }
}
```

We gave this local inner class (I like to think of it as an inner-*er* class) the name Happy. This class cannot be accessed from any other classes or methods. We used a local class only because we wanted to implement the Smiler interface (which was defined within the Happiness class). For many situations, it's not even necessary to give a local inner class a name—it can remain *anonymous*. Anonymous classes are very useful for implementing interfaces that have only one or two methods, especially if we need to create an instance that is used only once. Normally you cannot directly instantiate an interface. For example, you could not call the constructor of the Runnable interface (the interface used by a Thread). It would be illegal to use:

```
Runnable runner = new Runnable();   // not allowed!
```

But Java does allow you to create an instance of an anonymous local class that implements the interface. There is a special syntax for creating an instance of an interface:

```
Runnable runner = new Runnable() {
   public void run() {
      for (int i=0; i<10000000; i++) {
         countSheep();
      }
   }
};
```

This creates a local anonymous class, instantiates it, and assigns the new instance to the runner variable. You'll need to make sure that your class definition (the code between the outer curly braces) implements all the methods of the interface. You can also create subclasses this way. The code below instantiates an anonymous subclass of Object and assigns it to a variable:

```
Object timePrinter = new Object() {
   public String toString() {
      return String.valueOf(System.currentTimeMillis());
   }
};
System.out.println(timePrinter);
```

Anonymous classes are a useful tool in the Java developer's bag of tricks. Consider using them whenever you need to implement an interface (or a subclass) on a one-time basis. They are best used with smaller interfaces that have only one or two methods.

Equals Rights: == != .equals

Here's an issue that crops up in Java programs quite often. It's 3 A.M., after your fourth cup of coffee, and you're trying to find the right logic to solve some complex programming problem. By now, you're almost incapable of thinking about String and Object references, because the pillow is calling. And then the worst happens. . . . No, it's not a "Java" spill, but this:

```
String name = getName();
if (name == "Sleepy")   // oops!
```

```
{
    doSomething();
}
```

You quickly compile and test the code, and it seems to work. Finally! Time to go home and celebrate by snoring! Unfortunately, some time later, application testing uncovers an intermittent bug and traces it to exactly this section of code.

"What?" you say indignantly. "I tried a String comparison like this the other day and it worked just fine!" Possibly. But first, let's revisit Java object reference concepts. An object variable is a reference (pointer) to the real object, which is stored in the *heap memory*. When you assign one variable to another, you are really assigning the reference, not the actual object (Figure 1-1):

```
String a, b, c, d;
a = "123";
b = a;
c = new String("123");
d = "WCJ";
```

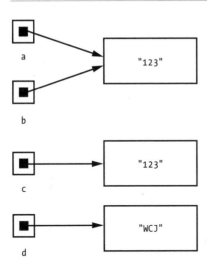

Figure 1-1: Object references

Java uses the == operator to compare two references to see if they point to the same memory object. For String instances, the runtime does its best to make sure that any two String literals with the same character data point to the same internal object. This is called *interning*, but it will not help with every String comparison. One reason is that an interned value could possibly be removed by the garbage collector thread. Another reason is that the place where the String was generated may have created a new instance using one of the String constructors. If so, the == comparison will always return false.

The equals method is designed to compare the *state* of two objects, or what is inside each object. For your own classes, you must override this method for it to work properly. But String instances will always compare properly if you use the equals method. This next code segment illustrates the problem with assuming that all String values are interned:

```
String name1, name2, name3;
name1 = "123";

name2 = name1;
if (name1 == name2) {}          // true
if (name1.equals(name2)) {}  // true

name2 = "123";
if (name1 == name2) {}          // usually true
if (name1.equals(name2)) {}  // true

name3 = new String("123");
if (name1 == name3) {}          // false
if (name1.equals(name3)) {}  // true
```

NOTE *Rule of thumb: Always use .equals to compare two String values, even though using the == operator may seem to work. For most applications, even if it works, the == code is simply a "wrong" that only equals would "right!" So tell all your developer friends to support equals rights for Strings! (Yes, that's probably the worst pun in this book.)*

Resources

Vladimir Roubtsov, "Does an Object Exist If You Can't Test Its Identity?" *Javaworld* (December 12, 2003). See www.javaworld.com.

Chapter Summary

In this chapter, we've discussed some of the new features that are available in Java 5 and some useful older API classes that are often overlooked by developers. In the next chapter, we'll focus exclusively on String processing. We'll look at some text-related classes in the Java core as well as some useful String-processing classes from open-source APIs.

2

STRING UTILITIES

Strings are a very important part of most Java programs. They are used for text display, data representation, lookup keys, and many other purposes. In this chapter we describe some useful utilities and techniques for String processing. We'll be using regular expression patterns to compare Strings, split delimited Strings, find substrings, and perform substitutions. We will also consider utilities for String randomization, formatting, and conversion.

Staying Regular: Using Regular Expressions to Search Text

JAVA 1.4+

Unix administrators like to keep themselves "regular," at least according to an old programming joke. Don't worry; this section is not about dietary fiber but about a type of pattern matching known as *regular expressions*, or *regex*. For a long time, Unix power users have worked with commands or programs that are based on regular expressions, such as grep, perl, sed, and awk. Because this is such a powerful way of searching and manipulating Strings, Java 1.4 added the java.util.regex package to the core API. Of course, Java is platform-independent, and these regular expressions will work on any system, not just Unix. The regex package has been in the JDK for a while, but I still find that many Java programmers have never used it. Regex patterns are a valuable starting point for many types of text processing: matching, searching, extracting, substituting, and parsing of structured content.

In Java, you can easily determine whether a String matches a pattern, using the appropriately named Pattern class. Patterns can be as simple as matching a specific String value. Or they can be much more complex, with grouping and character classes such as whitespace, numbers, letters, or control characters. Because they are Java Strings and are based on Unicode, regular expressions will also work with internationalized applications.

The simplest pattern exactly matches a given String; in other words, the pattern is the same as the text that we want to compare. The static Pattern.matches method is a convenient way to compare whether a String matches a given pattern. The following will check to see if the value of the variable data matches the word *Java*:

```
String data = getStringData();    // populate the String somehow
boolean result = Pattern.matches("Java", data);  // is it "Java"?
```

For directly matching a String against a pattern this simple, you probably wouldn't use a regular expression, since this is really just a less-efficient version of "Java".equals(data). The real power of regex comes from using more-complex patterns involving character classes and quantifiers (*, +, and ?). There are already many excellent books on regular expression patterns, so we'll look at only a few of the basic features of patterns and focus on Java's regex classes and methods instead. To give you a quick start, here are some of the special characters that you can use in regular expressions. Each of these represents a category of characters, which in regex terminology is called a *character class*:

\d   Digits

\D   Non-digits

\w   Word characters (0–9, A–Z, a–z, _)

\W   Non-word characters

\s   Whitespace (space, line feed, carriage return, tab)

\S   Non-whitespace

[]   Custom character classes, created by a list of characters within brackets

.   Match any single character (except newlines)

Most characters match themselves in a pattern expression, but some have special meanings. The backslash ("escape") character used above is one example. The following characters control how many times a subpattern is applied to the matching process. These are special characters that are treated differently than others:

- ? Repeat the preceding subpattern zero or one times
- * Repeat the preceding subpattern zero or more times
- + Repeat the preceding subpattern one or more times

The following regular expression matches the title of any ancestor, such as "father," "great-great-grandmother," or "great-great-great-grandfather." As you can see from this example, it's possible to make more-complex regular expressions by using parenthetical subexpressions:

```
((great\s)*grand)?(mother|father)
```

This next pattern expression will match anything beginning with a digit plus zero or more non-whitespace characters (for example, "3," "5x," and "56abcd9" would match, but not "8 5" or "hello"):

```
\d\S*
```

Be careful with the regex backslash character, since it is also the String literal escape character in Java. If you are using a String literal to hold the regular expression, you will need to escape the backslash character itself by using a double backslash. Yes, that's right, you're escaping the escape:

```
String digitNonSpacePattern = "\\d\\S*";
String data = getStringData();
boolean isMatch = Pattern.matches(digitNonSpacePattern, data);
```

Pattern matching is also built into the String class itself. There is a new convenience method within the String class: matches. You could rewrite the above code as:

```
boolean isMatch = getStringData().matches("\\d\\S*");
```

The Pattern.matches method and the matches method of String are fine for one-time use, but for repeated use they are less efficient. You can get a more efficient "compiled" version of the pattern for performing multiple matches by creating a Pattern instance using the static Pattern.compile method. The Pattern object works together with the java.util.regex.Matcher class. To do anything complex, you'll need to create a Matcher. The Matcher ties a pattern expression to a specific String, for performing more-advanced matching operations. The following code snippet compiles a pattern for matching text made of "word" characters only:

```
String data = getStringData();
Pattern namePattern = Pattern.compile("\\w+");
```

```
// get a Matcher to apply the pattern to the data
Matcher nameMatcher = namePattern.matcher(data);
boolean isMatch = nameMatcher.matches();
```

Remember that the matches method will match the entire input String against the pattern. If you want to check whether the String only *begins* with the pattern, use the lookingAt method instead:

```
boolean startsWith = nameMatcher.lookingAt();
```

We'll discuss some other matching techniques in the next few sections, including finding substrings that match a pattern and performing text substitutions.

Resources

Jeffrey E. F. Friedl, *Mastering Regular Expressions*, 2nd ed. O'Reilly, 2002.

Splitsville: Using the String.split Method

JAVA 1.4+ Developers sometimes need to split a String into substrings using a delimiter such as a comma, tab, or whitespace. As we discussed in the previous section, Java 1.4 added the Pattern class for performing text comparisons with regular expressions. In addition to pattern matching, a Pattern object can split a String into an array of substrings, using the regular expression as the delimiter. For example, a one-line comma-delimited list can be split into an array of Strings, using a comma as the pattern:

```
String data = "Australia,Fiji,New Zealand,Papua New Guinea";
Pattern comma = Pattern.compile(",");
String[] countries = comma.split(data);
```

Splitting Strings is even more convenient than that—there is a split method in the String class. Let's rewrite the above code using this method. This time, we'll also change the separator to include any whitespace before and after the comma so that it doesn't become part of the substring values:

```
String data = "Australia, Fiji, New Zealand , Papua New Guinea";
String[] countries = data.split("\\s*,\\s*");
```

The same regular expression syntax applies here as in the Pattern object described earlier, so the split method can be used for much more than commas and spaces. For help in processing complete *comma-separated value (CSV)* files, see the book's website, http://wickedcooljava.com.

Smartly Subbing: Finding Substring Patterns Within a String

JAVA 1.4+ The section "Staying Regular: Using Regular Expressions to Search Text" at the beginning of this chapter describes how to use a regex pattern to compare whether a String matches (or partially matches) a given pattern, starting from the beginning of the input String. In this section, we'll be using regex patterns to find multiple matching values within a String. As an example, we'll search within a document to find any URLs embedded in the text. First, we'll need a pattern String that matches URLs. Here is one pattern that will match most URLs in common usage:

```
String urlString = "(http|https|ftp)://[/\\w\\.\\-\\+\\?%=&;:,#]+";
```

This pattern is not completely sufficient to describe a URL, because it also matches some Strings with invalid URL syntax, such as http://////////. It will also grab extra characters in some cases, such as a comma or semicolon that might follow a URL embedded in text. These are characters that sometimes will appear in a URL, but they are also things that you might *not* want to capture as part of the URL if it appears in text! However, the pattern is relatively short and will work well enough to demonstrate searching for URLs embedded in a text document. The parts of this pattern expression are as follows:

- http or https or ftp
- ://
- One or more of the following: / 0-9 A-Z a-z _ . - + ? % = & ; : , #

Remember that a Matcher applies a pattern to a particular input String. To find multiple substring matches using the urlString pattern defined earlier, we must call the find method of a Matcher. To find each occurrence of the pattern within the input String, we repeatedly call the find method to locate the next match. The find method returns false when there are no more matches. To retrieve the current match, we can use the start and end methods to get the index to matching data within the input text. The following code will print all the URLs found within the data:

```
String urlString = "(http|https|ftp)://[/\\w\\.\\-\\+\\?%=&;:,#]+";
Pattern urlPattern = Pattern.compile(urlString);
// get the data (somehow)
String data = getStringData();
// get a matcher for the data
Matcher urlMatcher = urlPattern.matcher(data);
// iterate through the matches
while (urlMatcher.find()) {
    int startIndex = urlMatcher.start();    // index of start
    int endIndex = urlMatcher.end();        // index of end + 1
```

```
    // retrieve the matching substring
    String currentMatch = data.substring(startIndex, endIndex);
    System.out.println(currentMatch);
}
```

This code will not match *relative URLs* (such as /images/picture.jpg) that are often found in an HTML document or incomplete URLs that are missing the leading http:// (such as wickedcooljava.com). To know when something is supposed to be treated as a relative URL, your program would need to have an understanding of the structure of an HTML file. (It's still possible to do this with a regex but more difficult.) You would need to know the *context* of each match, and for that you must parse the document with an understanding of its *grammar*. See Chapter 3 for more information.

Resources

For references on URI/URLs, HTTP, and HTML see this book's companion website at http://wickedcooljava.com.

Getting Captured: Using Regex Capturing Groups

JAVA 1.4+ In the previous section, we saw how to use a regular expression to search within a document to retrieve all the URLs inside it. We were able to retrieve the matching URL Strings using the find, start, and end methods of the Matcher class. Sometimes it's necessary to further process the results of a matching substring, perhaps looking for an additional subpattern. For example, you might decide not to process URLs from particular domains. The brute force approach is to use another Pattern and Matcher object for this purpose, by writing code something like this:

```
// assume urlMatcher instance as in the previous example
while (urlMatcher.find()) {
    int startIndex = urlMatcher.start();
    int endIndex = urlMatcher.end();
    String currentMatch = data.substring(startIndex, endIndex);
    // the brute force approach, using a new pattern!
    Pattern restricted = Pattern.compile(".*(abc|cbs|nbc)\\.com.*");
    Matcher restrictMatcher = restricted.matcher(currentMatch);
    if (!restrictMatcher.matches()) {
        System.out.println(currentMatch);
    }
}
```

It's not a very efficient way to match domain names within the captured URL. We have already done the hard work of extracting the URL, with the find method. We shouldn't have to write another regex just to get a subsection of the result. And we don't have to, either. Regular expressions give us the power to break the pattern into *subsequences* of data. By placing parentheses around portions of the pattern that we want to remember later, we can read these values separately from the rest. Let's rewrite the URL pattern to make the domain name available separately from the other parts of the URL:

```
String urlPattern =
    "(http|https|ftp)://([a-zA-Z0-9-\\.]+)[/\\w\\.\\-\\+\\?%=&;:,#]*";
```

When you have parenthetical groups in the pattern, you can retrieve the value that matches each group separately from the rest of the matching String. The group corresponding to each opening parenthesis is numbered, starting from 1 for the leftmost group. In the above pattern, group 1 is the protocol (for example, http) and group 2 is the domain name. To get the groups out of the matching String, use the Matcher's group method. This sample code retrieves the domain name from each URL and prints out the value:

```
String data = getStringData();     // load the document
String urlString =
    "(http|https|ftp)://([a-zA-Z0-9-\\.]+)[/\\w\\.\\-\\+\\?%=&;:,#]*";
Pattern urlPattern = Pattern.compile(urlString);
Matcher urlMatcher = urlPattern.matcher(data);
// print out the domain from each URL
while (urlMatcher.find()) {
    String domain = urlMatcher.group(2);  // 2nd group is the domain
    System.out.println(domain);
}
```

Every matching group is saved so that the pattern can make a reference to it later. Referencing an earlier matching group within a pattern is called a *backreference*. To use a backreference to the third group, include \3 in the pattern. This will match only an exact repeat of the data that matched the earlier group. To illustrate this, let's consider a common mistake in text documents—accidentally repeating a common word such as *the* or *of* within a sentence.

```
"  The the water molecules are made of of hydrogen and oxygen."
```

Let's write a pattern to find these problems in a document. We can capture the first word, followed by some whitespace, followed by a repeat of whatever matched the first word:

```
String wordPattern = "\\s(of|or|the|to)\\s+\\1[\\s\\.,;]";
```

The pattern matches the following: a whitespace character, one of a specific list of words, more whitespace, the same word repeated again (using the \1 backreference), and whitespace or punctuation. This match should be done in case-insensitive mode so that we'll catch "The the" and similar variants. The following code fragment finds occurrences of the pattern in a String, using a case-insensitive match:

```
String data = getStringData();
String patternStr = "\\s(of|or|the|to)\\s+\\1[\\s\\.,;]";
Pattern wordPattern =
    Pattern.compile(patternStr, Pattern.CASE_INSENSITIVE);
Matcher wordMatcher = wordPattern.matcher(data);
while (wordMatcher.find()) {
    int start = wordMatcher.start();
    String word = wordMatcher.group(1);
    // print the index location of the repeated word
    System.out.println("Repeated " + word + " starting at " + start);
}
```

For a convenient and powerful way to match text in a document that allows you to use more than one regular expression to process the document, see the section "Partially Parseable: Parsing with the Scanner Class" later in this chapter. For an even more sophisticated text-searching solution with built-in indexing, see the Chapter 3 section titled, "What's Lou Seen? Searching with Lucene."

A String of Substitutes: Substituting with Regular Expressions

JAVA 1.4+   In the previous section, we created regular expressions for matching patterns in a String and for retrieving data from a subpattern group. With a regex, we can also substitute new values for the matching patterns. One way to do this is with the replaceAll method of the Matcher class. It returns a String where all matching substrings are replaced with a given String parameter. To illustrate, let's find all occurrences of the word *repetition* within a document and replace them with the word *duplication*:

```
String data = getStringData();
Pattern repPattern = Pattern.compile("(\\s)(repetition)([\\s;\\.,])");
Matcher repMatcher = repPattern.matcher(data);
String newData = repMatcher.replaceAll("$1duplication$3");
```

To find the word, we need to capture the whitespace (or punctuation) before and after it. Note that the code as shown above does not match the word if it occurs at the very beginning of the data String, because we are assuming that some whitespace exists. We want everything in the replacement text, except for the word *repetition*, to be the same as the original. This includes the surrounding whitespace characters. The dollar signs ($) here obviously don't represent money! They are references to captured groups 1 and 3 from the regex pattern, containing the whitespace or punctuation of the original match. The corresponding values will be inserted into the replacement text.

The `String` class (in JDK 1.4 and higher) has a `replaceAll` method that works like the one in the `Matcher`. This makes it very easy to replace substrings that match a pattern:

```
String data = getStringData();
String result =
  data.replaceAll("(\\s)(repetition)([\\s;\\.,])", "$1duplication$3");
```

The `replaceAll` method returns a new `String` with all the matching patterns replaced with the new value. However, there are still many advantages to using the `Matcher`, since it has much more flexibility than a `String` does.

You can use a `Matcher`'s find loop to substitute values individually for each match within the loop. This gives you more control over the substitution process. You can apply logic during each match and even substitute different values each time. A `StringBuffer` holds the updated text, and the `Matcher` appends to this buffer whenever you call the `appendReplacement` method. After processing each match and performing the substitutions, you'll still need to place the last portion of the input `String` (the tail end without any matches) into your output buffer by using the `appendTail` method. Figure 2-1 shows the relationship between substring matches and these two methods.

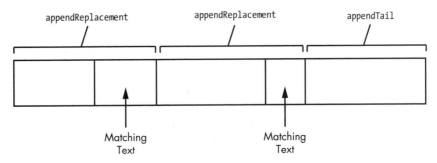

Figure 2-1: The Matcher append methods

A `Matcher` has an *append cursor* associated with it. The cursor starts at zero initially and moves forward with each call to `appendReplacement`. This is designed to be used within a `find` loop. For each match, you call the `appendReplacement` method, and the `Matcher` incorporates the unchanged text, between the last position of the cursor and just before the current match, into the `String-Buffer`. Then the `Matcher` substitutes the replacement value for the matching text and places this new value into the `StringBuffer`. Next, the `Matcher` moves the append cursor to the first character after the end of the current match, and the process repeats until there are no more matches. There will probably be one last unmatching part of the input text after all the matches are found. To add this portion of text to the output `StringBuffer`, use the `appendTail` method.

Now we'll rewrite the earlier substitution example as a loop using these methods. But this time, for every match we'll replace the word *repetition* with a random choice of suitable synonyms (*repetition, duplication, copying, reiteration, recurrence,* or *redundancy*):

```
StringBuffer result = new StringBuffer();
String[] wordChoices = new String[]
    {"repetition", "duplication", "copying",
     "reiteration", "recurrence", "redundancy"};
Random rand = new Random();
String data = getStringData();
Pattern repPattern = Pattern.compile("(\\s)(repetition)([\\s;\\.,])");
Matcher repMatcher = repPattern.matcher(data);
while (repMatcher.find()) {
    // pick a word at random
    int wordIndex = rand.nextInt(wordChoices.length);
    String replacement = "$1" + wordChoices[wordIndex] + "$3";
    repMatcher.appendReplacement(result, replacement);
}
repMatcher.appendTail(result);
System.out.println(result);
```

You can replace the logic within the find loop with any processing that you wish to perform for every match. You also have access to the methods of the Matcher that we discussed earlier: group, start, and end. You can use a combination of these techniques to selectively modify or remove each section of matching text within a document.

Partially Parseable: Parsing with the Scanner Class

JAVA 5+   Java 5 added the java.util.Scanner class, a new utility for scanning input text. It's something of a cross between the older StringTokenizer and the Matcher class. In previous sections we used a Matcher to search within a String to find data that matched a given pattern. This was useful, but we were limited to matching only a single pattern. Any data had to be retrieved by capturing groups within the same pattern or by using an index to retrieve portions of the text. We used a combination of regular expressions and methods that retrieve items of specific types from an input stream. In addition to regexes, the Scanner class can arbitrarily parse Strings and primitive types (such as int and double). With the Scanner, you can write custom parsers for any text content that you would like to process.

Let's use the Scanner class to read from an input source and programmatically select items from the text. As an example, we will read data from a file format used by the U.S. Census Bureau (see this book's website to obtain the data). This data summarizes the statistical distribution of the top 90 percent of first and last names (separately, so that individuals cannot be identified) from the 1990 census. The Census Bureau provided the list to the public for use by genealogists and statisticians. The data contains three separate files: surnames (dist.all.last), female given names (dist.female.first), and male given names (dist.male.first). Each file has lines of text with the following data separated by whitespace:

- Name
- Frequency in percent
- Cumulative frequency in percent
- Rank

Here are the first two lines of text in the surname file:

```
SMITH         1.006  1.006      1
JOHNSON       0.810  1.816      2
```

This shows that Smith was the last name of 1.006 percent of the population, and Johnson of 0.81 percent. This is a simple file structure. We could read each line of this data using a Matcher and the following regex with capturing groups:

```
(\S+)\s+(\S+)\s+(\S+)\s+(\S+)
```

Or by using String's split method:

```
// for each line of text, assume it's in a variable called line
String[] dataArray = line.split("\\s+");
String name = dataArray[0];
String frequency = dataArray[1];
String cumulativeFrequency = dataArray[2];
String rank = dataArray[3];
```

We could then convert the String for each data item into float and int types if necessary. If each line has the same structure, we can process every line using the same regex, and it's easy to use a Matcher or the String split method to read the data (see later sections in this chapter for more detail). But there is a disadvantage in using the split method of a String for this surname example, because it creates an unnecessary array of Strings as we process each line. Using a Matcher on the entire input text would be more efficient, but to do this we would first need to buffer the entire input stream into a String. With the Scanner class, we can accomplish several things at once: read the data from a live input stream, parse each line of text efficiently, scan with more than one regular expression, and retrieve the data elements directly into variables of the desired primitive type. The following code reads the surname data file using the Scanner class (and since the first name files also use the same structure, we can read these files in the same way).

```java
import java.io.FileReader;
import java.util.Scanner;

public class SurnameReader {
    public ArrayList<String> getNames() throws IOException {
        ArrayList<String> surnames = new ArrayList<String>();
        FileReader fileReader =
            new FileReader("/census/dist.all.last");
        // create a scanner from the data file
        Scanner scanner = new Scanner(fileReader);
        // repeat while there is a next item to be scanned
        while (scanner.hasNext()) {
            // retrieve each data element
            String name = scanner.next();
            float frequency = scanner.nextFloat();
            float cumulativeFrequency = scanner.nextFloat();
            int rank = scanner.nextInt();
            surnames.add(name);
        }
        scanner.close();       // also closes the FileReader
        return surnames;
    }

    public SurnameReader() {
        for (String s : getNames()) {
            System.out.println(s);
        }
    }
}
```

The Scanner uses whitespace as a default delimiter, although you can easily change the delimiter pattern. The default delimiter is convenient for our purposes. The hasNext method in this while loop checks to see if the input has another *token* to be processed. Besides whitespace, there are only four items in each line. We are consuming each of them, and therefore we can assume that the next method will also move the input to the next line as it retrieves each name. Be careful here, because if the file doesn't match what the code expects (for example, data is missing or of the wrong type), then the Scanner will throw an exception.

In the above example, we populated the ArrayList with a new name each time we passed through the loop. This surname data, plus the male and female first names, is very useful in populating test databases with realistic data. (You can find a link to the data on this book's website.) Once you have the data in an ArrayList, you can randomly select names from the list. For information on how to randomly select data from a list, see the section "Making It All Up: Generating Random Text."

Scan-Do Attitude: Parsing Complex Syntax with the Scanner Class

JAVA 5+

In the previous section, we read a data file using the Scanner class in Java 5. It was simple enough, because each line had the same structure. What if we wanted to read a data file that has a structure that is different for each line of text? A Matcher wouldn't work, because it can use only a single regex. The Scanner can be used for these kinds of tasks, because you can use regular expressions on the input text to look ahead for patterns in the upcoming text. Because you can read the input on a token-by-token basis, you can write custom parsers for any kind of text. Let's illustrate by inventing an imaginary file format for a log of building security events. Each line of this log file has the following structure:

```
eventType year month day time type-dependent-data
```

The structure of the last part of each line is dependent on the event type. For structures like this, you would need logic to read the appropriate tokens depending on the event type. Let's create a simple file with the following event types: building entry, building exit, and alarms. Here's a sample file:

```
entry 2005 04 02 1043 meeting Smith, John
exit 2005 04 02 1204 Smith, John
entry 2005 04 02 1300 work Eubanks, Brian
exit 2005 04 02 2120 Eubanks, Brian
alarm 2005 06 02 2301 fire This was a drill
```

Each type of event requires reading a different structure. In the first line of this file, John Smith entered the building at 10:43 A.M. to attend a meeting. He exited the building at 12:04 P.M. Brian Eubanks then entered the building at 1:00 P.M. to do some work and left at 9:20 P.M. A fire alarm later occurred at 11:01 P.M. and was noted along with the comment, "This was a drill." We can read this file using a Scanner, with the following code:

```java
Scanner scanner = new Scanner(new FileReader("logfile.txt"));
while (scanner.hasNext()) {
    String type = scanner.next();
    int year = scanner.nextInt();
    int month = scanner.nextInt();
    int day = scanner.nextInt();
    int time = scanner.nextInt();
    if (type.equals("entry")) {
        String purpose = scanner.next();       // purpose of visit
        // get the rest of the line and move to start of next line
        String restOfLine = scanner.nextLine();
    } else if (type.equals("exit")) {
```

```
        String exitName = scanner.nextLine();   // rest of the line
    } else if (type.equals("alarm")) {
        String alarmType = scanner.next();
        String comment = scanner.nextLine();   // rest of the line
    }
}
scanner.close();
```

Another trick you can use with the Scanner class is the findInLine method. It can be used to look ahead to find a pattern within the current line. A similar method, findWithinHorizon, can look for patterns farther ahead in the stream beyond the current line. This type of parsing requires us to know the *grammar,* or the syntax and structure, of the document in order to process it. In the code that we just wrote, there is an implicit knowledge of the grammar built into the system—we are essentially writing a parser for this "logging" language. For more complex grammars, such as one you would use in processing a scripting language, writing your own parser from scratch is very likely to result in logical errors. For larger and more complex grammars, it's far better to describe the grammar itself in a grammar description language such as the one in JavaCC (see the Chapter 3 section titled "Sin Taxes: Generating Parsers for Anything with JavaCC"). A parser generator uses a grammar metalanguage to generate parser classes that can process the grammar.

Resources

A detailed treatment of parsing and compiler theory is beyond the scope of this discussion. See the classic compiler book by Alfred V. Aho, Ravi Sethi, and Jeffrey D. Ullman, *Compilers: Principles, Techniques, and Tools.* Addison-Wesley, 1986.

Making It All Up: Generating Random Text

JAKARTA COMMONS

JAVA 5+

When you're testing Java programs, you may need to randomly generate String data to place into a database or use as test parameters for a method. One way to do this is by generating random int values and using them to index into an array to create each character, as in the following code:

```
public String getRandomString(int length) {
  StringBuffer result = new StringBuffer();
  Random rand = new Random();
  char[] letters = "abcdefghijklmnopqrstuvwxyz".toCharArray();
  for (int i=0; i<length; i++) {
     result.append( letters[rand.nextInt(26)] );
  }
  return result.toString();
}
```

The open-source Jakarta Commons Lang project contains utilities for working with classes in the java.lang package, such as String. There is a class in this project, org.apache.commons.lang.RandomStringUtils, that has a number of static utility methods for generating random text. The randomAlphanumeric method creates random alphanumeric text of a specified length. The most generic random method of this class can create text using your own source of randomness and an array of characters from which to select. The following code generates a random alphanumeric String and a random semi-pronounceable password (cvcvcv).

```
import org.apache.commons.lang.RandomStringUtils;

// create a 100-character alphanumeric string
String tenAlphaNums = RandomStringUtils.randomAlphanumeric(100);
// create a semi-pronounceable password
String consonants = "bcdfghjklmnpqrstvwxz";
String vowels = "aeiouy";
String password =
  RandomStringUtils.random(1, consonants) +
  RandomStringUtils.random(1, vowels) +
  RandomStringUtils.random(1, consonants) +
  RandomStringUtils.random(1, vowels) +
  RandomStringUtils.random(1, consonants) +
  RandomStringUtils.random(1, vowels);
```

I ran this code several times to produce the following values: pafesu, bydiro, nomyme, wosaha, and hofojy. (Any resemblance to real words or phrases in any language is purely accidental!)

Sometimes random text must contain values taken from a specific list. You can add the items to an ArrayList and select a random item from the list by using the following code:

```
import java.util.*;

ArrayList<String> list = new ArrayList<String>();
list.add("Jim");
list.add("Bob");
list.add("Mary");
list.add("Tom");
Random rand = new Random();
String randomName = list.get(rand.nextInt(list.size()));
```

For applications that require unique values in some random ordering, you can easily do this with the shuffle method of java.util.Collections. Populate a List with String values, shuffle it, and use the items in their new order:

```
ArrayList<String> words = new ArrayList<String>();
words.add("shuffling");
```

```
words.add("randomness");
words.add("collection");
words.add("string");
Collections.shuffle(words);
System.out.println(words);
```

The shuffle method affects the original list, so if that's a problem, work with a copy instead! If you need to select from a list of common English words, given names, or surnames, see this book's website. You can obtain files containing these words and load them into an ArrayList from which you can select random entries. See the section "Partially Parseable: Parsing with the Scanner Class" for one way to read name distribution data from the 1990 U.S. Census into an ArrayList. You can then select names randomly from the list. Also see the Colt API discussed in Chapter 5 for classes that provide various types of random distributions.

Array of Hope: Displaying Arrays in Java 1.5

JAVA 5+ For quite some time, Java programmers have been writing their own utility methods to print the contents of an array. This is because the JDK didn't provide a convenient way to convert an array into a String value. To make matters worse, an array of Strings has always returned the following information from its toString method:

```
[Ljava.lang.String;@360be0
```

This information has not been very useful to any Java developer that I know of! The [character means that it's an array, Ljava.lang.String; is the internal name for the String class (the element type of the array), and @360be0 is the hashcode. None of this gives us any indication of the array's actual contents. A java.util.Collection has a much nicer toString value: a comma-separated list of its elements. In Java 1.2 or higher, you can display the contents of an array by invoking asList (using java.util.Arrays) before calling the toString method:

```
String[] stringArray = new String[] {"A", "String", "Array"};
String stringValue = Arrays.asList(stringArray).toString();
```

That code works, but it's wasteful to create a List object just for the String conversion. In Java 5, there are new methods in the Arrays class for getting a comma-separated list of an array's elements. There is one method that returns a *shallow* String representation, printing the toString of each element, which gives a result equivalent to calling Arrays.asList(stringArray).toString(). Another Arrays method does a *deep* toString conversion and prints the contents of any arrays contained within the array to any level of depth. The deep representation is designed for displaying multidimensional arrays.

The following code illustrates the conversion of an array into a `String` value and shows the difference between deep and shallow `String` representations of an array:

```java
Object[] multiDimensional = new Object[] {
    "mercury", new Object[] {},
    "venus", new Object[] {},
    "earth", new Object[] { "moon" },
    "mars", new Object[] { "phobos", "deimos" }
};
System.out.println(multiDimensional);
System.out.println(Arrays.toString(multiDimensional));
System.out.println(Arrays.deepToString(multiDimensional));
```

The program produces the following output:

```
[Ljava.lang.Object;@18d107f

[mercury, [Ljava.lang.Object;@1372a1a, venus, [Ljava.lang.Object;@ad3ba4,
earth, [Ljava.lang.Object;@126b249, mars, [Ljava.lang.Object;@182f0db]

[mercury, [], venus, [], earth, [moon], mars, [phobos, deimos]]
```

In the first `println`, the array's standard `toString` prints only the array type (which is `[Ljava.lang.Object`) and its hashcode. The shallow representation in the second line prints the `toString` of each element in the array, delimited by commas as if we had used `Arrays.asList(multiDimensional).toString()`. The third line, the deep representation, prints the `toString` of each element and of the elements inside any nested arrays. This new enhanced ability to display arrays is a very useful feature of Java 5. I've been waiting for this addition for a while!

No Bits Allowed: Encoding and Decoding Binary Data

COMMONS-
CODEC

If you are processing or generating binary data, you may need to place this data into a `String` at some time. Most in-memory binary data is stored within byte arrays but is often converted into hexadecimal (base 16) or binary (base 2) `Strings` for display, storage, or transmission. For example, you may want to include some binary data within a text-based document such as an XML file, send it within an email, or use it in other places where non-text characters would cause problems. A decimal (base 10) representation is less desirable than a hexadecimal, because a decimal number does not reflect the original binary structure until it is converted back into a base that is a power of 2. All of the following are equivalent:

```
binary: 10010000 00000000 00000000 10101010
hexadecimal: 900000AA
decimal: 2415919274
```

The problem with hex and binary display formats is that they are verbose. The binary encoding is the worst, requiring eight times the length of the original data. Hex Strings are a good compromise, using only twice the space, while still giving some idea of the pattern of bits within the data. It's a shame that hexadecimal characters are not displayed in a font that shows the binary structure of each digit! This would be very useful in analyzing some types of binary data.

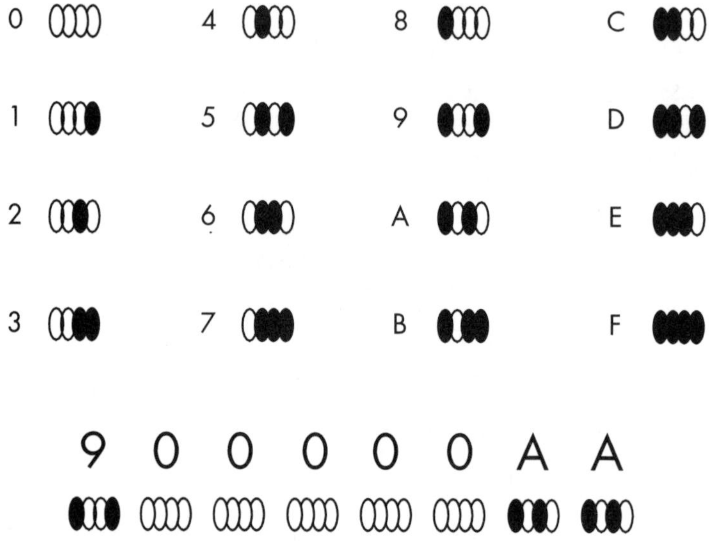

Figure 2-2: A hexadecimal font

There is another commonly used String representation for binary encoding. Base64 is a text representation that uses 4 bytes of text to represent every 3 bytes of the original binary data. It converts the data into a sequence composed of the following 64 printable characters:

```
ABCDEFGHIJKLMNOPQRSTUVWXYZabcdefghijklmnopqrstuvwxyz0123456789+/
```

The A character represents 000000 in binary, and the / character is 111111. Base64 is part of the Multipurpose Internet Mail Extensions (MIME) standard, and you may have seen mail messages that use this format to attach binary content such as images. Each character in the encoded version represents 6 bits of the original data, and there will be four characters for every 3 bytes of the original. If the length of the data is not a multiple of 3, there will be some padding characters required on the encoded String (the Base64 standard uses = for padding). The hexadecimal sequence 900000AA is encoded as kAAAAKo= in Base64. This is a more compact representation than hexadecimal, but because of the padding in this example, the difference will be more noticeable with longer data blocks.

Converting bits into a String is useful, especially if the data is going somewhere that doesn't allow "strange characters" (not the ones in your office—I mean the ones in your data!). But how do you go from byte[] to kAAAAKo= and 900000AA? You may think of simply using the default byte[]-to-String conversion as described earlier. Java 5 and higher can display items in an array by using the static `Arrays.toString` method:

```
byte[] data = readDataFromSomewhere();
System.out.println(Arrays.toString(data));  // in Java 5
```

But this will not help us much. It prints each byte of the data using the default toString for a byte, which is the two's complement decimal interpretation. Each byte is displayed as a number from -128 to 127. The code above prints the following result for the 900000AA data:

```
[-112, 0, 0, 0, -86]
```

Java treats each byte as a signed decimal number. Java does provide methods for converting values into hex and binary, but the data must first be converted into a single numeric type that contains all the bytes (such as a long or BigInteger). The open-source Jakarta Commons-Codec project from Apache provides classes that can convert between binary data and hexadecimal or Base64. To create a hexadecimal or Base64 String from byte array data, you can use the Hex and Base64 classes, in the org.apache.commons.codec.binary package.

```
import org.apache.commons.codec.binary.Hex;
import org.apache.commons.codec.binary.Base64;
import org.apache.commons.codec.DecoderException;

try {
    // the Hex class uses char arrays for String data
    // convert hex String to byte[] data
    byte[] dataArray = Hex.decodeHex("900000AA".toCharArray());
    // convert byte[] data to hex String
    char[] hexChars = Hex.encodeHex(dataArray);
    // the Base64 class uses byte arrays for both directions
    // convert base 64 String to byte[] data
    byte[] dataArray2 = Base64.decodeBase64("kAAAAKo=".getBytes());
    // convert byte[] data into base 64 String
    byte[] base64Bytes = Base64.encodeBase64(dataArray2);
    String base64Str = new String(base64Bytes);
} catch (DecoderException e) {
    e.printStackTrace();
}
```

To encode data to and from binary Strings, there is also a BinaryCodec in the same package, but it encodes the bits in the reverse order from the other codecs (BinaryCodec starts from the last byte, or in little-endian order). This can cause some confusion, so I recommend using the JDK's java.math.BigInteger class instead of the `BinaryCodec` class (unless `BinaryCodec` later switches to big-endian ordering). Converting raw data into a `String` of 1s and 0s is easy enough with the `BigInteger` class:

```
byte[] dataArray = readDataFromSomewhere();
// create a BigInteger with a positive (1) sign, using these bytes
BigInteger numeric = new BigInteger(1, dataArray);
System.out.println(numeric.toString(2));  // print as base 2 string
```

The `BigInteger` class also allows printing in other bases, such as hexadecimal. The maximum base that `BigInteger` allows is 36, so it's not possible to create Base64 `Strings` this way (and the characters in Base64 would not follow the same mappings anyway). There is a serious downside to using the `BigInteger` class to convert in the other direction, from a base 2 (or other base) `String` into a `byte[]`. A `BigInteger` includes a *sign bit*, and the conversion will sometimes introduce an extra byte of zero data at the beginning:

```
byte[] data = new byte[] {-112, 0, 0, 0, -86};
// create a BigInteger from the raw data (1 = positive sign)
BigInteger bigIntData = new BigInteger(1, data);
System.out.println(bigIntData.toString(2));
// BEWARE!!!!
// converting the data back into an array gives different data
byte[] converted = bigIntData.toByteArray();
// this example will print [0, -112, 0, 0, 0, -86]
System.out.println(Arrays.toString(converted));
```

Notice the extra zero byte created by the conversion process in this example! The highest bit of a two's complement number is used as the sign bit. Our example data had a 1 in that position, and the `BigInteger` added a zero byte internally to maintain the positive sign. If the highest bit of the first byte in the original data had been zero, the `byte[]` representation would have remained the same as the original. Most applications will not need to read binary data from a `String` of 1s and 0s, but it sometimes helps to be able to display data as a binary `String`. Just be careful to use `BigInteger` only as a way of displaying the raw data, not creating it. Better yet, use the `Hex` and `Base64` classes. See the online resources for more information on the Base64 standard and the Apache Commons-Codec project. We'll be working with binary structures again in Chapter 5, using a scientific API called Colt (see its `BitVector` class for more information).

A Message for Matt: Formatting Strings with MessageFormat

JAVA 1.1+   The `toString` method of an object converts the internal state of the object into a `String` representation. When we create the `toString` method for a class, this usually involves converting some of the class variables to `String` values and performing some data conversion. There are also many other times when programmers need to format text. Java developers may write their own methods for this or use the java.text.Format subclasses (which have been around since JDK 1.1):

ChoiceFormat
> Attaches a format to a range of numbers and is often used to pluralize Strings.

DateFormat
> Formats and parses date and time values.

DecimalFormat
> Formats decimal numbers.

MessageFormat
> Concatenates messages using the values of objects to be inserted into the text, as specified by a *format String*.

The MessageFormat class uses the other Format classes internally to produce its results, depending on the format String, so it's usually not necessary to directly use one of the others. The format String uses curly braces, { and }, as special characters to select items from the parameter list and apply formatting to them. You can call the static format method as shown in this example:

```
import java.text.MessageFormat;

Object[] dataArray = new Object[] {
    "Petunia",
    new java.util.Date(),
    new Double(13.685)
};
String result = MessageFormat.format(
        "{0} weighed {2,number,##.#} kg on {1,date}",
        dataArray);
System.out.println(result);
```

This code produces the following output:

```
Petunia weighed 13.7 kg on Dec 5, 2004
```

Our format String retrieves the first element of the array, the third element (after applying a numeric format), and the second element (after applying a default date format). These values are concatenated with the rest of the format String. See the MessageFormat class documentation for a complete description of the syntax and conversion options. You can also use the MessageFormat class for parsing text into variables; this is explained in the JavaDoc.

A completely different format String is used in the formatting class mentioned in the next section. It uses a different (and harder-to-read) syntax than the MessageFormat class does.

The Reincarnation of printf: Formatting Strings with Formatter

If you spent some time in a previous life as a C or C++ programmer, did you miss the printf function when you switched to Java? I did. Eventually I moved on, and I learned to love Java's MessageFormat, which I described in the previous section. (If you have no idea what printf is or does, then please skip this section before you get pulled into its disturbing world.) The functionality that the MessageFormat class provides is essentially the same thing but in an easier-to-read format than Formatter. Make sure not to confuse the two classes.

In Java 5, printf rises again from the ashes of C, and now there is yet another way to format text. For the "C captains" (arrrgh, bad pun!) among you, the new java.util.Formatter class provides the same functionality (and syntax) as printf. The String and java.io.PrintStream classes also have convenience methods that use a Formatter to produce output. These new methods use a format String and an argument list to produce a formatted String as output. Here is a short example that prints to System.out using a format that extracts the hour and minute from a Date object:

```
Date now = new Date();
System.out.format("The time is %tI:%tM", now, now);
```

The %tI prints the hour (12-hour clock) and the %tM prints the minute. The format String is very similar to printf's, and the Formatter documentation defines its syntax in great detail. The format String is not exactly the same as C's, but it is similar and can sometimes be useful in migrating C applications that have extensive printf code. And if you fell in love with printf and could never quite let go of C, you know you won't be able to resist! The syntax of this format String is obscure for many Java programmers, so use it with caution.

Resources

The Java 5 documentation has examples showing the syntax of the Formatter's format String.

Chapter Summary

In this chapter, we've looked at some of the String processing capabilities in Java. Besides what we've discussed here, there are many open-source projects with helpful utilities for working with Strings. On the book's website, you'll find links to some of these projects.

In the next chapter, we'll take String processing one step further. We will explore HTML, XML, and other structured text. We'll also look at some APIs that are part of the Java core, as well as some open-source text-processing tools that are written in Java.

3

PROCESSING XML AND HTML

In the previous chapter, we worked with utilities to create, read, and manipulate `Strings`. Using regular expressions and the `Scanner` class described in Chapter 2, we can now write custom parsing programs to extract data from structured text. This works well for simpler content, but using those techniques for very complex structures would involve a significant amount of coding. In this chapter, we will be working with a very common type of structured text—the Extensible Markup Language (XML). We will look at specific techniques for processing XML, generate a parser for a non-XML grammar, and convert an arbitrary grammar into an XML document. This chapter assumes a passing familiarity with XML, and we will not spend much time covering the basics of XML itself. We'll start with a very high-level XML refresher.

Quick XML Refresher

XML is a general-purpose markup language for describing structured, hierarchical data. The designers of XML intended for it to be readable by both computers and humans, rather than a binary format requiring special tools to process. XML is only a few years old, but it's already important for communicating between applications and in many other aspects of computing. Web development, semantic representations, configuration files, and business-to-business web services are just a few examples where XML is being used extensively. Here are some basic facts about XML:

- You can create and process XML documents from any programming language or computer platform, not just in Java.

- XML documents are highly structured, and all the data in an XML document must be placed in hierarchies under a single root element. If a document follows this rule and a few other syntax-related rules, it is called *well-formed*.

- *Elements* or *tags* contain the data, and the structure and names of these tags are application-specific. XML documents are machine-readable as long as the document is well-formed. The XML specification describes a generic syntax for separating a document into tokens, and each document type builds on this using its own tag names and hierarchical structure.

- *Simple API for XML (SAX)* is an API that reads XML documents at a low level. A SAX parser creates events that represent individual parts of the document (for example, start elements, character data, and end elements). Your program "listens" to these events through an *event handler*. SAX does not maintain a memory of previous events—that job belongs to your event handler.

- *Document Object Model (DOM)* is an API that reads a complete document into memory and stores it as a hierarchy of objects representing the data as a tree. Your program actively extracts or modifies data within the document tree by calling DOM methods, whereas SAX is a more passive process (your program waits to receive the data).

A sample XML document might look like the following text. The tag names and text content would be interpreted by an application in some way that makes sense to the application. In this case, the application is an imaginary pun-management system:

```
<?xml version="1.0" ?>
<programmingLanguages>
  <language name="Java">
    <pun>an island</pun><pun>a drink</pun>
  </language>
  <language name="C">
    <pun>to visualize</pun><pun>the ocean</pun>
    <pun>a note</pun><pun>yes</pun>
```

```
    </language>
  </programmingLanguages>
```

The example may be silly, but it does illustrate that you can make up your own tag names. However, you can share your data with other applications most effectively if you can describe it using a well-known XML-based standard. You can find links to some of the more common XML standards on this book's website, http://wickedcooljava.com. Much of the XML processing code in this chapter will also work with HTML—if the document is well-formed it can be processed as XML. For example, you may want to write a program that extracts data from a web page, or a *spider* that follows links in a document. Whether extracting data from an HTML document produces any usable data is another matter (as we'll see later in this chapter).

In this chapter, we will also discuss how to process complex structures that are not in XML or HTML format. We will write a parser for the simple log file format described in Chapter 2 and use this as a base to convert the file format into XML. You can apply these same concepts to convert other non-XML grammars into XML. Once your data is in an XML document, you can process the data using any of the tools and APIs available for XML.

Stop and XML the Rowsets: Using WebRowSet to Create XML

 In Java 5 and higher, there is a very convenient way to get data out of a database and into an XML document. This new addition to the *JDBC* family is called WebRowSet. It's an interface in the javax.sql.rowset package, and the core API has an implementation called WebRowSetImpl. With this class, you can easily convert a database query's ResultSet into an XML representation. From a JDBC result set, you can populate a WebRowSet by using the following:

```
import com.sun.rowset.WebRowSetImpl;

ResultSet rs = statement.executeQuery("select * from MyTable");
WebRowSetImpl data = new WebRowSetImpl();
data.populate(rs);
data.writeXml(System.out);
```

This example sends the XML-encoded data to the console, but you can send it to any Writer or OutputStream. Once you populate a WebRowSet, the data is disconnected from the original ResultSet and you can close the result set, statement, and database connection. I am assuming here that you already have connected to a database and created a Statement object. (If you are not sure how to do this, see one of the many websites and books that explain how to access a database with JDBC.) Once you have the data in XML, you can parse it using any of the XML processing techniques described in this chapter, share it with other applications, or style it into some other format using XSL-T. See the JDBC section of the Java 5 documentation for more details on the WebRowSet class and its XML format.

Stacks of SAX: Remembering Tag Relationships in SAX

If you wanted to be masochistic, you could write your own XML parser, reading each character and extracting the elements, text, and attributes from the input stream. Your program would have to know every detail about the syntax of XML. You would have to take into account things such as escaping characters, parsing elements and attributes, and making entity substitutions. But you don't need to do any of this, because there are many free (and good) XML parsers available for Java.

SAX is one type of XML parsing. With a SAX-based parser, you write an event listener class that receives data from the XML document via event callback methods that represent the tokens in the document. It's a relatively low-level interface, although not quite as low-level as reading on a character-by-character basis. The hardest part of writing SAX programs is keeping track of the hierarchy within the document. This is because the SAX parser does not remember tags and text that came earlier. Your program is like a horse wearing blinders, and it sees only a small part of the picture at a time. But SAX is useful because it can process very large documents that would not be possible using a tree-based approach such as DOM. To process more complex documents, you would probably want to use a tree approach because it is an easier and higher-level interface than SAX. But if you're working with a huge document, you have little choice. And if the program is reading the document over a network, it won't know ahead of time that the document is too large to fit in memory!

JDK 1.4 added a SAX parser to the Java core, so a parser is now available to all Java programs without installing anything extra. Let's take a peek at how SAX works, by writing a very basic SAX application. We'll just be looking at three methods that belong to the ContentHandler interface. This is the interface that programs implement if they want to be notified of events coming from the parser. There are other methods related to the more esoteric parts of a document's structure, but a large number of applications can get by with implementing just three ContentHandler methods. Here is a SAX event handler for processing XML content:

```java
import org.xml.sax.helpers.DefaultHandler;
import org.xml.sax.SAXException;
import org.xml.sax.Attributes;

/*
    DefaultHandler is a base implementation of ContentHandler,
    and by extending this class we don't need to implement all of
    the methods in the ContentHandler interface.
*/
public class SimplestContentHandler extends DefaultHandler {
  public void startElement(String uri, String localName,
                           String qName, Attributes attributes)
    throws SAXException {
      System.out.println("Opening tag " + localName + "");
```

```
  }

  public void characters(char[] ch, int start, int length)
  throws SAXException {
     String text = new String(ch, start, length);
     System.out.print(text);
  }

  public void endElement(String uri, String localName,
                           String qName)
  throws SAXException {
     System.out.println("Closing tag " + localName);
  }
}
```

As you can probably guess, these three methods correspond to starting an element (opening tag), character data, and ending an element (closing tag). I like to call this the "SAX-wich," because you could think of the opening and closing tags as being the bread that holds the meat (the text) in place. You will have to watch out for the cheese and mustard in this sandwich, however, because the characters method may be called more than once to represent a block of text! In other words, your event handler will need to collect the data from multiple characters method calls and place it into a String or StringBuffer somewhere. Here is where things can get a little tricky, because you'll need to know where you are in the document before you can assign the text to a particular tag. When the characters method is called, there is no contextual information carried with the character data. Many applications use boolean flags to represent the container element of the current text. We will be showing an example that uses a java.util.Stack to keep track of the most recent enclosing tags.

Be careful not to just grab everything inside that char array, because it may even contain the buffer for the whole document! You must use the start and length parameters to know how much of the data belongs to the current text. The easiest way to do this is with the String constructor that copies only a portion of a character buffer, as shown in our last bit of code. The StringBuffer class has an append method with similar parameters.

You won't normally run the ContentHandler by itself. You will need a driver program to create a parser instance, plug your handler into it, and stream a document through the parser. Here is some code that creates a parser, plugs in our handler, and reads a document from a URL:

```
import org.xml.sax.ContentHandler;
import org.xml.sax.XMLReader;
import org.xml.sax.helpers.XMLReaderFactory;

public class SimplestSAXDriver {
    public static void main(String[] args) throws Exception {
        XMLReader parser = XMLReaderFactory.createXMLReader();
        ContentHandler handler = new SimplestContentHandler();
```

```
        parser.setContentHandler(handler);
        String url = "http://docs.oasis-open.org/ubl/cd-UBL-1.0/" +
            "xml/office/UBL-Order-1.0-Office-Example.xml";
        parser.parse(url);
    }
}
```

Let's write a SAX-based program to process a document. As an example, we will extract some data from a *Universal Business Language (UBL)* document. UBL is a new XML-based standard for encoding business documents such as purchase orders, shipping notices, and invoices. (You can find a link to it on this book's website.) We will use one of the example files (the URL that we just used) from the UBL specification: a purchase order for office supplies from a vendor. Our example focuses on the line items of the purchase order, so I will leave out some details to avoid listing pages and pages of XML. Here are the general contents of the file:

```
<Order>
  <!-- Buyer ID, issue date, and total amount go here -->
  <!-- Buyer party's name and address go here -->
  <!-- Seller party's name and address go here -->
  <!-- Delivery date and address go here -->
  <!-- Delivery terms go here -->
  <OrderLine>
    <LineItem>
      <BuyersID>1</BuyersID>  <!-- line item number -->
      <Quantity quantityUnitCode="PKG">5</Quantity>
      <LineExtensionAmount>12.50</LineExtensionAmount>
      <Item>
          <Description>Pencils, box #2 red</Description>
          <SellersItemIdentification>
            <ID>32145-12</ID>
          </SellersItemIdentification>
          <BasePrice>
            <PriceAmount>2.50</PriceAmount>
          </BasePrice>
      </Item>
    </LineItem>
  </OrderLine>
  <OrderLine> .... </OrderLine>
  <OrderLine> .... </OrderLine>
</Order>
```

Imagine that you work for a company that has a policy requiring special approval for any extended line-item totals over $30 (I am assuming dollars in this example). We can write a program that prepares a report of items requiring a supervisor's approval by using SAX to read through the document and find any LineExtensionAmount values over 30. This would be simple enough, because we can look for the LineExtensionAmount tag and set a boolean flag when we encounter the open tag, resetting it to false when the tag closes. We then retrieve character data (in the characters method) only when the flag is true. This gives us the data for the dollar amount. However, if we want to capture other identifying information such as the item description, we need a better way to remember our current context within the document and to keep track of related data earlier in the document. For remembering tag hierarchies, we can push element names onto a Stack in the startElement method and pop them off in the endElement method. One simple way of capturing the text is to place it into a map with the tag name as a key. This won't work if the tag names are not unique within the document, however, and we haven't done anything with the attribute values either, but these problems are easily overcome. (Also note that the stack- and map-based approach is not safe for use by multiple threads.) Here's our new handler class:

```
public class LineItemReportHandler extends DefaultHandler {
  private java.util.Stack path = new java.util.Stack();
  private java.util.HashMap values = new java.util.HashMap();

  public void startElement(String uri, String localName,
                           String qName, Attributes attributes)
  throws SAXException {
    // push the element name on the stack
    path.push(localName);
    // values is the map that will collect our XML text
    // clear the text for this element when we open the tag
    values.put(localName, "");
  }

  public void characters(char[] ch, int start, int length)
  throws SAXException {
    String text = new String(ch, start, length);
    // what is the most recent tag?
    String currentTag = (String) path.peek();
    // what is the value of the text within it so far?
    String currentValue = (String) values.get(currentTag);
    // append the current text and add it back into the map
    currentValue = currentValue + text;
    values.put(currentTag, currentValue);
  }

  public void endElement(String uri, String localName, String qName)
  throws SAXException {
    path.pop();
    if (localName.equals("LineItem")) {
        String amount = (String) values.get("LineExtensionAmount");
        if (Double.parseDouble(amount) >= 30.0) {
            System.out.print("Quantity ");
            System.out.print(values.get("Quantity"));
            System.out.print(" of \"");
```

```
            System.out.print(values.get("Description"));
            System.out.print("\" costs $");
            System.out.println(amount);
        }
    }
}
```

This SAX handler produced the following results after processing the example UBL file:

```
Quantity 10 of "Photocopy Paper- case" costs $300.00
Quantity 10 of "Pens, box, blue finepoint" costs $50.00
Quantity 3 of "Tape, 1in case" costs $37.50
```

The above XML file was a simplification of UBL and did not include *namespace* or *schema* processing. For links to UBL and information on namespaces and schemas, see this book's online resources website.

Playing the SAX: Directly Feeding a ContentHandler

 We showed in the previous section that parsers generate SAX events based on input from an XML document. We also explored some of the methods that belong to the ContentHandler interface. In the example, we wrote a simple event handler to process XML content, using stacks and maps to collect the data. Sometimes you'll need to work in the other direction—firing your own SAX events to a ContentHandler. This is not the easiest way to create a document, but it may be your only choice for creating an extremely large document.

It's possible to feed a ContentHandler by creating an instance of it and calling its methods directly. Here's an example based on the simple handler we used earlier that creates a portion of the purchase order document by triggering SAX events:

```
ContentHandler handler = new SimplestContentHandler();
handler.startDocument();
// ... part of document omitted here
handler.startElement("", "Item", "Item", new AttributesImpl());
handler.startElement("", "Description", "Description",
        new AttributesImpl());
String text = "Pencils, box #2 red";
handler.characters(text.toCharArray(), 0, text.length());
// Don't forget to end the elements, and in the reverse order!
handler.endElement("", "Description", "Description");
handler.endElement("", "Item", "Item");
// ... part of document omitted here
handler.endDocument();
```

We begin the document processing by calling the startDocument method and then calling the startElement and endElement methods for the opening and closing tags. When we open a tag, we also need to pass an Attributes collection, which we can create by using the AttributesImpl class (Attributes is an interface and cannot be directly instantiated). Even if you are not adding any attributes, you still need to pass an empty Attributes object because the ContentHandler interface requires it. The empty String passed to the start and end elements is the XML namespace, which we are not using in this example, but the interface still requires an empty String for the value. The second copy of the tag name is the *qualified name*, or a tag name with a namespace prefix (which we aren't using). Real UBL uses namespaces and schemas, and you should familiarize yourself with them if you plan to use UBL in production. See the online resources website for more detail.

If you are generating a lot of SAX events, it can be helpful to write some convenience methods to make the code more readable, as in this example that creates a UBL document canceling an order. It may be a bit unconventional, but slightly indenting the code for each level of nested tags helps readability (and reminds you to close the tags!):

```
handler.startDocument();
open("OrderCancellation");        // open the OrderCancellation tag
  tagText("ID", "20031654-X");    // ID tag with embedded text
  tagText("IssueDateTime", "2003-03-09T09:30:47");
  tagText("CancellationNote", "order replaced");
  open("OrderReference");
    tagText("BuyersID", "20031654-1");
    tagText("IssueDate", "2003-03-07");
  close("OrderReference");
  open("BuyerParty");
    open("Party");
      open("PartyName");
        tagText("Name", "Bills Microdevices");
      close("PartyName");
    close("Party");
  close("BuyerParty");
  open("SellerParty");
    open("Party");
      open("PartyName");
        tagText("Name", "Joes Office Supply");
      close("PartyName");
    close("Party");
    open("OrderContact");
      tagText("Name", "Betty Jo Beoloski");
    close("OrderContact");
  close("SellerParty");
close("OrderCancellation");       // close the OrderCancellation tag
handler.endDocument();
```

For completeness, here is my definition of the open, close, and tagText methods:

```java
public class OurSAXGenerator {
    private ContentHandler handler;  // initialized earlier

    private void open(String tag)
    throws SAXException {
        handler.startElement("", tag, tag, new AttributesImpl());
    }

    private void close(String tag)
    throws SAXException {
        handler.endElement("", tag, tag);
    }

    private void tagText(String tag, String value)
    throws SAXException {
        open(tag);
        handler.characters(value.toCharArray(), 0, value.length());
        close(tag);
    }
}
```

You can create more sophisticated methods that make sense for your own application. In this example, we did not use any namespace prefixes or attributes, so using our own convenience methods removed some clutter from the code. Remember that there are easier ways to generate XML content than feeding your own SAX events to a ContentHandler, but for performance reasons or because of memory constraints with large documents, it's sometimes necessary. This works only where the XML does not cross boundaries from one system to another, since your generator code will need to have access to the handler instance. In the next section, we will discuss some other techniques for working with SAX events.

Mustard on a SAX-wich: Filter-Feeding a ContentHandler

JAVA 1.4+ Now that you can feed a hungry ContentHandler, as we did in the last section, you can let another part of the program call the SAX-wich methods, and then you can just add the mustard to it (or remove the mayonnaise). I'm not totally being facetious here, because there really is a kind of preprocessing that you can do to the XML data as it is being passed to a ContentHandler. In the previous section, you fired SAX events into a ContentHandler class directly, without using a parser. That may be useful in some applications, but a more common scenario involves reading data from an XML document and filtering or adding content before the document is processed.

The `org.xml.sax.XMLFilter` interface is a combination of `ContentHandler` and `XMLReader`—a parser and an event handler rolled into one. You can use this interface to implement a middle layer between the input events coming from an `XMLReader` and the output events going to a `ContentHandler`. To the `XMLReader` it looks like a `ContentHandler`, and to the `ContentHandler` it looks like an `XMLReader`. Figure 3-1 shows how the filter process works.

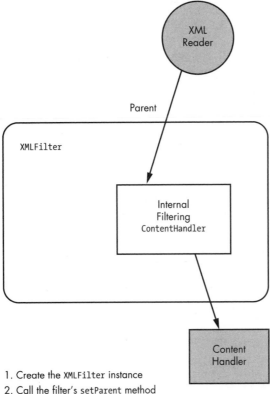

1. Create the `XMLFilter` instance
2. Call the filter's `setParent` method
3. Call the filter's `setContentHandler` method
4. Call the filter's `parse` method

Figure 3-1: XMLFilter flow

Since there are many methods in this interface, you'll probably want to extend the default implementation instead of writing everything from scratch; for this purpose, we have the `XMLFilterImpl` class in the `org.xml.sax.helpers` package. The default implementation sends any SAX methods directly to the attached event handler. This results in a document that is exactly the same as the input. To create a filter, extend the class by overriding the `ContentHandler` methods. When the overridden SAX methods in the filter are called by the parent `XMLReader`, the events are passed on to the destination handler only if you call the corresponding method in the superclass (for example, `super.characters`). In the same manner, you can create new content or modify existing content by calling the `super.startElement` and `super.endElement` methods with the data that you want to pass to the destination handler. In the following code, I've implemented a filter that ignores tags and text within an "ignore" tag:

```
import org.xml.sax.Attributes;
import org.xml.sax.SAXException;
import org.xml.sax.helpers.XMLFilterImpl;

public class IgnoringFilter extends XMLFilterImpl
{
  // Note that this filter will not work with nested ignore tags!
  boolean ignoring = false;

  public void startElement(String url, String localName,
          String qName, Attributes att) throws SAXException {
    if (localName.equals("ignore")) {
      ignoring = true;
    }
    if (!ignoring) {
      super.startElement(url, localName, qName, att);
    }
  }

  public void characters(char[] data, int start, int length)
  throws SAXException {
    if (!ignoring) {
      super.characters(data, start, length);
    }
  }

  public void endElement(String url, String localName, String qName)
  throws SAXException {
    if (localName.equals("ignore")) {
      ignoring = false;
    } else if (!ignoring) {
      super.endElement(url, localName, qName);
    }
  }
}
```

To plug in the filter, use the following:

```
XMLReader parser = XMLReaderFactory.createXMLReader();
ContentHandler handler = new SimplestContentHandler();
IgnoringFilter filter = new IgnoringFilter();
filter.setContentHandler(handler);
filter.setParent(parser);
filter.parse("C:/projects/wcj3/test.xml");
```

Note that since we implemented only those three SAX methods in the filter, there may be situations where the filter does not catch all of the events, such as with namespace prefix mapping and whitespace characters. For a complete filter that works in all cases, you may need to also implement other methods in the SAX interface. See the ContentHandler and XMLFilter documentation in the JDK for more details.

You can also chain filters together. Now we'll add in another filter that adds a signedBy attribute inside every element in the document. Here's the filter class:

```
import org.xml.sax.Attributes;
import org.xml.sax.SAXException;
import org.xml.sax.helpers.AttributesImpl;
import org.xml.sax.helpers.XMLFilterImpl;

public class SignatureFilter
extends XMLFilterImpl
{
  public void startElement(String url, String localName,
          String qName, Attributes att)
  throws SAXException {
    // start with the existing attributes, if any
    AttributesImpl moreAtt = new AttributesImpl(att);
    // add a new attribute:
    // type is CDATA, name is signedBy, value is SignatureFilter
    moreAtt.addAttribute("", "signedBy", "signedBy", "CDATA",
                    "SignatureFilter");
    // pass this on to the listener
    super.startElement(url, localName, qName, moreAtt);
  }
}
```

We chain this filter with the one that we created earlier, by using the following code:

```
XMLReader parser = XMLReaderFactory.createXMLReader();
IgnoringFilter filter = new IgnoringFilter();
SignatureFilter signer = new SignatureFilter();
signer.setContentHandler(new SimplestContentHandler());
filter.setContentHandler(signer);
filter.setParent(parser);
filter.parse("C:/projects/wcj3/test.xml");
```

This creates a two-stage filter, fed by the XMLReader (the parser), through the IgnoringFilter, into the SignatureFilter, and out to the destination content handler SimplestContentHandler. With process flows like this, you can build up complex XML content in multiple stages using SAX events. If you feed the filtered SAX events into a document tree, you can load selected portions of a very large XML document that would not otherwise fit in memory. We'll be exploring this option in a later section.

Easy Reading: Using DOM4J to Read XML Documents

DOM4J

DOM-based programs often turn out to be clumsy and hard to read. Some of the DOM methods for reading and manipulating XML are not the most desirable. The open-source DOM4J project provides a cleaner API that makes XML processing much smoother. It's not part of Java's core, so you'll need to download the DOM4J library and add it to your classpath. There are DOM4J objects that are analogous to each the DOM objects, but they have a different API and use different methods and classes. Unfortunately, they have the same names as some of the DOM classes. *Be careful that you don't get the DOM classes and packages in the Java core confused with the classes in DOM4J!* You'll find that the biggest difference between the two is in reading XML documents. To illustrate the difference, let's write some code to read data from a UBL purchase order (as discussed in earlier examples) using DOM and then show the corresponding DOM4J code. First, here's the DOM code to load the document and retrieve the BuyersID, IssueDate, and LineExtensionTotalAmount values:

```
// This is DOM code. Imports have been omitted for brevity
DocumentBuilderFactory fact = DocumentBuilderFactory.newInstance();
DocumentBuilder parser = fact.newDocumentBuilder();
String url = "C:/projects/wcj3/purchaseOrder.xml";
Document doc = parser.parse(url);
// get the root element
Element root = doc.getDocumentElement();
NodeList list = root.getElementsByTagName("BuyersID");
Element idElem = (Element) list.item(0);
String buyersID = idElem.getTextContent();
System.out.println("Buyers ID is " + buyersID);
list = root.getElementsByTagName("IssueDate");
Element issueElem = (Element) list.item(0);
String issueDate = issueElem.getTextContent();
System.out.println("Issue date is " + issueDate);
list = root.getElementsByTagName("LineExtensionTotalAmount");
Element totalElem = (Element) list.item(0);
String total = totalElem.getTextContent();
System.out.println("Total amount is " + total);
```

The first four statements load the parser and parse the XML document into a DOM Document object. We then get the root element. The code in boldface is the more complex part of DOM. For each of the three values, we need to first get the child element by its name and get its child text. For this,

DOM has a method that returns a node list, and we capture the first element in the list and get the text underneath it by calling the `getTextContent` method. The corresponding DOM4J code is much cleaner:

```
// This is DOM4J code.
String url = "C:/projects/wcj3/purchaseOrder.xml";
org.dom4j.io.SAXReader reader = new org.dom4j.io.SAXReader();
org.dom4j.Document doc = reader.read(url);
org.dom4j.Element root = doc.getRootElement();
String buyersID = root.elementText("BuyersID");
System.out.println("Buyers ID is " + buyersID);
String issueDate = root.elementText("IssueDate");
System.out.println("Issue date is " + issueDate);
String total = root.elementText("LineExtensionTotalAmount");
System.out.println("Total amount is " + total);
```

Note that the `org.dom4j.Document` and `org.dom4j.Element` classes used here are the ones from DOM4J and *not* the ones from DOM! The lines in boldface are equivalent to the boldface code from the DOM example. DOM4J has a very convenient way to retrieve the text from a child element, as you can see.

DOM4J has other methods that make it easy to process XML data. Here is an example that prints the buyer and seller information from the purchase order. Assuming the same DOM4J doc instance as before (`org.dom4j.Document`), we find the buyer's name, company, and address by traversing the tree:

```
// This is DOM4J code
Element root = doc.getRootElement();
// get the element for root->BuyerParty->Party
Element party = root.element("BuyerParty").element("Party");
// get the company name from Party->PartyName->Name
String company = party.element("PartyName").elementText("Name");
// Party->Address
Element address = party.element("Address");
// Address -> StreetName, BuildingNumber, etc
String street = address.elementText("StreetName");
String building = address.elementText("BuildingNumber");
String city = address.elementText("CityName");
String zip = address.elementText("PostalZone");
String state = address.elementText("CountrySubentityCode");
// Party->Contact->Name
String contact = party.element("Contact").elementText("Name");
```

If you have a choice in which API to use for processing XML, using DOM4J will make your code cleaner and more maintainable. DOM4J can also interface with DOM and SAX parsers, so you can easily plug your DOM4J-based program into existing code, and it has many other nice features. One of these features is described in the next section.

Eck's Path: Using XPath for Easy Data Extraction

DOM4J

In the last section, we showed how to use DOM4J to read data from an XML document. We used the `element` and `elementText` methods to extract data from items in the tree. There is another way of traversing a DOM4J tree, using an expression language called *XPath*. With XPath, we can follow a path from the root of the document to any point in the tree by using a shorthand expression that looks something like a Unix directory path. Let's use the purchase order XML as an example. We can find the terms of delivery by following the `Order` (root) element to its `DeliveryTerms` child element and to the `SpecialTerms` child element and its text. You can express this as the following XPath expression:

```
/Order/DeliveryTerms/SpecialTerms
```

In DOM4J, you can very easily get the value of this expression as a `String`, which returns the text underneath the `SpecialTerms` tag:

```
String terms = doc.valueOf("/Order/DeliveryTerms/SpecialTerms");
```

This method works on any type of DOM4J `Node`, such as `Element` or `Document`, and can even be a *relative expression* that finds a value relative to the current node. You can get the value of an XPath expression as a `Node` that holds text and possibly other child elements. There is a version that returns a single node and one that returns a `java.util.List` of nodes (for handling multiple matching results). To illustrate this process, we'll now read the line items within the purchase order document:

```
List items = doc.selectNodes("/Order/OrderLine");
Iterator iter = items.iterator();
while (iter.hasNext()) {
    Element orderLine = (Element) iter.next();
    String qty = orderLine.valueOf("LineItem/Quantity");
    String desc = orderLine.valueOf("LineItem/Item/Description");
    String price =
        orderLine.valueOf("LineItem/Item/BasePrice/PriceAmount");
    System.out.println(qty + " " + desc + " at " + price);
}
```

The first line of code reads the purchase order items into a `List` of nodes. We iterate through the list, using relative XPath expressions to extract the text for each item. Using XPath, we were able to read much of the document in just a few lines of code.

Creating XML (and HTML) within DOM4J is just as simple. For this next demonstration, we'll use DOM4J to create an XHTML page displaying the items that we just collected. XHTML is HTML content that is also proper XML (for example, tags are properly closed and attributes are quoted). When the program runs, it will create an HTML output file that looks like Figure 3-2.

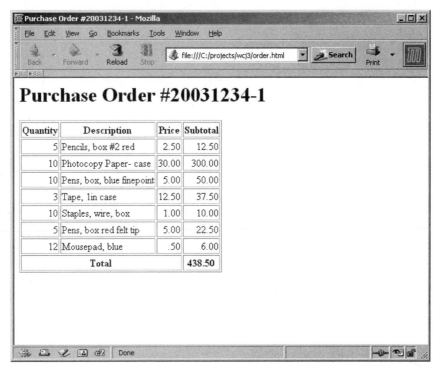

Figure 3-2: DOM4J HTML result

We first create a new document by using the `DocumentHelper`'s `createDocument` method. Then we can call the `addElement` and `addText` methods wherever necessary to create the HTML content. In this example, we are working with two DOM4J documents—one for reading the input XML and one for generating the HTML output file. Before we list the main program code, here are the imports that we are using:

```
import java.io.FileWriter;
import java.io.IOException;
import java.util.Iterator;
import java.util.List;
import org.dom4j.Document;
import org.dom4j.DocumentException;
import org.dom4j.DocumentHelper;
import org.dom4j.Element;
import org.dom4j.io.HTMLWriter;
import org.dom4j.io.OutputFormat;
import org.dom4j.io.SAXReader;
```

Leaving out exception handling, here is the code:

```
// Read the input XML document (purchase order)
String url = "C:/projects/wcj3/purchaseOrder.xml";
SAXReader reader = new SAXReader();
```

```java
Document po = reader.read(url);
// Create the output HTML document object
Document htmlDoc = DocumentHelper.createDocument();
// Add a title with the extracted Buyer ID
String buyerID = po.valueOf("/Order/BuyersID");
String title = "Purchase Order #" + buyerID;
// Create the root HTML element and document title
Element html = htmlDoc.addElement("html");
html.addElement("head").addElement("title").setText(title);
// Create a body tag and H1 heading for a title
Element body = html.addElement("body");
body.addElement("h1").addText(title);
// Create the HTML table, with border
Element table = body.addElement("table")
                        .addAttribute("border", "1");
// Create a header row
Element header = table.addElement("tr");
header.addElement("th").addText("Quantity");
header.addElement("th").addText("Description");
header.addElement("th").addText("Price");
header.addElement("th").addText("Subtotal");
// Get the list of line items in the document
List items = po.selectNodes("/Order/OrderLine");
Iterator iter = items.iterator();
while (iter.hasNext())
{
    Element item = (Element) iter.next();
    // Add a table row
    Element row = table.addElement("tr");
    // Add a cell containing the quantity
    row.addElement("td")
        .addText(item.valueOf("LineItem/Quantity"))
        .addAttribute("align","right");
    // Add a cell containing the description
    row.addElement("td")
        .addText(item.valueOf("LineItem/Item/Description"));
    // Add a cell containing the unit price
    String priceAmount =
        item.valueOf("LineItem/Item/BasePrice/PriceAmount");
    row.addElement("td")
        .addText(priceAmount)
        .addAttribute("align","right");
    // Add a cell containing the subtotal
    row.addElement("td")
        .addText(item.valueOf("LineItem/LineExtensionAmount"))
        .addAttribute("align","right");
}
// Produce the total row
Element totalRow = table.addElement("tr");
totalRow.addElement("th")
```

```
                    .addAttribute("colspan", "3")
                      .addText("Total");
String total = po.valueOf("/Order/LineExtensionTotalAmount");
totalRow.addElement("th").addText(total);
// Stream the output HTML document to disk
// We use "pretty printing" to produce easy-to-read HTML
// Without this, tags have no indentation or whitespace
OutputFormat format = OutputFormat.createPrettyPrint();
FileWriter file = new FileWriter("order.html");
HTMLWriter writer = new HTMLWriter(file, format);
writer.write(htmlDoc);
writer.close();
```

This code illustrates the unusual way in which DOM4J programs often chain their method calls when they create child elements. This chaining is possible because the addElement method returns the newly created element, and the addText and addAttribute methods return the original element (the one to which you added the text). If you haven't done HTML work before, you may need to look at an HTML reference (see this book's website) to understand the table tags and the attributes that affect a table's layout. To avoid confusion between Elements used in reading data and those used in creating output, I have extracted the data almost entirely by using XPath expressions (by calling the valueOf method on the po object). The only Element that represents input data is the item variable within the while loop, and it contains the current line item being processed. All of the other Element references are used in creating the output document. The HTML creation work that we just did could also have been done by an XSL stylesheet, without involving any Java code. On this book's website, you'll find links to information on how to use XSL for creating HTML from an XML file.

Invisible Tags: Filtering Documents Before Loading into DOM4J

DOM4J

JAVA 1.4+

When you load an XML document into DOM4J, the document needs to be small enough to completely fit into memory. However, for very large documents, it's possible to filter the document before reading it into memory. We did something like this in the section "Mustard on a SAX-wich: Filter-Feeding a ContentHandler," when we filtered out SAX events with a SAXFilter. But we didn't build a tree; instead, our program directly processed the SAX events. Most document object trees are initially built using SAX events. By placing an XMLFilter between the SAX events and the handler that creates the tree, you can make part of the content "invisible" to the building process.

We can demonstrate tree filtering with the purchase order example. We will load only the seller's information into a DOM4J tree, representing a small subset of the document. If you recall from the last few sections, a UBL purchase order contains buyer and seller information, delivery instructions, and order lines (line items). Here is an abbreviated version of the XML we've been using in this chapter, showing the high-level structure of the document:

```
<Order>
   <BuyersID>20031234-1</BuyersID>
   <IssueDate>2003-01-23</IssueDate>
   <LineExtensionTotalAmount>438.50</LineExtensionTotalAmount>
   <BuyerParty>
      <!-- buyer name, address, contact information -->
   </BuyerParty>
   <SellerParty>
      <!-- seller name, address, contact information -->
   </SellerParty>
   <Delivery>
      <!-- delivery date, time, and address -->
   </Delivery>
   <DeliveryTerms>
      <SpecialTerms>Signature Required</SpecialTerms>
   </DeliveryTerms>
   <OrderLine>
      <LineItem>
         <!-- line item details -->
      </LineItem>
   </OrderLine>
   <OrderLine>
      <LineItem>
         <!-- line item details -->
      </LineItem>
   </OrderLine>
   <!-- more line items.... -->
</Order>
```

Although it probably wouldn't happen in real life, imagine that we have an extremely large purchase order document, many gigabytes in size. (We're in the far future, and it's an order for replacement parts on a starship's warp drive.) Our boss wants to display only the seller information from this document and expects us to use a tree-based approach. We certainly can't just load the whole document into the tree (as of this writing, not on my machine, anyway). Besides possibly running out of memory, it's a waste of space to load the whole document when you need only part of it. Similarly to what we did earlier, we can create a filter that ignores everything except the seller information. We can do that by writing a subclass of `XMLFilterImpl` that sends output to the SAX handler only after it encounters a `SellerParty` start tag and until it encounters the matching end tag. Here is a simplistic version of it:

```
public class SellerFilter
extends XMLFilterImpl {
```

```
        private boolean ignoring = true;

        public void startElement(String url, String localName, String qname,
                                 Attributes att)
        throws SAXException {
            if (localName.equals("SellerParty")) {
                ignoring = false;
            }
            if (!ignoring) {
                super.startElement(url, localName, qname, att);
            }
        }

        public void characters(char[] arg0, int arg1, int arg2)
        throws SAXException {
            if (!ignoring) {
                super.characters(arg0, arg1, arg2);
            }
        }

        public void endElement(String url, String localName, String qname)
        throws SAXException {
            if (!ignoring) {
                super.endElement(url, localName, qname);
            }
            if (localName.equals("SellerParty")) {
                ignoring = true;
            }
        }
    }
}
```

This filter works by turning on a "faucet" when it encounters the right opening tag (SellerParty) and turning off the flow of data again when it sees the closing tag. To integrate this filter into the DOM4J builder, we need to place it between the SAX parser that reads the input stream and the builder that creates the tree. The SAXReader class in DOM4J has a wonderful setXMLFilter method to do this:

```
org.dom4j.io.SAXReader parser = new org.dom4j.io.SAXReader();
SellerFilter filter = new SellerFilter();
parser.setXMLFilter(filter);
org.dom4j.Document doc = parser.read("C:/projects/wcj3/test.xml");
```

DOM4J also has its own tree-pruning mechanism that is a little different than the SAX filtering process. The DOM4J documentation describes the other approach and provides some example code. In this section's example, we used the same filtering process that SAX uses, because it is a more general approach and the resulting filter could also be applied as part of a chain of SAX filters.

Sin Taxes: Generating Parsers for Anything with JavaCC

JavaCC
Sometimes you will be lucky enough to work with data that uses a well-known syntax, such as XML or HTML, as we have done so far in this chapter. In those cases, you can use an existing parser. For other structures, you may need to write your own parser. This is essentially what we did in Chapter 2, in the section "Scan-Do Attitude: Parsing Complex Syntax with the Scanner Class." We encoded the knowledge of our *grammar*, the relationship between all the parts of the data, into the program itself. If there are no errors in converting the grammar into program logic, this may work fine. But for complex grammars, the chances of logic errors are much higher, and the program is much harder to develop and maintain. This explains why just about everyone uses an existing parser for XML or HTML, rather than writing their own! If you want to process a grammar for something else, such as a custom language, it's better to first encode the rules of the grammar in a specification language. You can then build a parsing program around the grammar, after you've tested the grammar rules themselves. You will sleep much better at night, knowing that the grammar is correct before you've even started writing the logic of your program.

To process structured text, you first need to separate the text into *tokens*, or objects representing indivisible units of data. The process of creating tokens from input text is called *scanning* (also called *lexical analysis* or *lexing*). For example, in scanning a mathematical expression, each number, variable name, function name, parenthesis, and operator become separate tokens. We did a simple lexical analysis earlier when we retrieved the domain name from a URL by using a regular expression with capturing groups. You can think of each capturing group as creating a token.

Once an application tokenizes an input stream, it has a list of objects that represent the tokens in the order in which they occur in the text. The next step is to build a data structure, called an *abstract syntax tree (AST)*, that represents the relationship of each token to the others. A mathematical expression is one common type of syntax tree. An XML document is another. A *parser* processes an input stream to create an AST, based on a grammar that describes the allowed tokens and the rules for their use within the tree. Parsers are usually generated from a grammar specification rather than coded manually. A *parser generator* converts the grammar into a program that recognizes the grammar. Let's look at a simple grammar, the logging file described previously:

```
eventType year month day time type-dependent-data
```

We will use an open-source parser generator, JavaCC, that generates a Java-based parser from a grammar specification. Every grammar consists of a set of *production rules* that explain how to build the syntax tree out of tokens. The JavaCC compiler reads a .jj file describing the grammar rules and generates the Java source code for a parser. The input file also contains Java code for additional logic to include in the parser class. The first part of a .jj file defines the core of the parser class.

```
PARSER_BEGIN(LogParser)
public class LogParser {
    public static void main(String[] args) {
        try {
            LogParser parser = new LogParser(System.in);
            parser.allLines();
        } catch (ParseException e) {
            System.out.println("Error: This is not a valid file.");
        }
    }
}
PARSER_END(LogParser)
```

As you can see, this is not a normal Java source file but is instead a *metalanguage* that tells the code generator what to put in the generated parser class. The code that is generated by JavaCC will have a constructor that takes an input stream as a parameter. Our class has a main method that simply passes the standard input (System.in) to the constructor. The rest of the file contains the token definitions and production rules for the grammar. We will define the allLines method later; it represents the highest-level production rule and starts the parsing process. There is something of a science as well as an art to writing production rules, and the JavaCC documentation gives many examples of grammar specifications. You will want to read the book on compiler theory given under "Resources" at the end of this section for a more complete treatment of the parsing process.

Let's write the grammar by creating some production rules. The parser processes text recursively, by trying to match regular expressions for tokens in such a way that a complete tree can be built using the higher-level rules. We first define the lowest-level items, or *terminals*, and then we can build higher-level rules based on these. The TOKEN section of the file defines the tokens used within the grammar and gives each one's name and regular expression. They need names so that we can refer to them in other rules. Our main tokens for this grammar are the log's event names and the time and date numbers. Here is the TOKEN section:

```
TOKEN:
{       /* these < and > brackets have nothing to do with XML! */
    < ENTRY: "entry" >
  | < EXIT: "exit" >
  | < ALARM: "alarm" >
  | < NUM: ["0"-"9"]+ >
  | < CRLF: ["\r","\n"]+ >
  | < WORD: ["a"-"z", "A"-"Z", "0"-"9", ",", "-"]+ >
  | < SPC: ([" ", "\t"])+ >
}
```

The regular expressions are defined just a bit differently here than the ones we did in Chapter 2, and there are some additional special characters such as the angle bracket (not to be confused with XML tag delimiters). You must place the matching characters within double quotes, and since this is not a Java `String` literal expression, you don't need to escape backslash characters in each regex.

Now for the production rules. At the topmost level, we read lines of text, and to do this we need to look for a carriage return and/or line feed, or an end-of-file marker, as a terminator for each line. (To repeat: These angle brackets are *not XML tags* but instead delineate the token names.) We add the following production rules to read the lines of text:

```
void allLines():
{}
{
    ( anyLine() )*
}

void anyLine():
{}
{
    lineOfText() (<CRLF> | <EOF>)
}

void lineOfText():
{}
{
    entryLine() | exitLine() | alarmLine()
}
```

These production rules get turned into methods in the generated class. Each production has three sections: a rule name (method name); a Java section with code that runs when the rule is triggered; and a production that is a combination of tokens, other productions, and regular expressions. Remember that this is a recursive process. The `allLines` production is the topmost one. It has zero or more lines of text, where a line of text is defined as the `anyLine` production. The `anyLine` production looks for line terminators or an EOF (end-of-file) marker. The `lineOfText` represents one of the three log types: entry, exit, and alarm. The three specific types of lines in the log file are defined next:

```
void entryLine():
{}
{
    <ENTRY> <SPC> dateTime() <SPC> <WORD> <SPC> restOfLine()
}

void exitLine():
{}
```

```
{
    <EXIT> <SPC> dateTime() <SPC> restOfLine()
}

void alarmLine():
{}
{
    <ALARM> <SPC> dateTime() <SPC> <WORD> <SPC> restOfLine()
}
```

Notice how the tokens that we defined in the TOKEN section are being used here within the production rules and how the rules recursively define the grammar. There is just a little bit more to this grammar. Next we define the dateTime and restOfLine productions:

```
void dateTime():
{}
{
  <NUM> <SPC> <NUM> <SPC> <NUM> <SPC> <NUM>
}

void restOfLine():
{}
{
  ( <WORD> | <SPC> )*
}
```

Our grammar is now complete. We can use JavaCC to generate a parser for it. The javacc program (not to be confused with javac) processes the .jj grammar file and turns it into Java source code for the parser. Run it as shown here:

```
C:\projects\wcj3> javacc logfile.jj
Java Compiler Compiler Version 3.2 (Parser Generator)
(type "javacc" with no arguments for help)
Reading from file logfile.jj . . .
Parser generated successfully.
```

If there are no syntax errors in the grammar, you will now have some generated Java source code for your parser. Compile the source code using the JDK:

```
C:\projects\wcj3> javac LogParser.java
```

You can now run the parser. It will take its input from System.in, and you can either enter some log file data from the keyboard or redirect a file as the input. If the input does not follow the grammar, the parser will throw a

ParseException, which we catch in the main method. From the keyboard, enter the following:

```
C:\projects\wcj3> java LogParser
alarm 2005 06 02 2301 fire This was a drill
entry 2005 01 XYZ 1200 meeting This is a comment
Error: This is not a valid file.
```

To end the file when testing from the keyboard, you may need to use the CTRL-Z character in Windows systems (CTRL-D in Unix or Linux systems). In this test run, the program reported a problem with the file because XYZ is not a number. The exception's stack trace contains more information on where and why the input failed. With file redirection, we can run example files through the program to test our grammar:

```
C:\projects\wcj3> java LogParser < log1.txt

C:\projects\wcj3> java LogParser < badlog1.txt
Error: This is not a valid file.
```

Once you are confident that a grammar specification is correct, you can then expand the Java part of the grammar specification to further process the data. In the next section, we will build on this parser program to convert the log files into XML documents.

Resources

A detailed treatment of parsing and compiler theory is beyond the scope of this discussion. See the classic compiler book by Alfred V. Aho, Ravi Sethi, and Jeffrey D. Ullman: *Compilers: Principles, Techniques, and Tools.* Addison-Wesley, 1986.

See this book's website at http://wickedcooljava.com for links to the JavaCC page and example grammar specifications.

To XML and Beyond: Converting Other Grammars into XML

DOM4J

JavaCC

To process structured text that has an unusual format, we must write a parser for its grammar. This is what we did in the previous section, when we wrote a grammar specification in JavaCC for an arbitrary file format. Working with a non-XML grammar is much more difficult than processing XML, and being able to convert the data to an XML format is useful because the data can then be processed by one of the many XML parsers available. Once you've tested a grammar that you've written, you can expand the parser to extract and process your data. You could then have the parser create XML as an output. You wouldn't want to modify the Java source code that was generated by JavaCC, because that would make it harder to modify the grammar later. Instead, you would add the logic for creating XML into the .jj file and then regenerate the parser.

Every JavaCC production rule has a Java code block. This is the first section of curly braces, and it is where you add logic to execute when the production rule triggers during parsing. Recall the dateTime production rule from the previous example:

```
void dateTime():
{}
{ <NUM> <SPC> <NUM> <SPC> <NUM> <SPC> <NUM> }  /* NOT XML!!! */
```

So far, we do not have any Java code in our productions. Let's add some Java logic to the dateTime production. The second part of the production, also in curly braces, is the production block. It contains the rules for building a syntax tree based on the grammar. In this part of the grammar, the parser is looking for four numbers separated by spaces. As the parser grabs each token from the input text, you can also include Java logic to retrieve and process values from the tokens captured from the input:

```
void dateTime():
{
    /* This is the Java block. This code executes whenever the
       production rule is triggered. We need placeholders
       for any data that we wish to later retrieve from tokens.
     */
    Token year=null, month=null, day=null, time=null;
    System.out.println("Processing the date and time:");
}
{
    /* This is the production rule block.
       Retrieve the year, month, day, and time into Token variables
       and print them to System.out
       (Remember that these angle brackets describe tokens, not XML)
     */
    year=<NUM> <SPC>
        { System.out.println(" The year is " + year); }
    month=<NUM> <SPC>
        { System.out.println(" The month is " + month); }
    day=<NUM> <SPC>
        { System.out.println(" The day is " + day); }
    time=<NUM>
        { System.out.println(" The time is " + time); }
}
```

Notice that inside the production block we can run Java code after each token is captured. It's not terribly difficult to modify this program to generate an XML document, instead of simply printing out the values retrieved from the tokens. Let's expand our parser to convert the data from the log file into an XML format. We can use the DOM4J API, as described earlier in this chapter, to make the process of creating XML as simple as possible. We'll put the data into an XML file with the following structure:

```
<log>
  <entry>
    <year>2005</year><month>01</month><day>01</day><time>1000</time>
    <purpose>meeting</purpose>
    <comment>Jones, John Paul</comment>
  </entry>
  <exit>
    <year>2005</year><month>01</month><day>01</day><time>1105</time>
    <comment>Jones, John Paul</comment>
  </exit>
  <alarm>
    <year>2005</year><month>01</month><day>01</day><time>1105</time>
    <type>fire</type>
    <comment>This was a drill</comment>
  </alarm>
</log>
```

Rewriting the Rules

Let's modify the `.jj` file to generate an XML file from the input text. The JavaCC compiler creates static methods for each of the production rules; therefore, any class variables that we use within the productions need to be defined as static. First we create a static DOM4J `Document` variable and an `Element` variable for the root element (as a convenience). We will use another `Element` variable, called `current`, as a reference to the current element and change this reference as we move through the production rules. First we define the `LogParser` class and its `main` method:

```
PARSER_BEGIN(LogParser)
import org.dom4j.DocumentHelper;
import org.dom4j.Document;
import org.dom4j.Element;
import java.io.FileWriter;
import java.io.IOException;

public class LogParser {
    // create a new XML document with <log> as the root element
    static Document doc = DocumentHelper.createDocument();
    static Element root = doc.addElement("log");
    static Element current = root;

    public static void main(String[] args) {
      try {
        // parse the input file
        LogParser parser = new LogParser(System.in);
        // and construct the XML output document as we parse
```

```
      parser.allLines();
      // write the XML document to a file
      FileWriter file = new FileWriter("log.xml");
      doc.write(file);
      file.close();
    } catch (ParseException pe) {
      System.err.println("Syntax error in log file input");
    } catch (IOException ioe) {
      System.err.println("Unable to write the XML file");
    }
  }
}
PARSER_END(LogParser)
```

The rest of the .jj file contains the tokens and production rules of the grammar. In each production, we now add some code that populates the XML document. TOKEN, allLines, anyLine, and lineOfText all remain the same as before, but remember not to get confused between XML tags and the < and > used with token names. They are different animals!

```
TOKEN:
{
    < ENTRY: "entry" >
  | < EXIT: "exit" >
  | < ALARM: "alarm" >
  | < NUM: (["0"-"9"])+ >
  | < CRLF: (["\r","\n"])+ >
  | < WORD: (["a"-"z", "A"-"Z", ",", "0"-"9", "-"])+ >
  | < SPC: ([" ", "\t"])+ >
}

void allLines():
{}
{ (anyLine())*  }

void anyLine():
{}
{ lineOfText() (<CRLF> | <EOF>) }

void lineOfText():
{}
{ entryLine() | exitLine() | alarmLine() }
```

In the entryLine production, we create a new "entry" element and hang it onto the root. We set the current element to be the one that we just created, because we will need to add subelements to it in other production rules. The dateTime production runs first, which will add subelements (relative to the new current element) for the year, month, day, and time. We'll take a look at that in a moment. The purpose token is a single word that represents the purpose from the entry line in the input file. There is a small block of Java code that adds a "purpose" subelement and adds the token's String value as the element's text. Everything on the input line after the purpose is considered a comment and is handled by the restOfLine production:

```
void entryLine():
{
  Token purpose = null;
  current = root.addElement("entry");
}
{ /* ENTRY, WORD, and SPC are token names, not XML tags! */
  <ENTRY> <SPC> dateTime() <SPC>
  purpose=<WORD>
      { current.addElement("purpose").setText(purpose.toString()); }
  <SPC> restOfLine()
}
```

The exitLine and alarmLine productions work very similarly to entryLine. The main difference between them is the use of different element names:

```
void exitLine():
{
  current = root.addElement("exit");
}
{  /* EXIT and SPC are token names, not XML tags! */
  <EXIT> <SPC> dateTime() <SPC> restOfLine()
}

void alarmLine():
{
  Token alarmType = null;
  current = root.addElement("alarm");
}
{  /* ALARM, SPC and WORD are token names, not XML tags! */
  <ALARM> <SPC> dateTime() <SPC>
  alarmType=<WORD>
      { current.addElement("type").setText(alarmType.toString()); }
  <SPC> restOfLine()
}
```

The only two productions left to write are dateTime and restOfLine. The dateTime production works by adding year, month, day, and time tags to the parent element stored in the current variable. If we are currently parsing an alarm line, for example, the current element was previously set to the new alarm element created within the higher-level alarmLine production. The values for the text in these tags come from the corresponding input tokens. In the restOfLine production, we capture each token left in this line of text, which will be either a word or spaces, and append that token's text to a new comment element.

```
void dateTime():
{ Token year=null, month=null, day=null, time=null; }
{ /* NUM and SPC are token names, not XML tags! */
  year=<NUM> <SPC> month=<NUM> <SPC> day=<NUM> <SPC> time=<NUM>
  {
    current.addElement("year").setText(year.toString());
    current.addElement("month").setText(month.toString());
    current.addElement("day").setText(day.toString());
    current.addElement("time").setText(time.toString());
  }
}

void restOfLine():
{
  Token word = null;
  current = current.addElement("comment");
}
{
  (  /* WORD and SPC are token names, not XML tags! */
     word=<WORD> { current.addText(word.toString()); }
|    word=<SPC>  { current.addText(word.toString()); }
  )*
}
```

If you use a process like this to generate XML, you'll need to be careful that the variables you are using to create your XML are assigned and used within the correct production rules and in the right order within the hierarchy of the grammar.

Once we have something in XML, we can parse the data and move or transform it into other XML documents (or HTML) much more easily than we could with the original non-XML grammar. The tag names and even the hierarchy can be changed through XSL transformations. The process that we used in this section is helpful for converting legacy data into XML for further processing.

Scraping the Sun: Screen Scraping HTML Pages for Data

Although you won't see any fingernail marks on my computer monitor, I have been doing some *screen scraping*. This is a colloquial name for extracting data from HTML pages, named for the fact that HTML is designed for displaying on browser screens rather than processing by other programs. Ideally, all the data on the Web would also be available in XML, with excellent documentation, and published as a web service with complete metadata. Of course, that's not going to happen very soon, so our programs may occasionally have to read data directly from an HTML document. This is not as trivial as it may sound, for several reasons.

- Websites often change the layout of their pages (the HTML structure).
- Websites often change the location or URL of the data.

- The HTML may not be in a sensible structure or even well-formed.
- The data may be in a format, such as an image, that the program cannot use.

If I haven't convinced you to give up this quixotic pursuit, let's begin by reading the contents of an HTML document into memory and extracting some data from it.

Because we have no guarantee that the HTML will be well-formed (browsers are more tolerant than XML parsers), it doesn't even make sense to try to read the document as a tree. Please tell all your friends to use XHTML for their web pages! It is still possible to do some parsing of ill-formed HTML documents using SAX. You could write a simple parser that looks for certain text keywords or tag combinations to look for the data. One problem with using SAX in this way is that the characters method may be called more than once, and your ContentHandler would need to take this into account when matching text.

Because HTML documents are structured for presentation, rather than as a data hierarchy, most extraction processes are probably better done via String regex. Before I get out my scraper code, I'll often strip any tags out of a document and replace them with whitespace. You can do this with a SAX ContentHandler, as we discussed earlier in this chapter. There can be some difficulty in getting this to work for reading HTML files, due to *extended ASCII* characters in the document that are invalid in the default *Unicode* character encoding of *UTF-8*. You can preprocess the stream and ignore any unusual characters (like the author!) before the parser gets them.

As we discussed in Chapter 2, Java has regular expressions that are an extremely useful way of extracting text from a String. We did some of this when we extracted URLs from a text document and when we used the Scanner class to find data within some text. We'll use the Scanner class here too, as a simple illustration of how you might extract data from a document. Take the following web page (Figure 3-3) as an example.

Wikipedia is a free online encyclopedia where the entries are created by a community process. The entry for the Sun (that's our star, the one that Earth revolves around, not Sun, the creator of Java) has some useful data that an application may want to extract. Unfortunately, it's embedded in the text and in HTML tables, and the document also has some characters that violate the normal Unicode character encoding. After stripping out all the tags and normalizing the whitespace into single spaces, we would end up with a portion of the document that looks something like this:

```
Sun Observation data Mean distance from Earth 149.6 ×10 6 km
(92.95×10 6 mi ) Visual brightness (V) ?26.8 m Absolute magnitude
4.8 m Orbital characteristics Mean distance from Milky Way centre
~2.5×10 17 km (26,000  light-years ) Galactic  period ~2.26×10 8 a
Velocity ~217 km/ s Physical characteristics Diameter 1.392 ×10 6
km (109 Earths ) Oblateness ~9×10 -6 Surface area 6.09 × 10 12
km² (11,900 Earths) Volume 1.41 × 10 18 km³ (1,300,000 Earths)
Mass 1.9891 × 10 30 kg (332,950 Earths) Density 1.408 g/cm³ Surface
gravity 273.95 m s -2 (27.9  g ) Escape velocity from the surface
```

```
617.54 km/s Surface temperature 5780 K Temperature of corona 5 M K
Approximate core temperature 13.6×10 6 K
```

This data was originally within a table, but we are in luck here, because the names are right next to the corresponding values. With the java.util.Scanner, you can write your own custom parsing process to extract the data, such as this code that displays the surface temperature of the Sun:

```
XMLReader reader = XMLReaderFactory.createXMLReader();
// the TagStripper ContentHandler removes any tags from the input
// and places it into a buffer
// TagStripper code is on http://wickedcooljava.com
TagStripper strip = new TagStripper();
reader.setContentHandler(strip);
// read the URL into a string, through a utility method
// I am doing this to avoid character encoding issues in the HTML
String all = readFully("http://en.wikipedia.org/wiki/Sun");
StringReader strRdr = new StringReader(all);
InputSource src = new InputSource(strRdr);
reader.parse(src);
// scan the contents of the buffer
Scanner scanner = new Scanner(strip.getBuffer());
// find the first match of "Surface temperature"
scanner.findWithinHorizon("Surface temperature", 0);
String surfTemp = scanner.next();
String units = scanner.next();
System.out.println(surfTemp + " " + units);
```

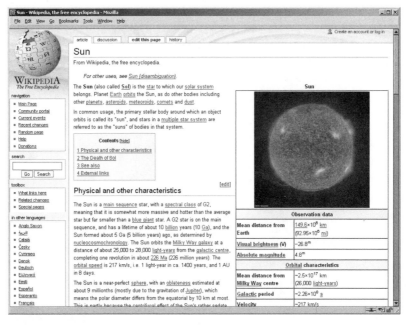

Figure 3-3: The Sun

As of the time of this writing, the program prints the value 5780 K. We are assuming a lot about the ordering, placement, and patterns in the text. This is a messy process, and the document can change at any time. Not that the Sun is going to suddenly gain a lot of additional mass or temperature, but the document structure could certainly change at any time, and screen scraper programs need to be flexible in how they extract data. It may be worthwhile to manually check the automated results. See this book's companion website for links to screen scraping utilities. In the next section, we discuss Lucene, a powerful open-source tool for indexing and searching text within many types of documents.

What's Lou Seen? Searching with Lucene

LUCENE

Most large websites have a search capability of some kind. You can add sophisticated search functions to your own applications, using a powerful API called Lucene. This is an open-source API from Apache's Jakarta project that can automatically index documents and process search queries. Besides keyword searches, Lucene can do *fuzzy searches* based on word similarity. It also handles logical connectives such as OR and AND within searches and is capable of handling many types of documents besides HTML. To index documents, you can use the IndexWriter class in the org.apache.lucene.index package. This example indexes the contents of a single file and programmatically creates another document for indexing. Lucene uses the documents to create an index directory:

```
import java.io.BufferedReader;
import java.io.FileInputStream;
import java.io.InputStreamReader;
import java.io.Reader;
import org.apache.lucene.analysis.standard.StandardAnalyzer;
import org.apache.lucene.document.Document;
import org.apache.lucene.document.Field;
import org.apache.lucene.index.IndexWriter;

StandardAnalyzer analyzer = new StandardAnalyzer();
IndexWriter writer = new IndexWriter("index", analyzer, true);

// create a Lucene document
Document doc = new Document();
// read a file into the document object
FileInputStream is = new FileInputStream("c:/wcj/sample.txt");
Reader reader = new BufferedReader(new InputStreamReader(is));
doc.add(Field.Text("contents", reader));
doc.add(Field.Text("name", "sample.txt file"));
writer.addDocument(doc);

// create a document programmatically
Document doc2 = new Document();
doc2.add(Field.Text("contents", "This is some more data to index"));
```

```
doc2.add(Field.Text("name", "some data"));
writer.addDocument(doc2);
writer.optimize();
writer.close();
```

Here we go again: yet another type of Document object! This time, it's a Lucene document, representing some content to be indexed. Lucene uses the StandardAnalyzer class to look at the document and decide what to include in the index. The IndexWriter creates the actual index entries. Because we told it to use the name "index," the IndexWriter will create a directory called index in which to store its files. You can place any type of data into the index, as we did with the second document in the previous example.

Let's look at the searching side of Lucene. Here's some code that searches through the index for either of two keywords:

```
Searcher searcher = new IndexSearcher("index");
Analyzer analyzer = new StandardAnalyzer();
String searchText = "word or data";
Query query = QueryParser.parse(searchText, "contents", analyzer);
Hits hits = searcher.search(query);
for (int i = 0; i < hits.length(); i++) {
    Document doc = hits.doc(i);
    System.out.println(doc.get("name"));
}
searcher.close();
```

In this case, we searched through the contents field of the index for *word* or *data*. If you would like to search through multiple fields, there is a QueryParser subclass that can do this, called MultiFieldQueryParser. The Lucene distribution comes with a sample web application that demonstrates more of what Lucene can do. There is much more to Lucene, and its indexing and searching capabilities can work with more than documents. You can populate the index with data from any source and create multiple searchable fields similar to what we did above with the contents and name fields. For more information on Lucene's advanced features and a link to download the required library files, see this book's website.

Chapter Summary

In this chapter, we've looked at ways of processing XML, HTML, and other structured text. It's particularly important to be able to work with XML, because it is used by so many different kinds of applications and APIs. Many of the projects explored in the rest of this book use XML for configuration files and data exchange formats. Knowing how to extract data and manipulate XML documents is an essential part of working with these APIs. In the next chapter, we will discuss the development of next-generation web applications built on semantic relationships between logical entities: a web of concepts.

4

CRAWLING THE SEMANTIC WEB

In this chapter, we examine techniques for extracting and processing data in the World Wide Web and the Semantic Web. The World Wide Web completely changed the way that people access information. Before the Web existed, finding obscure pieces of information meant taking a trip to the library, along with hours or perhaps days of research. In extreme cases, it meant calling or writing a letter to an expert and waiting for a reply. Today not only are there websites on every imaginable topic, but there are search engines, encyclopedias, dictionaries, maps, news, electronic books, and an incredible array of other data available online. Using search engines, we can find information on any topic within a few seconds. The Google search engine has even become so well known that it is now often used as a verb: "I Googled a solution." Online information is growing exponentially, and because of it we have a completely new problem on our hands that is not solved by simply using keyword searches to find our data. The problem is infoglut. Keyword searches return too many documents, and most of those documents don't have the information that we want.

Suppose that we wanted to search for a Java class library that converts data from one format to another. With all the open-source projects out there, someone may have already solved the problem for us, and we'd rather not reinvent the wheel. In theory, we should be able to search for matching projects that meet our needs. But running a query on related keywords may give us many results that are not related to what we really want. In an ideal world, we should be able to ask the computer a question: "Is there an open-source Java API that converts between FORMAT1 and FORMAT2?" The computer should then search the Web and give us the name of a suitable API if it exists, along with a short description of the standard and links to more detailed information. For this to happen, information about a hypothetical "J-convert-1-2" API would need to be encoded in such a way that the computer can find it easily without performing a keyword search and extracting data from the text results.

Information on the World Wide Web is mostly free-form text contained in HTML pages and is mostly not organized into categories and structures that search programs can easily query. At the very least, all web content ought to have subject indicators similar to the Library of Congress and Dewey Decimal codes for books. This is not yet the case, although it will most likely happen soon. Several new standards are rapidly leading us in that direction. So far, all of these standards rely on web content developers adding special tags to their data, and few developers know about these standards at the present time. In short, it's a mess out there, and we're trudging through this messy data looking for nuggets of gold.

The *Semantic Web* is the next-generation web of concepts linked to other concepts, rather than a collection of hypertext documents linked by keywords. If you think about it, an HTML anchor tag (link) is a keyword reference to another document. It supplies a word or phrase that links to another document, usually displayed as underlined text on a browser. But the link doesn't exactly say *how* the two documents are related to each other. HTML hyperlinks don't give any real indication about relationships between files, and the text in the link may be extremely vague. A new standard, the *Resource Description Framework (RDF)*, makes it possible to be much more specific about how things are related to each other. In fact, RDF describes much more than documents—any entities or concepts can be linked together. This is the basic idea behind the Semantic Web—that concepts, rather than documents, can be linked together.

As Java developers, how can we participate in building the Semantic Web? First, you'll need to know something about official standards such as RDF. You will then need to tag your documents appropriately. Many sites are already starting to do some of this by creating *RDF Site Summary (RSS)* feeds. An RSS feed syndicates the content from a website so that it can be combined with information from other sites and delivered to the users as *aggregated content*. RSS makes a small portion of a site available as a summary, similar to what you see in an article or news abstract. However, RSS enabling is only the first step in moving toward a Semantic Web. In this chapter we'll discuss enough to get you started working with RDF, and we'll introduce some APIs that help in producing or consuming content.

This *Somethings* That: A Short Introduction to N3 and Jena

JENA The theory behind the RDF standard is actually quite simple. Everything has a Uniform Resource Identifier (URI), and by this I mean *everything*: not only documents but also generic concepts and relationships between them. Even though you are not a document (or are you?), there could be a URI assigned to represent you as an entity. This URI can then be used to make connections to other things. For the "you" URI, these connections might represent related organizations, addresses, and phone numbers. URIs do not have to return an actual document! This is what sometimes confuses developers when they see a URI referenced somewhere and find that there is nothing at the location. These addresses are often used as markers or unique identifiers to represent concepts. We make links between URIs to represent relationships between things. This functions much like a simple sentence in English:

```
Programmers enjoy Java.
```

To begin with, let's use a shorthand notation, called *N3*, to encode this as an RDF graph. N3 is an easy way to learn RDF because the syntax is only slightly more complex than the sentence above! In essence, N3 is merely a set of *triples*, or "subject predicate object" relationships. Here is the N3 version of the sentence:

```
@prefix wcj: <http://example.org/wcjava/uri/> .
wcj:programmers wcj:enjoy wcj:java .
```

We first define a prefix to make the N3 code less verbose. The prefix is used as the beginning part of a URI wherever it is found in the document, so that `wcj:java` then becomes `http://example.org/wcjava/uri/java` (the value is also placed within < and > markers—these have nothing to do with XML). The three items together are called a *triple*, and the verb is usually called a *predicate*. RDF makes a link by stating that a *subject URI* is related by a *predicate URI* to an *object URI*. The predicate represents some relationship between the subject and object—it tells *how* things link together. This is very different than an anchor in HTML, because here a relationship type is clearly defined. Remember that URIs in RDF could be anything: concepts, documents, or even (in some cases) `String` literals. In theoretical terms, we are creating a labeled directed graph of the relationship. A graph representation of the above might look like Figure 4-1.

Figure 4-1: RDF subject, predicate, and object

As you might expect, there is a Java API for creating and managing RDF and N3 documents. *Jena* is an open-source API for working with RDF graphs. Here is one way to create the graph in Jena and serialize it to an N3 document:

```
import com.hp.hpl.jena.rdf.model.*;
import java.io.FileOutputStream;

Model model = ModelFactory.createDefaultModel();
Resource programmers =
    model.createResource("http://example.org/wcjava/uri/programmers");
Property enjoy =
    model.createProperty("http://example.org/wcjava/uri/enjoy");
Resource java =
    model.createResource("http://example.org/wcjava/uri/java");
model.add(programmers, enjoy, java);
FileOutputStream outStream = new FileOutputStream("out.n3");
model.write(outStream, "N3");
outStream.close();
```

Here, Jena is using the term *property* to refer to the predicate and *resource* to refer to something used as a subject or object. The model's write method also has options to write out the document in other formats besides N3. With the Jena API, you can connect many entities together into very large *semantic networks*. Let's make some additional relationships using the entities and relationships that we just created. We will produce the graph shown in Figure 4-2.

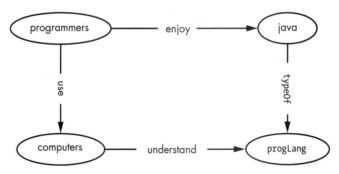

Figure 4-2: An RDF graph with multiple subjects

Here is the additional code to produce the network in Figure 4-2:

```
Property typeOf =
    model.createProperty("http://example.org/wcjava/typeOf");
Property use =
    model.createProperty("http://example.org/wcjava/use");
Property understand =
    model.createProperty("http://example.org/wcjava/understand");
```

```
Resource computers =
    model.createResource("http://example.org/wcjava/computers");
Resource progLang =
    model.createResource("http://example.org/wcjava/progLang");
model.add(java, typeOf, progLang);
model.add(programmers, use, computers);
model.add(computers, understand, progLang);
model.write(new java.io.FileOutputStream("out2.n3"), "N3");
```

The N3 output of this code is the following:

```
<http://example.org/wcjava/uri/java>
        <http://example.org/wcjava/typeOf>
                <http://example.org/wcjava/progLang> .

<http://example.org/wcjava/computers>
        <http://example.org/wcjava/understand>
                <http://example.org/wcjava/progLang> .

<http://example.org/wcjava/uri/programmers>
        <http://example.org/wcjava/uri/enjoy>
                <http://example.org/wcjava/uri/java> ;
        <http://example.org/wcjava/use>
                <http://example.org/wcjava/computers> .
```

The semicolon in the N3 document is a shortcut that indicates we are going to attach another property to the same subject ("programmers enjoy java, and programmers use computers"). The meanings of elements within a document are often defined in terms of a predefined set of resources and properties called a *vocabulary*. Your RDF data can be combined with other data in existing vocabularies to allow semantic searches and analysis of complex RDF graphs. In the next section, we illustrate how to build upon existing RDF vocabularies to build your own vocabulary.

Triple the Fun: Creating an RDF Vocabulary for Your Organization

An RDF graph creates a web of concepts. It makes assertions about logical relationships between entities. RDF was meant to fit into a dynamic knowledge representation system rather than a static database structure. Once you have information in RDF, it can be linked with graphs made elsewhere, and software can use this to make *inferences*. If you define how your own items are related in terms of higher-level concepts, your data can fit into a much larger web of concepts. This is the basis of the Semantic Web.

Every organization has relationships between information that is held in a data store such as a database or flat file (or human memory!). If your data is in a relational database, your data items probably have relationships between them that are hidden or implied within the database structure itself.

Your data may not be completely accessible, because there are relationships that an application cannot query. As an example, suppose that we have a relational database containing employees and departments within a company. A common approach is to create an Employee table, with columns for employee information such as ID number, date of birth, name, hire date, supervisor name, and department. There are many relationships hidden within the table and column names, and it is up to an application to know these relationships and take advantage of them. Column names alone would not give you the following information:

- A and B are employees.
- An employee is a person.
- A supervisor is an employee who directs another employee.
- C is a company.
- A company is an organization.
- A and B work for C.

Column and table names in a database are simply local identifiers and don't automatically map to any concepts that might be defined elsewhere. But this is domain knowledge that could be used more effectively by the application if it were defined in an extensible and machine-readable way. Having such information available would give our applications more flexibility, and this knowledge could also be reused elsewhere. How can we encode this information so that applications can make use of these relationships? And how can our application relate this to other information that we might find on the Semantic Web?

It may not make sense to put this metadata in your database, but you can create an RDF mapping outside the database schema that describes each item relative to the Semantic Web as a whole. We can represent some of these concepts using existing vocabularies. The rest of them we can define in our own terms. If you don't know where to connect a concept to an existing vocabulary, you can always define a URI for that concept now and make the connection to other systems later. At least you can use it to share data within your own organization if your vocabulary is well documented and the meaning of each item is clear. There are many basic vocabularies that RDF applications can use, and new ones are constantly being created (like yours!). The online resources page for this section has an updated listing of some existing vocabularies that you can use in defining your data.

The first step is to define a URI for each concept that is even remotely related to your application. This is much like the object-oriented development process, but these entities may also be things that are not directly used by the application. By defining your terms within a larger context, you can later map these entities to existing concepts on the Web. Let's try it with our employee example, by first listing some related concepts and their meanings (in English text). Here is a simplistic attempt to define some terms:

- http://example.org/wcjava/employee = an employee
- http://example.org/wcjava/person = a person

- http://example.org/wcjava/organization = an organization
- http://example.org/wcjava/employer = an organization that employs an employee

The important point is to make sure that each concept has a unique identifier. Make sure that the URIs will still be around a few years from now; you are building a complete concept space around these identifiers! If you have control over your domain name, it might be wise to have a policy that forbids anyone placing actual content under URIs beginning with some prefix (such as http://yourdomain/uri). We are using these names as globally unique identifiers, not as URLs for retrieving documents. There is nothing wrong with a document being there, but it could lead to confusion between the concept and the document. In this example, we are using the example.org domain, which is reserved solely for illustrative purposes within documentation. If you want to define a permanent URI, there are sites that will let you define your own permanent URI independent of future domain name ownership changes. (For more information on this, see this book's companion website.) The best known of these is http://purl.org.

After you have identified some concept URIs, it's time to define relationships between them. In the previous section, we showed how to do this in Jena using our own relationships. Now let's use some predefined relationships created by others and apply them to our entities. Adding another entity that was defined elsewhere is easy: just add its URI to the graph we are building. But if we want to do anything useful with these entities, we will also need to import the statements that define its related properties and resources. In our example, we will use the subClassOf property defined in the RDF schema, which works similarly to a subclass relationship in object-oriented programming. The graph in Figure 4-3 shows the relationships between our resources.

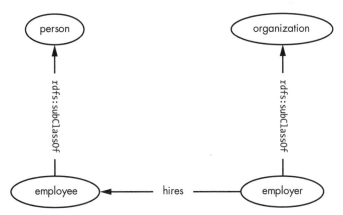

Figure 4-3: Using the subClassOf property from RDF schema

At first, you should do this mapping with pen and paper (archaic, but always accessible) or using an RDF visualization tool. This book's website has a list of some free tools that can be used for this purpose. When you have finished, you will have a graph of the relationships between entities in your system. Once you've created a hierarchy and vocabulary, you can create

N3 or RDF/XML files that you can use as metadata. Most RDF visualization tools will do this for you automatically. You'll want to familiarize yourself with some of the existing RDF vocabularies on which you can base your own hierarchy. Our resources page has links to some of these and examples of using them. Once you have designed a hierarchy, you can create and manipulate it from Jena. The next section shows how to do this.

Who's a What? Using RDF Hierarchies in Jena

Earlier we created a hierarchy of terms to use for our metadata. We used the word *vocabulary* to refer to this collection of terms, but it is often called an *ontology* if it defines relationships between the terms. According to the Wikipedia definition, an ontology (in the computer science sense) is a "data structure containing all the relevant entities and their relationships and rules (theorems, regulations) within a domain."

In Jena, there are built-in helper classes for working with commonly used ontologies. The RDF schema is one of these. Jena has a helper class called RDFS, which has a static variable for the subClassOf property. You can create the graph in the previous section by using this code:

```
Model model = ModelFactory.createDefaultModel();
model.setNsPrefix("wcj", "http://example.org/wcjava/");
Resource employee = model.createResource("wcj:employee");
Resource person = model.createResource("wcj:person");
Resource employer = model.createResource("wcj:employer");
Resource organization = model.createResource("wcj:organization");
Property hires = model.createProperty("wcj:hires");
model.add(employer, hires, employee);
model.add(employer, RDFS.subClassOf, organization);
model.add(employee, RDFS.subClassOf, person);
model.write(new FileWriter("ourEntities.rdf"), "RDF/XML");
```

The second line sets a namespace prefix for our graph, which makes the code easier to read because we can describe the URIs in a simpler way. There is nothing special about the choice of "wcj" as our prefix. It could have been any String of letters, but whichever value is used becomes the prefix that is sent to the output file. The RDF/XML output type is the XML representation of our RDF graph. Most applications will exchange RDF graphs using the XML format rather than N3. As you can see, Jena's RDF model can work with either type.

Once you have an RDF vocabulary defined for your data, you will want to put it onto a website so that applications can use it. You can use your new vocabulary to semantically tag any components within applications. For the database example above, you might create a new table to hold metadata linking each column and table name to their RDF types. It could be as simple as an entry for each table/column name and the corresponding URI from your RDF vocabulary that describes its meaning. You might use this for automatically generating documentation or in analyzing and reusing application code. Using RDF for this type of metadata is a convenient way to tag the data without changing anything in the existing data structures. For our Java classes, we could also add code annotations or JavaDoc tags to semantically mark up our code to facilitate its reuse.

There are some well-known standard RDF vocabularies that you can use to build your own vocabulary. The first one to consider using is a vocabulary extension to RDF, created by the W3C, called the *OWL Web Ontology Language*. It includes vocabulary along with formal semantics that you can use in your own definitions. OWL builds on the framework created by the RDF and RDF schema vocabularies. Although we used the RDF schema's subClassOf property, OWL has a much more comprehensive version that adds formal semantics such as property restrictions and set operations. Jena has an OWL helper class with static variables for each of the OWL resources and properties. Another common RDF standard is the *Dublin Core (DC)*, an element set for describing metadata about information resources of any kind. It defines generic properties such as title, creator, type, format, language, and rights. The type property uses values from the *Type Vocabulary*, part of the Dublin Core. Some examples of types are collection, dataset, interactive resource, and software. In Jena, there is a DC class with static Property variables for each of the Dublin Core properties. You can add a type property to an item within a model by using:

```
model.add(myDatabaseResource, DC.type, DCTypes.Dataset);
```

This marks the resource myDatabaseResource as being a type of Dataset. Combining with RDF schema or OWL, you can create your own hierarchy of terms using these as a baseline. For example, you might create terms for "JDBC-accessible database," "relational database table," and "relational database column" that are RDF subclasses of Dataset. You could then define unique URIs for specific instances of these and make statements about them in RDF: "MySQL instance #743234 at OurOrganization contains data about employees, stored in the table named Employee." Having such metadata available can make managing IT resources much easier.

Eventually there will probably be a standard upper-level ontology for all information technology terms. Many groups are working to create standard vocabularies for various domains. One effort, the *Suggested Upper Merged Ontology (SUMO)*, aims to develop an upper-level hierarchy for all abstract concepts. Future applications that use ontologies based on this may be able to make high-level inferences using data from entirely different domains. There are some domain-specific hierarchies that are also based on SUMO. In this section's resource page, there is an updated list of some existing vocabularies that you can use. In the next section, we attach an RDF document as metadata for an HTML document.

Getting Attached: Attaching Dublin Core to HTML Documents

One of our original reasons for exploring RDF (besides it being cool!) was because of the limited linking capability of HTML. We'd like web browsers to still be able to display our HTML and web content, yet also have metadata available for processing by search engines and automated knowledge discovery systems. Given that most websites are probably still going to be using HTML for many more years, has RDF solved our link metadata problem yet? In some ways it has. There are several ways of marking up HTML documents with Dublin Core or other RDF metadata. The method I'll be using here is the method suggested by the Dublin Core, and it also embeds the metadata without affecting the browser's view of the data and without breaking the XHTML validation.

The browser may or may not know how to do anything with our RDF data, but we are assuming that other programs may be able to process it. We will need to embed the metadata so that it doesn't interfere with the browser's understanding or rendering of the HTML. We can do this by using link and meta tags in our HTML. Any programs that read this data should have a way to discover which technique we are using. Rather than let programs make assumptions (which could be wrong), we place a marker as an attribute of the head tag of the HTML, telling any programs how to retrieve this metadata:

```
<head profile="http://dublincore.org/documents/dcq-html/">
```

The profile URI means that there is metadata in the HTML document and that it should be interpreted in the manner associated with the given profile. Any software processing this document will also need to know the schemas for RDF prefixes used in the metadata. We do this by placing link tags in the head section:

```
<link rel="schema.DC" href="http://purl.org/dc/elements/1.1/" />
<link rel="schema.DCTERMS" href="http://purl.org/dc/terms/" />
```

You can now add the actual Dublin Core properties to meta tags in the head section. It's the same as using RDF triples, but the implicit subject of each triple is the current HTML document. Here is an example showing how to attach title and subject metadata to a document:

```
<meta name="DC.title" xml:lang="en"
      content="The World is Full of RDF" />
<meta name="DC.subject" content="earth" />
```

See this book's website for more information on HTML metadata and the Dublin Core.

What's the Reason? Making Queries with Jena RDQL

JENA You've built the perfect ontology for your organization's knowledge base. You've encoded it in RDF based on standard vocabularies, so you can exchange data with other applications. And now you have a large amount of data encoded using this vocabulary. "But what can I do with all this data?" you think to yourself. "It's not like I can just use a query language like SQL!" Well, actually, you can—not specifically with the SQL language but with a similar structured language designed for querying knowledge bases. In this section, we'll use an RDF query language to retrieve information from an existing knowledge base.

Because RDF data is not organized into tables, columns, and rows like a relational database, SQL won't work for querying RDF graphs. Instead, we need to search within a graph to find subgraphs that match some pattern of RDF nodes (subject, predicate, and object). For instance, you might ask a knowledge base whether a particular employee is a supervisor. In this case, you know the subject, predicate, and object that you are looking for. You can directly ask whether the given structure exists in the RDF. However, most often you won't know every part of the target structure, such as when you want a list of supervisors having a salary less than $100,000. Because we don't know the URI of each item, we will have to use variables to represent the unknown items in the query. In this type of query, we are asking: "Show me all X where X is a supervisor, and X has salary Y, and Y < 100000." The response will list all the possible values for X that would match the desired properties. Jena's built-in query language is called *RDF Data Query Language (RDQL)*. An RDQL query has several parts:

- What values the query should return
- The RDF sources to query
- The query predicates
- Optional namespace prefixes

RDQL will let us declare the RDF source (where the data is coming from) directly within the query String, but that is very inefficient for multiple queries against the same source. It's usually better to run the query from an RDF model already in memory. Let's run a query on the Suggested Upper Merged Ontology (SUMO), a very high-level ontology created by the IEEE. SUMO has standard names for high-level abstractions such as Process, Organization, and GeopoliticalArea. These are not Java classes; they are classes in the mathematical sense: a set whose members share one or more properties in common. We'll look at Organization and find all of its direct subclasses, using the RDQL query:

```
SELECT ?x
WHERE (?x <rdfs:subClassOf> <sumo:Organization>)
USING rdfs FOR <http://www.w3.org/2000/01/rdf-schema#>
      sumo FOR <http://reliant.teknowledge.com/DAML/SUMO.owl#>
```

The ?x in this query is a variable representing something that we want the query to locate. The query engine will try to substitute a value for ?x wherever it finds a subclass of Organism. Remember that all entities in RDF are URIs. The rdfs and sumo prefixes make the URIs in the query much shorter and less awkward. To run the query in Jena, we first load the SUMO ontology into memory. Then we run the query using the static exec method of Jena's Query class and process the results. The following code performs this query:

```
Model sumo = ModelFactory.createOntologyModel();
String sumoURL = "http://reliant.teknowledge.com/DAML/SUMO.owl";
sumo.read(sumoURL);
sumo.setNsPrefix("sumo", sumoURL + "#");
String rdq = "SELECT ?x " +
    "WHERE (?x <rdfs:subClassOf> <sumo:Organization>) " +
    "USING rdfs FOR <http://www.w3.org/2000/01/rdf-schema#> " +
        "sumo FOR <" + sumoURL + "#>";
QueryResults results = Query.exec(rdq, sumo);
RDFVisitor aVisitor = new SysoutVisitor();
while (results.hasNext())
{
    ResultBindingImpl binding = (ResultBindingImpl) results.next();
    RDFNode node = (RDFNode) binding.get("x");
    node.visitWith(aVisitor);
}
```

This matches the known subclasses of the Organization entity in SUMO. To visit each node and display its URI, you'll need to write a visitor, using Jena's RDFVisitor interface. My SysoutVisitor class prints out the URI of each node that it visits. You can do more interesting things with a visitor besides just printing a node's value, such as visiting nodes connected to it by a particular property. Here is the code for SysoutVisitor:

```
public class SysoutVisitor implements RDFVisitor {
    public Object visitBlank(Resource r, AnonId id) {
        System.out.println("anon: " + id);
        return null;
    }

    public Object visitURI(Resource r, String uri) {
        System.out.println("uri: " + uri);
        return null;
    }

    public Object visitLiteral(Literal l) {
        System.out.println(l);
        return null;
    }
}
```

There is a feature of the Visitor pattern that lets a visitor return a value, but we are not using that feature here. To make the program do something else instead of print each node's value, all you need to do is plug in a different visitor. The previous query matches the following nodes:

```
http://reliant.teknowledge.com/DAML/SUMO.owl#Corporation
http://reliant.teknowledge.com/DAML/SUMO.owl#PoliticalOrganization
http://reliant.teknowledge.com/DAML/SUMO.owl#EducationalOrganization
http://reliant.teknowledge.com/DAML/SUMO.owl#JudicialOrganization
http://reliant.teknowledge.com/DAML/SUMO.owl#ReligiousOrganization
http://reliant.teknowledge.com/DAML/SUMO.owl#GovernmentOrganization
http://reliant.teknowledge.com/DAML/SUMO.owl#Organization
http://reliant.teknowledge.com/DAML/SUMO.owl#MercantileOrganization
http://reliant.teknowledge.com/DAML/SUMO.owl#Manufacturer
http://reliant.teknowledge.com/DAML/SUMO.owl#Government
http://reliant.teknowledge.com/DAML/SUMO.owl#PoliceOrganization
http://reliant.teknowledge.com/DAML/SUMO.owl#MilitaryOrganization
http://reliant.teknowledge.com/DAML/SUMO.owl#MilitaryForce
http://reliant.teknowledge.com/DAML/SUMO.owl#ParamilitaryOrganization
```

Jena can also make rule-based inferences. You can create a knowledge base, combine it with SUMO facts, and query the model while applying matching rules. See the documentation and tutorial links on the resource page for more details. The W3C recently created its own query language called SPARQL, which works very similarly to Jena's. See this book's website for updated information on this and other query languages.

Simply Logical: Lojban, RDF, and the Jorne Project

Lojban (www.lojban.org) is an artificial spoken and written language based on the concepts of predicate logic. While it was designed to be used by human beings, it has a parseable grammar and structured semantics that make it ideal for processing by computers. Lojban defines words based on predefined predicate root words called *gismu*. Each root word has a specific structure associated with it, containing one to five slots that can be filled with nouns (Lojban calls these items *sumti*). For example, the Lojban predicate "bevri" means the act or process of carrying something, and it functions much like a verb. Within its structure are also contained five other related concepts: carrier, cargo, delivery-destination, delivery-source, and delivery-path. While in English and most other languages these may be separate words, in Lojban they are references to positions within the bevri structure.

There are over 1,300 root gismu in the Lojban vocabulary, and these structures form a very interesting ontology of their own. Each of them has between one and five slots. Most of the gismu don't have five slots like bevri does. In fact, there are only a few gismu with five parameters. Table 4-1 shows the number of gismu of each *arity*, or parameter count, and the total number of slots as of this writing.

Table 4-1: Gismu Count, by Arity

Gismu Arity	Gismu Count	Total Slots
1	73	73
2	555	1110
3	535	1605
4	171	684
5	18	90
Total		**3562**

The slots in the root predicates give us 3,500+ base concepts. These can be combined in many different ways by using compound words and logical connectives, but for our purposes here we are looking at the root words only as base concepts. Perhaps you are now wondering, "So what does all this have to do with the Semantic Web?" In an earlier section, we discussed some existing ontologies with built-in relationships that we might use to describe our own entities. Lojban has a convenient set of base concepts that could be used in creating an ontology.

Lojban fits in very well with RDF, which also maps verbs as predicates, although RDF uses graphs of "subject verb object" predicates, and Lojban uses a slot-based approach. There is some mapping required in order to integrate the two, and although it can be done, no standard RDF ontology exists for Lojban—yet. In January 2005, I created an open-source project called Jorne to define standards for combining Lojban with the Semantic Web. Once these standards are complete, the project will release Java software to convert Lojban text to and from RDF triples. One of the goals of this project is for a human to be able to write Lojban text and have the computer automatically convert it into RDF statements for running queries against knowledge bases.

Published ontologies such as SUMO are great for mapping terms from one vocabulary to another, such as in creating dictionaries. The Jorne project is working to map Lojban terms onto well-known vocabularies, so that Lojban documents can share a common semantic space with RDF documents. When the Jorne project completes its first standards, the Jorne project page (www.jorne.org) will hold the latest RDF files along with some sample documents. For creating terms in your own vocabularies, you may want to build upon the SUMO vocabulary, since it is already linked to many others. In Chapter 5, we will discuss a dictionary standard based on English word senses, called *WordNet*, and a Java API for working with it. WordNet has also been mapped to RDF and SUMO. See this book's website for more information on these and other ontologies.

Guess What? Publishing RSS Newsfeeds with Informa

RDF Site Summary (RSS) is a standard for summarizing content on a web server. An RSS feed is stored in an XML file, and it might include items such as recent news, changes to a website, or new *blog* entries. A client program called an *aggregator* collects RSS feeds from multiple web servers and displays them in summary form, sorted by category. The user then chooses to view the full content of any summaries that are of interest. The summary has metadata, such as its subject, encoded along with a text summary. Over time I expect that document metadata will have much more than the Dublin Core and other terms that RSS currently uses. In theory, you could plug into other ontologies such as SUMO, and the meaning of an entire article could be encoded using RDF. This is possible only if you are using an ontology that is expressive enough. This is certainly a lot of effort, but the long-term advantage is that machines would have access to the fully encoded semantics of the text. This probably won't happen for a while, but adding metadata such as RSS descriptions is a good start in that direction and has an immediate benefit of giving us more accurate categorization of content.

There are several standards named RSS, all of them XML-based and used for similar purposes. Unfortunately the different standards not only have different XML structures but even use different definitions for the RSS acronym. Most aggregators are able to understand all RSS flavors, though. The version we discuss here, RDF Site Summary 1.0, uses RDF and is most closely related to the semantic work we've done so far in this chapter. However, it's still better to use *something* rather than encoding no metadata at all. There are ways to map between the semantics of each standard, although all of them are not equally expressive. One common practice is to use XSL-T stylesheets to transform between the different forms of RSS.

Because RSS 1.0 is built on RDF and XML, there are several ways of creating feeds: a DOM parser, an RDF API, or an RSS-specific API. DOM is more low-level than is necessary for creating RDF. Jena has RSS support through its RSS class, which has static objects that represent RSS properties you can use in building an RSS-compatible RDF graph. But if you're going to be working a lot with RSS, you'll want to use an RSS-specific API that can understand the different RSS versions that are commonly used.

Informa is an open-source API for reading and writing RSS in Java. One of its most powerful features is the ability to persist the feed metadata in a database. Informa can also read data from external feeds (as described in a later section), perform text-filtering tasks, and update RSS content on a periodic schedule. Let's use it to create a feed using the basic in-memory builder—the ChannelBuilder class from the de.nava.informa.impl.basic package. In RSS terminology, a *channel* is another name for metadata about some content (such as a website) and is the main entity in a newsfeed. Each RSS file defines a channel and items belonging to the channel. Rather than work with the XML directly, which can be somewhat tedious, we'll use a ChannelBuilder to create the RSS file.

```
ChannelBuilder builder = new ChannelBuilder();
ChannelIF myChannel = builder.createChannel("Latest Bug Fixes");
// This is the URL for which we are describing the metadata
URL channelURL = new URL("http://example.org/wcj/bugs.rss");
myChannel.setLocation(channelURL);
myChannel.setDescription("The latest news on our bug fixes");

// We create a first item
String title = "Annoying Bug #25443 Now Fixed";
String desc = "A major bug in OurGreatApplication is fixed. " +
  "Bug #25443, which has been annoying users ever since 3.0, " +
  "was due to a rogue null pointer.";
URL url = new URL("http://example.org/wcj/bugfix25443.html");
ItemIF anItem =
  builder.createItem(myChannel, title, desc, url);
anItem.setCreator("Ecks Amples");

// We create a second item
title = "Bug #12121 not Fixed in 7.1";
desc = "Bug #12121 will not be fixed in OurGreatApplication " +
  "release 7.1, so that developers can focus on adding " +
  "the WickedCool feature.";
url = new URL("http://example.org/wcj/bugfix12121.html");
anItem = builder.createItem(myChannel, title, desc, url);
anItem.setCreator("Dee Veloper");

// export the document to disk, in RSS 1.0 format
ChannelExporterIF exporter = new RSS_1_0_Exporter("bugs.rss");
exporter.write(myChannel);
```

You can place the XML-encoded RSS feed anywhere on your site. The main page of your site should include a link to the feed. For automated discovery by RSS crawlers such as Syndic8, you can do this with a link tag in the page's head section:

```
<link rel="alternate" type="application/rss+xml"
title="Bugs" href="http://your-site/bugs.rss" />
```

You'll also want a hypertext link for human visitors, so they can add your site to their aggregator. If you are going to be creating large feeds that change often or working with many feeds simultaneously, use the *Hibernate*-based version of the builder, which will persist the RSS metadata in a database. Hibernate is an API for mapping Java objects to relational database structures and automatically translating data between them. See the Informa documentation, and this section's resource page, for more information. In the next section, we'll see how to read newsfeeds with Informa.

What's Up? Aggregating RSS Newsfeeds

INFORMA

JAVA 5+

In the previous section, we used the Informa library to create RSS content, so that visitors with content aggregators can be automatically informed about updates to your site. Another great use of RSS within your site is displaying recent news related to your industry. You can get these newsfeeds from many sources, such as news sites, websites in your industry, and aggregator sites like Syndic8. Make sure to check whether the sites you are syndicating will allow you to incorporate items from their feeds into your site. Usually this is the case, but not always.

Let's start by reading items from a newsfeed and displaying them as text. Using Informa, reading an RSS feed is easy. You can populate the same ChannelBuilder object that we used in the previous section with data from an existing RSS feed. The FeedParser class has a parse method that returns a ChannelIF instance containing the channel data from the RSS feed. The RSS standards may be in a state of confusion, but the Informa API reads all of them and gives us a common object model for working with them.

```java
import de.nava.informa.impl.basic.Channel;
import de.nava.informa.impl.basic.ChannelBuilder;
import de.nava.informa.impl.basic.Item;
import de.nava.informa.parsers.FeedParser;

ChannelBuilder builder = new ChannelBuilder();
String url = "http://wickedcooljava.com/updates.rss";
Channel channel = (Channel) FeedParser.parse(builder, url);
System.out.println("Description: " + channel.getDescription());
System.out.println("Title: " + channel.getTitle());
System.out.println("===================================");
// using Java 5 syntax in this for loop
for (Object x : channel.getItems())
{
    Item anItem = (Item) x;
    System.out.print(anItem.getTitle() + " - ");
    System.out.println(anItem.getDescription());
}
```

This will print some basic information about the channel and its items. If you want to include these in a web page, it's now just a matter of wrapping HTML tags around the text. If you are including RSS files that are outside your control, you may want to filter data from the channels before displaying them. We'll discuss this in a later section.

Heading to the Polls: Polling RSS Feeds with Informa

INFORMA

We just showed how Informa can retrieve data from an RSS channel, using the ChannelBuilder class. Ideally, updating your copy of the feed should be an automated process, and Informa can also do this. The Poller class (located in the de.nava.informa.utils.poller package) can periodically poll a Channel object's RSS feed and trigger some action whenever there are changes. By default, this polling occurs every 60 minutes but can be configured to use longer or shorter periods. The Poller class works by notifying an observer object whenever something changes in the feed. To use this process, you must first create a class implementing the PollerObserverIF interface. This interface has methods for poll tracking, error handling, and feed change notification.

Let's look at an example of a PollerObserverIF that uses the newItem method, which the Poller calls whenever the feed has a new item. However, the new item will not be added to the copy in your Channel object unless the observer explicitly adds it. Here is a PollerObserverIF implementation that does not add feed changes to the Channel object but instead prints a notification message to the console:

```
public class AnObserver
implements de.nava.informa.utils.poller.PollerObserverIF
{
   public void itemFound(ItemIF item, ChannelIF channel) {
      System.out.println("New item found");
      channel.addItem(item);
   }

   public void pollStarted(ChannelIF channel) {
      System.out.println(
         "Started poll with " + channel.getItems().size() +
         " items in channel");
   }
      public void pollFinished(ChannelIF channel) {
      System.out.println(
         "Finished poll with " + channel.getItems().size() +
         " items in channel");
   }
      public void channelChanged(ChannelIF channel) {}
   public void channelErrored(ChannelIF channel, Exception e) {}
}
```

This observer will print information about the beginning and end of each polling event, list any new items in the feed, and add new items to the object model. Warning: An observer does not add new items to the Channel object unless you explicitly call the addItem method. If you have more than one observer attached, one of them should be assigned the task of adding the new item to the Channel. With real RSS feeds, you'll want to set a polling frequency that doesn't clog the network or the site with unnecessary traffic. A polling period of 60 minutes (the default) or longer should be frequent enough for most sites. The following code fragment uses the observer that we just defined and polls the RSS feed for a previously loaded Channel object every 60 minutes.

```
Poller poller = new Poller();
poller.addObserver(new AnObserver());
poller.registerChannel(channel);
```

To use a three-hour interval instead of the default, you can call:

```
poller.registerChannel(channel, 3 * 60 * 60 * 1000);
```

Make sure to remember that the polling interval is specified in milli-seconds! If you are going to filter items from the feed, the observers should not be doing the filtering. There is a separate component that can approve polled changes prior to observer notification. This keeps the observers focused on their task of propagating changes rather than filtering data. The process is more scalable that way, as you may want many observers to receive approved changes. This filtering and approval process is described in the next section.

All the News Fit to Print: Filtering RSS Feeds with Informa

INFORMA   In the previous section, we polled an RSS feed and wrote some code that automatically updates our copy of the Channel object whenever the feed changes. Our PollerObserverIF implementation added the item to a Channel object. You may think that the observer would be a good candidate for doing some filtering of the feed content, such as deciding whether to add new items to our copy. This could work, but since there can be more than one observer connected to a Poller, it's better to have a separate object do the filtering. By doing this, we won't need to duplicate any filtering functions, and all the observers can benefit equally from the filtering process.

Informa implements filters through an approval process. You can add one or more approvers to a Poller. The observers will see a new item only if all of the approvers accept it. The approval must be a unanimous vote or the change will remain invisible to the observers (that is, the observers' newItem method is not called). To add an approver, implement the PollerApproverIF interface and pass it to the Poller's addApprover method. By making fine-grained approvers, you can use them in a plug-and-play manner. For example, you could have a NoBadWordsApprover that checks for the existence of words that you don't want to appear on your website or to be added to the Channel. In a similar way, a RelevancyApprover class could check for keywords that are relevant to your intended usage of the feed.

Approvers check properties within each item, such as the category list and subject, to determine whether an item should be approved. Poller-ApproverIF has only a single method, as indicated in this example that checks the title and the description of each item using regular expressions (as discussed in Chapter 2). Here is the approver class:

```
public class RelevancyApprover
implements PollerApproverIF {
```

```
public boolean canAddItem(ItemIF item, ChannelIF channel) {
    String title = item.getTitle();
    String description = item.getSubject();
    if (title.matches(".*Java.*") || description.matches(".*Java.*"))
    {
      return true;
    } else  {
      return false;
    }
  }

}
```

As you might guess, this approver accepts only items that have "Java" some-where in the title or description. The next code fragment adds this approver to a `Poller`. The approver should be added before the observer, and the observer added before registering the channel:

```
Poller poller = new Poller();
poller.addApprover(new RelevancyApprover());
poller.addObserver(new AnObserver());
poller.registerChannel(channel);
```

There is another class similar to the `Poller`, the `Cleaner`, that can per-iodically remove unwanted items in a channel. It uses a similar process: `CleanerObserverIF` observers are added to a `Cleaner`, and `CleanerMatcherIF` instances decide what should be removed. Perhaps these interfaces should be called "JuryMember" and "Executioner," because that is a very good meta-phor for what they do! You might use the `Cleaner` to remove items that are older than a few days or meet some other criteria for removal. For both the `PollerApproverIF` and `CleanerMatcherIF` decision making, you might want to integrate Lucene text matching, as described in Chapter 3. This would give much more sophisticated text-matching abilities, such as similarity ("fuzzy") matches.

Chapter Summary

The techniques of semantic tagging that we've described in this chapter are quickly becoming popular in large published data sets, and in the next few years the Semantic Web will see an exponential growth. The latest news and website updates, along with what your colleagues are *blogging*, are already being gathered automatically by RSS aggregators and organized by category. In business-to-business transactions, common high-level ontologies are beginning to connect domains with completely different terminology in ways that were impossible before. For example, within highly specific scientific disciplines, new discoveries often use domain-specific terms to describe their findings. This information could lead to breakthroughs in other disciplines, if it were only translated into the appropriate terminology.

Structured newsfeeds are already bringing current news and other information to anyone with an aggregator and a network connection. Using more detailed semantic markup (with SUMO or other high-level ontologies), information could be made even more accessible to everyone—even if the original document uses obscure terminology or a foreign language. We will soon see new types of aggregators and intelligent agents that make logical inferences based on the news and perhaps act on our behalf. Organizations that are properly prepared for this will be able to use the Semantic Web much more effectively. One way to start preparing now is by identifying each type of data with a URI, adding a machine-readable RDF type description (for example, that the item is a person, hardware, software, or some other entity), and using standard ontologies where possible. Jena, Informa, and the ontologies discussed in this chapter are some tools that can help you with this process. In the next chapter, we discuss intelligent software agents and explore some of the scientific and mathematical APIs for Java.

5

SCIENTIFIC AND MATHEMATICAL APPLICATIONS

Amazingly, in some scientific communities, the Fortran programming language still rules supreme (I know, it makes me cringe too). The reason is not because Fortran is necessarily a fantastic programming language. Rather, it is the large set of built-in mathematical operations that come with the Fortran core libraries and the large base of existing programs using these APIs. Java has been around for a decade, runs on many more platforms, has some core APIs that Fortran doesn't, and does some things that are not even possible in standard Fortran. So why isn't Java more popular for writing math and science applications? There is a perception that there are no good Java mathematical libraries. The java.lang.Math class is very limited in its scope, but since it is in the core, some developers of scientific software may not want to be bothered with searching for additional libraries. Perhaps many developers think "what you see is what you get." The picture is slowly changing, as new APIs come onto the scene and more high-profile projects use Java. But Java is more than its core APIs, and there are many open-source projects that do some incredible things. In this chapter, we discuss some of the scientific and mathematical libraries that are available for Java. Among the topics we'll be exploring in this chapter are functors, truth tables, graph theory, physical quantities, neural networks, genetic algorithms, and intelligent agents.

Fun-Tors: Creating and Applying Functors

JGA

JAVA 5+

According to the Merriam-Webster Online Dictionary, a *functor* is "something that performs a function or an operation." From a programming point of view, a functor is a function that can be passed as a parameter and manipulated like other values. Many languages, such as C, have *function pointers* that hold the actual memory address of a function. In these languages, you can pass a function to another function and then apply it to different arguments. You can use this to apply a function to each member of a collection or create pluggable composite functions. Languages such as Scheme, Lisp, and Haskell use a purely functional programming style, which is very powerful for some types of applications (particularly in artificial intelligence). Java doesn't have either Lisp-style or C-style functions, but we can implement the same behavior using interfaces and base classes. There are several implementations of functor APIs for Java, and you can find references to some of these on this book's website.

Generic Algorithms for Java is a flexible open-source implementation of function objects. There are classes for zero-, one-, and two-argument functors:

Generator   A zero-argument functor

UnaryFunctor   A one-argument functor

BinaryFunctor   A two-argument functor

These functors are designed to work closely with the generics in Java 5 (as discussed in Chapter 1). Generator is actually defined as Generator<R>. It has a method called gen that takes no arguments and returns an object of a type R that is defined when you construct the Generator. To create a zero-arity functor that returns Double objects, you can do the following:

```
import net.sf.jga.fn.Generator;
public class CubeGenerator extends Generator<Double> {
    double current = 0;
    public Double gen() {
        current = current + 1;
        return current * current * current;
    }
}
```

Now you can see why it's called a Generator. This one generates cubes of the positive integers. Besides letting you create your own generators, JGA has some built-in generators for creating random, constant, or constructed values. The values returned by a Generator do not have to be numeric.

The single-arity functor class is UnaryFunctor<T,R>. It has an fn method with a parameter of type T and that returns an R. We can create a predicate by creating a functor that returns a Boolean. Let's make a UnaryFunctor<Number, Boolean> that returns true for all even numbers:

```
public class EvenNumber extends UnaryFunctor<Number,Boolean> {
   public Boolean fn(Number x) {
      return (x.longValue() % 2) == 0;
   }
}
```

So far it may seem to be a lot of extra work for no reason. But the advantage is that we can now write methods that take arbitrary functors as parameters. The following code shows how this can be done:

```
public void removeMatches(List<Number> aList,
                          UnaryFunctor<Number,Boolean> functor) {
   for (Number num : aList) {
      if (functor.fn(num)) {
         aList.remove(num);
      }
   }
}
```

The method removes any items in the list for which a Number-to-Boolean functor returns true. Consider two alternative ways of writing code to remove the even numbers from a list:

```
List<Number> numbers = ....   // populate the list somehow
// the first way
for (Number aNumber : numbers) {
   if (aNumber.longValue() % 2 == 0) {
      numbers.remove(aNumber);
   }
}
// the second way
removeMatches(numbers, new EvenNumber());
```

Having a removeMatches method is a very useful part of a general-purpose library. This allows us to successively apply different UnaryFunctor<Number, Boolean> operations to the list:

```
removeMatches(numbers, lessThan30000);
removeMatches(numbers, greaterThan10000000);
```

You can do the equivalent of this through the Iterables utility class that works with the Java 5 for loop. On the JGA site there is a more detailed tutorial on filtered iteration. Here is a short example using a for loop that iterates through only the even numbers in a List:

```
UnaryFunctor<Number,Boolean> even = new EvenNumber();
List<Number> numbers = ....; // populate the list somehow
for (Number aNumber : Iterables.filter(numbers, even)) {
   System.out.println(aNumber);
}
```

The Algorithms class has implementations of some common algorithms that use functors. The next example uses two of these methods: transform applies a unary functor to each element in a list, and removeAll removes all elements that match a predicate:

```
import net.sf.jga.util.Algorithms;
List<String> aList = ....;    // populate me
// remove all nulls
UnaryFunctor<Object,Boolean> isNull =
  new UnaryFunctor<Object,Boolean>() {
    public Boolean fn(Object o) { return o == null; }
};
Algorithms.removeAll(aList, isNull);
// trim Strings
UnaryFunctor<String,String> trimmer =
    new UnaryFunctor<String,String>() {
      public String fn(String s) {
          return s.trim();
      }
};
Algorithms.transform(aList, trimmer);
```

If you don't want to modify the list itself, you can create an iterator that iterates over the original values and returns the transformed value for each item or ignores nulls. Functional programming techniques are a very useful tool in the Java programmer's bag of tricks. In the next section we'll use some more advanced features of the API.

Funkier Functors: Using Composite Functors

In the previous section, we used functors to filter the input to a for loop, thereby removing any need for filtering code in our processing loop. JGA has utilities for creating composite functors, and they are automatically built into every unary and binary functor. A UnaryFunctor has a compose method that returns a new functor that is a composition of an inner functor. When you

see the `compose` method, think about the word *of*: `f.compose(g)` is like saying
"f of g." In other words, you can create a functor h from two existing functors
f and g, such that h=f(g(x)), with the following code:

```
UnaryFunctor<Object,Object> f,g;
UnaryFunctor<Object,Object> h = f.compose(g);    // h = f of g
```

When you call the `fn` method of h, it will use the composite function on
its parameter. A `BinaryFunctor` has similar `compose` methods for combining it
with other unary and binary functors. You can create a chain of processors in
this way, as many as you would like. You can also send the output of a `Generator`
through a composed function by using the `Generate` class. Now let's use this
process to create a complex `Generator`. This one will generate a series of logarithms of the square of every 30th integer starting at 99. We can start with a
`Generator` for every 30th integer and build our other functionality on top of it:

```
Generator<Number> every30thFrom99 = new Generator<Number>() {
    long count = 99;
    public Number gen() {
        long result = count;
        count += 30;
        return result;
    }
};
UnaryFunctor<Number,Number> log =
    new UnaryFunctor<Number,Number>() {
        public Number fn(Number in) {
            double val = in.doubleValue();
            return Math.log(val);
        }
};
UnaryFunctor<Number,Number> square =
    new UnaryFunctor<Number,Number>() {
        public Number fn(Number in) {
            double val = in.doubleValue() ;
            return val * val;
        }
};
Generate<Number,Number> logOfSquareOfEvery30thFrom99 =
    new Generate(log.compose(square), every30thFrom99);
```

Function chaining is not limited to numeric processes. Composite
functions can work with objects of any type (for example, `String`, `Employee`,
`Automobile`, `WebRowSet`). You can see now why it is important to create low-level
functors, so that you can combine and reuse them within other contexts.
Before you build a new functor, see if there is a way to accomplish the same
thing by combining existing ones. At the current time (late 2005), the API
is still in a beta development status and may be subject to change. See the
documentation for more information (links are on this book's website).

High-Caliber Bits: Using Colt's BitVector

What do math, pistols, horses, and alcohol have to do with one another? Colt! In addition to a gun manufacturer, a malt liquor, and a young male horse, Colt is also the name of a scientific and mathematical API. It was created by the same place where the Web started—the CERN particle-physics laboratory in Switzerland. CERN's website describes Colt as "efficient and usable data structures and algorithms for Off-line and On-line Data Analysis, Linear Algebra, Multi-dimensional arrays, Statistics, Histogramming, Monte Carlo Simulation, Parallel & Concurrent Programming."

In this section, we'll take a look at one of the Colt utility classes, BitVector. We'll model a digital logic function by creating a functor (as discussed earlier) that works with BitVector values. This is different than the boolean predicates that we discussed before, because we will be modeling a function with multiple input and output bits. A logic function takes an ordered set of bits as the input and produces another ordered set of bits as the output. The Java core provides a BitSet class for working with collections of bits. While it can be useful to some applications, it has disadvantages when used to model logic functions. First, it does not have a fixed size associated with it. For example, modeling a function with 5 bits of input and 3 bits of output requires separate values to keep track of the input and output vector sizes. Second, a BitSet does not have methods for mapping subsets of its bits to and from integer values. The BitVector class from the Colt API is more flexible and well suited to modeling truth functions. Let's start with a basic BitVector example to show some of its capability:

```
BitVector vec1000 = new BitVector(1000);   // size = 1000 bits
// initially the bits are all set to 0 (false)
vec1000.set(378);                          // set bit 378 to 1 (true)
System.out.println(vec1000.get(378));      // prints "true"
vec1000.replaceFromToWith(1, 40, true);    // sets bits 1-40 to true
// get the bits from 38 to 50 (inclusive)
BitVector portion = vec1000.partFromTo(38, 50);
// get the long value of bits 3 to 10 of the portion BitVector
long longValue = portion.getLongFromTo(3, 10);
```

We can use these methods to simulate hardware logic gates, which are the basic components that make up a computer. Some low-level examples of these are the AND, OR, and NOT gates. We can model a generic logic gate by using BitVector instances as the input and output of a functor. Although Colt has its own general-purpose functors, I'll use the API from the previous sections to avoid confusion. A BitVector functor for an AND gate might look like this:

```
public class UnaryBitVectorAndFunction
extends UnaryFunctor<BitVector,BitVector> {
    public BitVector fn(BitVector in) {
        int oneBits = in.cardinality();    // how many bits are 1
        int size = in.size();              // the vector size
        BitVector outVec = new BitVector(1); // a one-bit output
        outVec.put(0, size == oneBits);    // AND = all ones
```

```
        return outVec;
    }
}
```

Using this process in combination with a functor API allows you to create any type of Boolean function. Let's do another example, this time with more than one output bit. A 1-of-4 decoder (*demultiplexer*) is a logic component with three inputs and four outputs. It sends an input data signal (D) to one of four outputs (Q0, Q1, Q2, Q3), based on a 2-bit selector code (S0, S1). Table 5-1 shows the output bits resulting from each combination of inputs to the decoder. This type of table is called a *truth table*.

Table 5-1: Two-Bit Demultiplexer Truth Table

D	S1	S0	Q0	Q1	Q2	Q3
0	0	0	0	0	0	0
0	0	1	0	0	0	0
0	1	0	0	0	0	0
0	1	1	0	0	0	0
1	0	0	1	0	0	0
1	0	1	0	1	0	0
1	1	0	0	0	1	0
1	1	1	0	0	0	1

The first three columns represent the inputs, and the others are the output values. The selector bits S0 and S1 decide which output gets the current value of D, and all other outputs receive the default value of 0. Let's create a model of this circuit. In the model discussed here, we reference the inputs by their index within the input BitVector. For the inputs, I am assuming that bit 0 is D, bit 1 is S0, and bit 2 is S1. The UnaryFunctor below creates a 4-bit BitVector containing the output values:

```
public class QuadDemuxer
extends UnaryFunctor<BitVector,BitVector> {
    public BitVector fn(BitVector in) {
        // a 4-bit output vector, defaults to all 0
        BitVector outVec = new BitVector(4);
        // get the input data
        boolean data = in.get(0);
        if (data) {
            // get the selector bits as an int
            int selector = (int) in.getLongFromTo(1,2);
            outVec.set(selector);
        }
        return outVec;
    }
}
```

In the next section, we'll extend this process to create a generic truth table implementation of a logic function.

The Truth Is in There: Creating Truth Tables from a BitMatrix

In the previous section, we created a demultiplexer, a specific type of Boolean function that has several input and output bits. To explain how it works, we used a truth table to show the corresponding output for every possible combination of input bits. A truth table works like a lookup table for binary inputs. You may have noticed that it looks a lot like a matrix of bits. We can use this observation to write a generic truth-table model. In this section we'll create a generic truth table using the Colt API's BitMatrix, a 2D cousin of the BitVector.

The input combinations are listed in binary ascending order: 000,001,010, 011.... Because the ordering of input bits in a truth matrix always follows the same pattern regardless of the input size, this part of the table is redundant. We can work with just the output part of the matrix. The number of rows and columns is directly related to the number of input and output bits of the function. In the example from the last section, a three-input/four-output function, there were four columns and eight rows. The number of columns is the same as the number of output bits. The number of rows for n input bits is 2^n, because we need to account for every possible combination of inputs. Obviously, a single truth table will not work for a large number of input bits. But complex systems can be created by wiring together many simpler components, so this is not a real limitation.

As long as you remember how you've ordered the input bits, you can convert them into an integer value and use that as an index to the row containing the output bits. We can demonstrate by making a BitMatrix for the truth table shown in Table 5-1:

```
int inputSize = 3;
int rows = 1L << inputSize;    // 2**n rows, for n bits in the input
int outputSize = 4;
int columns = outputSize;
// this is the truth table matrix: all bits default to 0
BitMatrix matrix = new BitMatrix(columns, rows);
// set output mappings for the demultiplexer example
matrix.put(0, 4, true);        // column 0, row 4 = true (1)
matrix.put(1, 5, true);
matrix.put(2, 6, true);
matrix.put(3, 7, true);

// get the output bits for an input value of 101 (5)
boolean Q0 = matrix.get(0, 5);    // column 0, row 5
boolean Q1 = matrix.get(1, 5);    // column 1, row 5
boolean Q2 = matrix.get(2, 5);    // column 2, row 5
boolean Q3 = matrix.get(3, 5);    // column 3, row 5
```

To look up an input/output mapping in the truth table, convert the input bits into an integer value and use it as an index to the row that contains the output bits. You can read each output bit individually as a boolean or convert it into an int or long to use all the bits at once. This truth table was easy to create because it had only a few 1 bits. You will probably want to have a utility method that sets an input/output mapping in a single method call. The following methods implement generic storage and retrieval for a truth table mapping:

```java
public void store(int inputVal, long out) {
    int start = inputVal * outSize;
    int end = start + outSize - 1;   // inclusive
    matrix.toBitVector().putLongFromTo(out, start, end);
}

public long retrieve(int inputVal) {
    int start = inputVal * outSize;
    int end = start + outSize - 1;   // inclusive
    long out = matrix.toBitVector().getLongFromTo(start, end);
    return out;
}
```

We could also write BitVector versions of these methods, using what we did in the last section. The above code works by accessing the internal backing bits (a BitVector) of the BitMatrix. (I've done this because the BitMatrix class does not have a convenient accessor for a complete row of bits.) Remember that the number of input bits should be kept small, because the size of the truth table grows exponentially. There is no check on the input value, and an invalid input value will cause an exception. Unused bits in the output value are ignored because of the way that the BitVector transfers bit values from a long. Keep in mind that the input and output values are processed with the least significant bit counted as the zeroth. We'll explore truth tables again later, when we create a connected network of processing components, each with its own truth table.

Two Terafurlongs per Fortnight: Using JScience Quantities

JScience is an open-source API for scientific and mathematical processing. One of its goals, and an extremely lofty one, is to create a common API for Java programming within all the sciences. One of its coolest features is a units framework for physical quantities (for example, mass, velocity, temperature, distance). In JScience, you can work with values of physical constants, such as the speed of light and Planck's constant, and not care about which units are used internally. Conversion between different units is extremely easy, and you can even define your own custom units. In this section, we show how to access the built-in constants, create your own units, and work with quantity classes.

In the United States, outside of scientific usage, most people are still using non-metric (non-SI) units such as Fahrenheit, feet, and pounds. This frequently causes a lot of confusion and even caused the loss of an unmanned spacecraft! Maybe we can't completely solve the problem of mismatched units, but at least in a Java program we can define quantities in such a way that we don't care about the units. In JScience, the basic physical quantities have their own classes and are all subclasses of the Quantity class. Here are some of these classes, along with their SI unit of measurement:

- Length, in meters
- Duration, in seconds
- Mass, in kilograms
- Temperature, in degrees Kelvin

The Quantity classes are in the org.jscience.physics.quantities package. A quantity says something about the property that you are measuring and is much more specific (with less potential for error) than just using a double to represent the numeric value. In any type of application that tracks a common physical quantity such as length, you can use one of the built-in JScience quantities. Each Quantity class has a system unit associated with it and can perform automatic type conversion. If you are writing an application to track computers, you might write a class that represents a particular configuration:

```java
public class ComputerConfig {
    double length, width, height;
    double mass;
    int ram, rom, network;
}
```

In this ComputerConfig class, the units are not part of the variable definitions, and the quantities themselves are not typesafe. Nothing in its definition prevents us from trying to do the following:

```java
length = mass;
```

There has been a lot of work done on unified theories of physics, but I don't think we're quite *that* far along! We can rewrite ComputerConfig so that it uses classes that represent real physical quantities:

```java
import org.jscience.physics.quantities.*;
public class ComputerConfig {
    Length length, width, height;
    Mass mass;
    DataAmount ram, rom;
    DataRate network;
}
```

Now the program knows that there are three length values, one mass, two data amounts, and one data rate. This has another advantage, too, because we can set and get the value with any units of a Quantity and still have the value stored internally as an SI unit. Let's use mass as an example, by setting a Mass variable as 20 pounds and then displaying it in kilograms:

```
Mass mass = (Mass) Quantity.valueOf(20, NonSI.POUND);
System.out.println(mass.toText(SI.KILOGRAM));
```

As you might expect, if you try to use a unit that is incompatible with the quantity, the toText method will throw an exception. You'll find the SI-based units in the SI class and many of the non-SI units in the NonSI class. For units that are not already part of JScience, you can create your own derived unit based on existing ones.

One of the more obscure English units is called a *furlong*, and it is equal to an eighth of a mile, or 220 yards. This is not one of the built-in units of JScience, but you can easily create a derived unit for it. This code creates the unit, along with a systemwide alias so that it can be used elsewhere in the application:

```
Unit furlong = NonSI.MILE.multiply(0.125);
furlong.alias("furlong");
furlong.label("furlong");
Quantity fiveFurlong = Quantity.valueOf("5 furlong");
```

Setting the alias for a unit allows us to use it for parsing quantities. The label is used when you display a quantity. Quantities and units can be multiplied and divided to create combined quantities such as acceleration ($m*s^{-2}$). In this next example, we derive a new velocity unit and use it to display the speed of light (c):

```
Velocity c = Constants.c;
// A fortnight is an old English unit of 14 days
Unit fortnight = NonSI.DAY.multiply(14);
fortnight.alias("fortnight");
fortnight.label("fortnight");
Unit furlongperfortnight = furlong.divide(fortnight);
System.out.println(c.toText(furlongperfortnight));
```

The new unit is a velocity unit, because it is defined as a length/duration. Running this program shows that the speed of light in a vacuum is 1,802,617,499,785.253 furlong/fortnight, or a little less than 2 Terafurlongs/fortnight.

Fractious Fractions: Arbitrary-Precision Arithmetic

JScience

Two times two is 3.9999999998, if you believe the results of some calculations using double values. Most Java developers have worked with the double and float data types. Perhaps you have also used some of the methods in the java.lang.Math class. This class is part of the Java core and includes methods for operations such as logarithms, exponents, and trigonometric functions. The precision of a double is sufficient for most needs, but for scientific and theoretical applications its 11-bit exponent and 52-bit mantissa (based on IEEE 754 double-precision floating point) can cause subtle errors that quickly grow into larger problems. This is particularly true when performing iterative calculations, where the output of one calculation is used as the input to the next.

To solve the problem of rounding errors in mathematical applications, Java includes two classes for arbitrary-precision math: BigDecimal and BigInteger. The BigInteger class is great for working with extremely large numbers. (Yes, I do realize that the name gives a hint of that!) The size of these numbers is limited only by available memory and processing speed. An integer such as 9^{700} is too large to represent in a double or long variable but fits very comfortably within a BigInteger. Similarly, the BigDecimal class can exactly represent numbers such as 0.012345678987654321234567890123456 that a 52-bit mantissa can't handle. The following short code sample uses the BigInteger and BigDecimal classes to represent these quantities:

```
BigInteger nine = new BigInteger("9");
BigInteger nineToSevenHundredth = nine.pow(700);
BigDecimal exactNumber =
    new BigDecimal("0.012345678987654321234567890123456");
```

The BigDecimal class can exactly represent any number that has a finite decimal expansion. This works for fractional numbers with multiples of 2 and 5 in the denominator, such as 1/2, 15/4, or 127/20, but not for numbers such as 1/3 (0.333333 . . .) or 5/7. This can cause cumulative rounding errors in more complex calculations. In fact, all of the BigDecimal methods for division require a scale parameter, describing the number of digits to the right of the decimal to keep in the result. Consider the following example, which calculates 1/3 to 15 decimal places (and rounding as necessary):

```
BigDecimal one = new BigDecimal("1");
BigDecimal three = new BigDecimal("3");
BigDecimal third = one.divide(three, 15, BigDecimal.ROUND_HALF_UP);
```

When performing arbitrary-precision division, it's best to maintain the numerator and denominator as separate values. Since there are no objects in the Java core for arbitrary-precision fractions, you may have thought about writing your own class. Many people have built something like the following:

```
public class HugeFraction
{
    private BigInteger numerator, denominator;

    // methods for operating on fractions
```

```
    public HugeFraction divide(HugeFraction other) {
        // calculate result
        return result;
    }
}
```

In the JScience API, there are several classes for doing arbitrary-precision calculations. The first is a `LargeInteger` class that is similar to the `BigInteger` class in the Java core. `LargeInteger` is optimized for speed and real-time performance and implements an `Operable` interface for use in number theory and matrix operations. It also has an XML format associated with it. A `Rational` class builds upon this to allow infinite-precision representations of a/b, where a and b are non-zero integers. The `Rational` class is immutable, and all its methods return the result rather than affect the original. It works as you would expect it to:

```
Rational oneThird = Rational.valueOf("1/3");
Rational nine87654321 = Rational.valueOf("987654321/1");
Rational msixteen = Rational.valueOf("-16/1");
Rational msixteenOver987654321 = msixteen.divide(nine87654321);
Rational aNumber = oneThird.multiply(msixteenOver987654321);
```

There won't be any rounding errors as long as you stay within the `Rational` domain (addition, subtraction, multiplication, division, and integer exponentiation). Another class that you'll want to know about is `Real`. (Yes, that's its real name.) It represents an arbitrary-precision real number that has a guaranteed uncertainty. The API also has a `Complex` class, but it's not arbitrary-precision because it uses `double` values for the real and imaginary parts. In the next section, we take a look at algebraic and polynomial functions.

Proudly Polynomial: Using Algebraic Functions in JScience

JScience

Earlier in this chapter we showed the benefit of being able to manipulate functions as objects and pass them as parameters to a method. In this section, we look at functions from a mathematical point of view. JScience, Colt, and JGA (discussed earlier) all have their own functor implementations, and each of them has certain advantages. The JGA implementation is great for general-purpose functional programming because of its simplicity and generality. Colt includes more built-in mathematical functors (see the `Functions` class) but doesn't provide arbitrary-precision calculations. In this section, we discuss JScience because it has a general algebraic and *polynomial* framework that can be used with anything that implements the `Operable` interface (such as `Real` and `Rational` or your own *ring* or *number* classes).

An `Operable` is anything that has multiplicative and additive operations and an inverse for each operation. The `Polynomial` class is "a mathematical expression involving a sum of powers in one or more variables multiplied by coefficients" (from the JScience documentation). You can create polynomials that work with any `Operable`. For this section's examples, we'll define a polynomial of `Rational` variables. We'll start with a constant polynomial. The `org.jscience.mathematics.functions.Constant` class is a subclass of `Polynomial` that represents a polynomial of degree 0. Create one using the `valueOf` method:

```
Constant sixty = Constant.valueOf(Rational.valueOf("60/1"));
```

Let's use this to create a polynomial of $(7/15)\ x^5 + 9xy + 60$. We need to first create each term and then multiply by the coefficient. Then we can add the terms together to create the final polynomial. This code creates a polynomial, assigns values to x and y, and prints the result:

```
Function.Variable x = Function.Variable.X;
Function.Variable y = Function.Variable.Y;
Polynomial xpoly = Polynomial.valueOf(Rational.ONE, x);
Polynomial ypoly = Polynomial.valueOf(Rational.ONE, y);
Rational nine = Rational.valueOf("9/1");
Rational sixty = Rational.valueOf("60/1");
Rational seven15ths = Rational.valueOf("7/15");

Polynomial seven15X5 =
    Polynomial.valueOf(seven15ths, Polynomial.Term.valueOf(x, 5));
Polynomial nineXY = (Polynomial)
    Constant.valueOf(nine).times(xpoly).times(ypoly);
Polynomial poly = (Polynomial)
    seven15X5.plus(nineXY).plus(Constant.valueOf(sixty));
Function.Variable.X.setValue(Rational.valueOf("5/7"));
Function.Variable.Y.setValue(Rational.ONE);
System.out.println(poly);
System.out.println(poly.evaluate());
```

The code prints the following result for ($x=5/7$, $y=1$):

```
[7/15]x5 + [9/1]xy + [60/1]
479110/7203
```

You can also take derivatives or integrals of a polynomial. JScience has many other powerful features. You can find links to JScience documentation at this book's companion website.

Connecting the Nots: Connecting Truth Tables Using Ports

In the early twentieth century, the philosopher Ludwig Wittgenstein wrote the book *Tractatus Logico-Philosophicus*, in which he outlined the concept of a *truth function*, a higher-level abstraction of a logical proposition. His truth functions work like our truth tables, but they connect statements consisting of other functions and have only a single `Boolean` output value. In our truth table implementation from the section "The Truth Is in There," we had a number of inputs and a number of outputs, and we didn't connect them to other functions. If you were building a digital logic simulator, you would want to connect many components together into a complex system. To build logical components and connect them together, we need to write code that connects each output to an input.

We can connect arbitrary objects into a graph by joining them with edges that work much like wires in a digital circuit. But we wouldn't want to connect each component with an edge leading directly to another component. Instead, we need to associate an output on one component with a specific input on another, which we can accomplish by connecting the graph's edges to ports on the components. You can think of the ports as being input or output pins on an IC chip. Connecting ports makes it easier to know which of a component's inputs and outputs are being connected to where. Let's use port-edge connections to build a Component class that can be combined into more complex systems. Figure 5-1 shows a block diagram of this component.

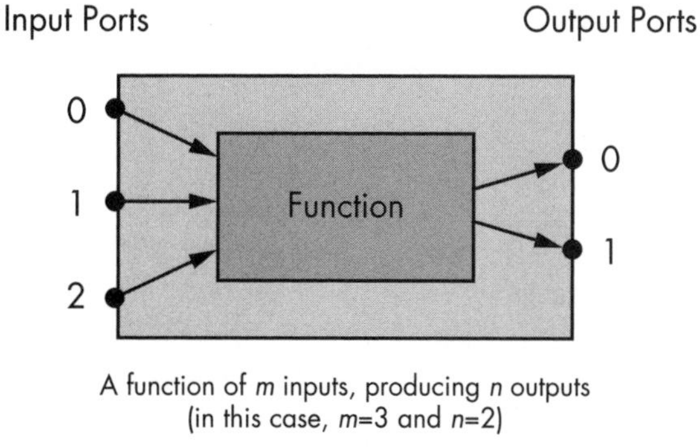

Input Ports   Output Ports

A function of *m* inputs, producing *n* outputs
(in this case, *m*=3 and *n*=2)

Figure 5-1: Generic processing component

Our Component class is a generalization of the "function with ports" idea that could be applied to any function with a set of inputs and outputs. We'll use this to write an expansion of the truth table store and retrieve methods we created earlier. We will add some input/output ports and accessor methods to the class. Since an input port can connect only to an output port, we first create a separate interface for each (and an implementation that can serve as either one):

```
public interface Port {
    public TruthComponent getParent();
}
public interface InputPort extends Port {
    public void setValue(Object value);
}
public interface OutputPort extends Port {
    public Object getValue();
}
public class PortImpl implements InputPort, OutputPort {
    private Component parent;
```

```
    private Object value;
    public PortImpl(Component parent) {
        this.parent = parent;
    }
    public Component getParent() { return parent; }
    public Object getValue() { return value; }
    public void setValue(Object value) { this.value = value; }
}
```

InputPort and OutputPort are the interfaces that are used externally to
a component. Sending data to an input port requires a method to set the
value, and reading from an output port needs a method to get the value.
A component has an input and output size and a Object[] -> Object[] function
to calculate the output values from the inputs. Component is designed as an
interface, to make it flexible enough for any application:

```
public interface Component {
    // get the number of input ports
    public int getInputSize();
    // get the number of output ports
    public int getOutputSize();
    // get an input port by its index
    public InputPort getInputPort(int index);
    // get an output port by its index
    public OutputPort getOutputPort(int index);
    // perform the component's function: outputs = f(inputs)
    public void process();
}
```

At this point, we have a very generic framework for connected components that have input and output ports. I've assumed that the component's
unary function will process an Object[] and return an Object[]. If you wish,
you can also make the process method flexible enough to send any single
Object value to the first output port and null to the rest. On the book's website
you'll find an implementation of the Component class that is enhanced to
support Java generics. An external process controls the components and
manages the connectivity between them, and we'll implement this later by
using a graph API. But before we do that, we need to turn this into a bit-
processing unit that uses a truth table.

We can write a UnaryFunctor that processes an array of objects as bits, by
applying some basic conversion rules. The function should be flexible enough
to interpret each Object in the array as a bit in some consistent way (Boolean,
nonzero, or non-null). (We'll assume for this example that an arrayToBits
method converts an array into bits.) The converted bits are sent through a
truth-table function to produce the output bits. The output bits are returned
as a Boolean[] so the component can send the results to its output ports.
(Assume that a bitsToArray method does this.) The following is a simplified
example of a "truth" function that might be used with our Component class.

```
public class UnaryTruthTableFunction
implements UnaryFunctor<Boolean[],Boolean[]> {
    public Boolean[] fn(Boolean[] in) {
        // convert the objects into bits -- somehow
        int convertedInput = arrayToBits(in);
        // lookup the output from the truth table
        // see the section "The Truth Is In There"
        long result = retrieve(convertedInput);
        // convert the output bits into a Boolean[] -- somehow
        return bitsToArray(result);
    }
}
```

A more complete implementation is available on this book's companion website. In the current component design, results must be evaluated in a feed-forward manner (that is, only from inputs to outputs). If components are wired together in any type of cycle, you would need a synchronization framework. In the following sections, we introduce a graph API and then use it to connect ports between components and run a simulation.

The Knee Bone's Connected to the . . . : Connecting with JGraphT

JGraphT

JAVA 5+

In Chapter 4, we explored the Semantic Web and linked concepts together to form semantic networks. The RDF standard that we discussed in Chapter 4 models these networks as *labeled directed graphs*. Note that we are not talking about "graphing" or "charting" here but using the mathematical sense of a graph as a network of nodes or *vertices*. In graph theory, a labeled directed graph means that each link, or *edge*, has a label and a direction. The Jena and RDF graphs that we used before are a special-purpose implementation of directed graphs, but some applications may want to model other types of graphs and be able to perform mathematical operations on them. For this purpose you can use *JGraphT*, an easy-to-use API for working with many different types of graphs. It focuses on the graph model itself, its connectivity, and performing operations on the graph rather than displaying or visualizing it. In Chapter 6, we'll discuss another API that focuses on the visualization of graph models. But for now, we will be building the graph model itself.

The nodes within a JGraphT graph can be any Java objects. The graph model describes how objects are interconnected. By using this type of model, you can treat the relationships between the objects independently from the objects themselves. This is very similar to the Model-View-Controller (MVC) pattern used in Swing and many other Java frameworks. This process can be used for modeling all sorts of real-world situations. Graph theory is useful in simulating and analyzing many types of complex systems, such as computer networks, digital circuits, highway traffic, and data flow.

Creating a graph in JGraphT is easy. First you create an instance of the desired type of graph. Then you call the graph's addVertex method to add each Java object as a vertex. Once an object is in the graph, you can call methods to connect it with other vertices. Here is an example that models the interconnectivity of some organs and systems in the human body. Figure 5-2 shows the relationships of items within the graph.

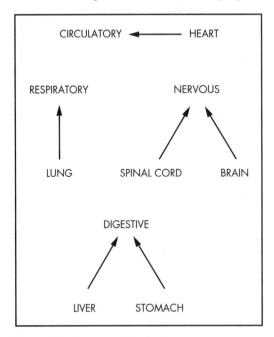

Figure 5-2: Organs and body systems

We will use a Java 5 enum (see Chapter 1) to represent each organ and system that will be in the graph. We can create an undirected graph to hold the relationships between these parts:

```
import org._3pq.jgrapht.graph.SimpleGraph;

enum Organs {HEART, LUNG, LIVER, STOMACH, BRAIN, SPINAL_CORD};
enum Systems {CIRCULATORY, DIGESTIVE, NERVOUS, RESPIRATORY};

SimpleGraph graph = new SimpleGraph();
graph.addVertex(Organs.HEART);
graph.addVertex(Organs.LUNG);
graph.addVertex(Organs.BRAIN);
graph.addVertex(Organs.STOMACH);
graph.addVertex(Organs.LIVER);
graph.addVertex(Organs.SPINAL_CORD);
graph.addVertex(Systems.CIRCULATORY);
graph.addVertex(Systems.NERVOUS);
graph.addVertex(Systems.DIGESTIVE);
graph.addVertex(Systems.RESPIRATORY);
```

```
graph.addEdge(Organs.HEART, Systems.CIRCULATORY);
graph.addEdge(Organs.LUNG, Systems.RESPIRATORY);
graph.addEdge(Organs.BRAIN, Systems.NERVOUS);
graph.addEdge(Organs.SPINAL_CORD, Systems.NERVOUS);
graph.addEdge(Organs.STOMACH, Systems.DIGESTIVE);
graph.addEdge(Organs.LIVER, Systems.DIGESTIVE);
```

You'll need to be careful that each item has been added as a vertex before you add it as an edge, or an Exception will occur. This code does not display anything; in fact, it does nothing except create an internal graph of relationships between the objects. Essentially, it creates a list of "neighbors" (edges) for each object. In this particular example, all the edges are treated equally. You can use labeled edges to differentiate between types of neighbors.

You can find the neighbors of a given object by calling methods on the graph. Let's find the edges for a vertex in the body systems example and print what is on the other side of each edge. We can find the nodes that are directly connected to the DIGESTIVE node by the following:

```
import org._3pq.jgrapht.Edge;

List digestiveLinks = graph.edgesOf(Systems.DIGESTIVE);
for (Object item : digestiveLinks) {
   Edge anEdge = (Edge) item;
   Object opposite = anEdge.oppositeVertex(Systems.DIGESTIVE);
   System.out.println(opposite);
}
```

The technique we used here is to obtain the list of edges, and for each edge find the vertex that is not the DIGESTIVE node (that is, find the "opposite" vertex). Edge is the interface that all edges implement, and it associates a target vertex with a source vertex. You can use one of the default implementations that come with JGraphT or write an Edge class to meet specific needs.

JGraphT has implementations of other operations that you can perform on graphs. You can find more information on these in the JGraphT documentation. We'll be working more with JGraphT in the next section. In Chapter 6, we will use a different API to visualize graphs.

Tied Up in Meta-Nots: Connecting Generic Processing Units

JGraphT

JAVA 5+

In the section "Connecting the Nots," we created a generic processing unit with input and output ports, and in the section "The Knee Bone's Connected to the . . .: Connecting with JGraphT," you saw how to connect arbitrary Java objects together into a graph structure. In this section, we'll connect component input and output ports using JGraphT. Using this design, we can maintain the port connections (the wiring) separately from the component implementations. In fact, we don't really care what the components are doing, or even whether they are processing boolean values. Each component has a process method that grabs the data from its input ports, processes the data, and moves the results to the output ports. We can run each component's process method, which performs the component's function and sends the result to the output ports. If we have used a directed graph to connect the ports, we can propagate each output to the next stage by iterating through all the edges. For each edge, we call getValue on the source vertex (an Output-Port) and setValue on the destination vertex (an InputPort). Now we can write a class that manages components using a graph API:

```java
public class MetaComponentSimple {
    private ListenableDirectedGraph graph;

    public MetaComponentSimple() {
        graph = new ListenableDirectedGraph();
    }

    public void connect(OutputPort out, InputPort in) {
        Component source = out.getParent();
        Component target = in.getParent();
        // add parent components to graph
        if (!graph.containsVertex(source)) {
            graph.addVertex(source);
        }
        if (!graph.containsVertex(target)) {
            graph.addVertex(target);
        }
        // add ports to graph
        if (!graph.containsVertex(in)) {
            graph.addVertex(in);
        }
        if (!graph.containsVertex(out)) {
            graph.addVertex(out);
        }
        // add an edge from out parent to output port
        graph.addEdge(source, out);
        // add an edge from output port to input port
        graph.addEdge(out, in);
        // add an edge from input port to target component
        graph.addEdge(in, target);
    }

    public void process() {
        processSubComponents();
        propagateSignals();
    }

    private void propagateSignals() {
        for (Object item : graph.edgeSet()) {
            Edge edge = (Edge) item;
            Object source = edge.getSource();
```

```
        Object target = edge.getTarget();
        if (source instanceof OutputPort) {
            OutputPort out = (OutputPort) source;
            InputPort in = (InputPort) target;
            in.setValue(out.getValue());
        }
    }
}

private void processSubComponents() {
    for (Object item : graph.vertexSet()) {
        if (item instanceof Component) {
            ((Component) item).process();
        }
    }
}
}
```

To use this class, you would make connections between ports by calling the connect method. The method adds each port's parent component to the graph, so that the component can later call the process method of its sub-components. The manager itself has its own process method, which first processes all the components and then propagates each output value to the next input stage. It's no accident that I chose the same name for the process method in the manager class. If you would also implement the other methods of the Component interface, you could use this class to build a more complex component from other components. The book's website has a more complete example of this. Here is some code that uses our new class to implement the function y=and(or(a,b),or(c,d)):

```
MetaComponentSimple manager = new MetaComponentSimple();
// Assume that we have created an AND gate Component,
// using techniques discussed earlier. This one has 2 inputs.
Component and = createAndGateComponent(2);
OutputPort y = and.getOutputPort(0);
// We'll use a couple of OR gates, each with 2 inputs
Component or1 = createOrGateComponent(2);
InputPort a = or1.getInputPort(0);
InputPort b = or1.getInputPort(1);
Component or2 = createOrGateComponent(2);
InputPort c = or2.getInputPort(0);
InputPort d = or2.getInputPort(1);
manager.connect(or1.getOutputPort(0), and.getInputPort(0));
manager.connect(or2.getOutputPort(0), and.getInputPort(1));
// set the input values
a.setValue(true);
b.setValue(false);
c.setValue(false);
d.setValue(false);
```

```
manager.process();
// we need to process twice, because there are two component stages
manager.process();
System.out.println(y);       // this prints false
```

Note that a signal may take more than one processing cycle to reach the other "end" of the circuit. This is also true in real circuits, because every component has a processing delay, but it is usually so short that we don't notice it. We'll discuss time-dependent processes in Chapter 7. In the next section we work with another network, a brain-like system called a neural network.

Joone Bugs: Building Neural Networks in Joone

JOONE

Log4J

Did you ever feel like building a brain? Well, you can do it in Java without feeling too much like Dr. Frankenstein. In computer science jargon, an *artificial neural network* is a group of simple processing cells that are highly connected and work together to form a larger computing system. Some people use the term *neural network* to refer to any type of *connectionist* system. In this section, however, we are discussing systems that have an architecture roughly similar to the brain's neurons. These systems are often used in tasks such as speech recognition, computer vision, and machine learning.

In a neural net, an individual node is called a *neuron*. Despite the name, these neurons are only superficially similar to human or animal neurons. A neuron works by receiving inputs from neighboring neurons, with each of these connections having a *weight* associated with it. The connections in a neural network are called *synapses*. The weight of each synapse is combined with the input value to determine the weighted input value that is sent to the target neuron. Neural nets are very useful because they can be trained to recognize patterns within data. You actually "teach" the network how to do its job.

Joone is an easy-to-use API for working with neural networks in Java. It has a GUI editor for creating and training neural networks. There is also a core engine for embedding networks within applications. While it is possible to create and train a network entirely from the engine, using the editor is the easiest way. Once you have used the GUI to create and train a network, you can embed the trained network and the core engine within your own application. Figure 5-3 shows the GUI editor in operation, editing one of Joone's sample networks.

Within the editor, you can create, train, and run neural networks. By exporting a trained neural network to a serialized file (using the menu File ▸ Export NeuralNet), you can then use the network within your own applications. The Joone editor creates a serialized file containing the network, which you can read into the engine and run by using the following code:

```
import org.joone.net.NeuralNetLoader;
import org.joone.net.NeuralNet;
import org.joone.engine.Monitor;
import org.joone.io.FileOutputSynapse;
```

```
NeuralNetLoader netLoader =
    new NeuralNetLoader("/projects/nn/mynetwork.snet");
NeuralNet myNet = netLoader.getNeuralNet();
// get the output layer of the network
Layer output = xorNNet.getOutputLayer();
// add output synapse (connection) to the output layer
FileOutputSynapse myOutput = new FileOutputSynapse();
// set the output file as mynetwork.out
FileOutput.setFileName("/projects/nn/mynetwork.out");
output.addOutputSynapse(myOutput);
Monitor monitor = myNet.getMonitor();
// execute for one cycle
monitor.setTotCicles = 1;
// not in learning mode
monitor.setLearning(false);
// start the neural net's layers
myNet.start();
// start the monitor
monitor.Go();
```

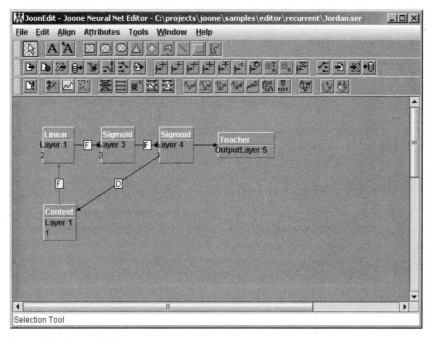

Figure 5-3: Joone GUI

The above example loads the serialized network into a NeuralNet instance, using the NeuralNetLoader utility class. We then create a FileOutputSynapse that will capture the output generated by the network. The inputs and outputs of a network are arrays of double values. The Monitor class manages the neural network, allowing you to stop and start it and set parameters that control its behavior. I've left out the exception-handling code to keep this short and simple and to focus on the operation of the neural network itself. If all you want to do is run a neural network and capture its output to a file, you don't need to write an application to do this. There is a `NeuralNetRunner` class with a command-line interface, or you can execute the network from within the Joone editor.

Follow the links from this book's website to the Joone documentation for a discussion of its more advanced features. The documentation has many samples to experiment with: image recognition, time-series analysis, charting, stock forecasting, and much more. Because networks can be serialized, there is also a framework for creating distributed neural networks. This framework is suitable for creating global brains that would have made Dr. Frankenstein very happy! Neural networks are a powerful technique to use in many types of pattern-recognition tasks, and Joone makes it easy to create and embed them in your own applications.

It's Alive! Using JGAP for Genetic Algorithms

JGAP

COLT

For some tasks, it's not always easy finding the correct algorithm or sequence of steps to perform the work. This is especially true for processes that require frequent changes to an algorithm to match changing circumstances in the program's environment. In situations like these, you may be able to write a program that evolves a solution. This is called a *genetic algorithm (GA)*. This type of programming works by trying many possible solutions and selecting the ones that perform the best. In each round of trials, the best-performing members of the population (according to some *fitness function*) are chosen to "breed" and create the next generation of programs. When a new generation is created, the best-performing programs are randomly mutated and combined with other programs, making many slightly different versions. Then the process repeats for many generations.

Sometimes this process creates finely tuned algorithms after only a few generations. It may be very difficult for a human being to understand how a particular individual performs its task. The steps taken may not be the ones that you would select if you were coding it by hand. Since the fitness function chooses based not on readability but on performance, it will select individuals that match those characteristics the most.

There are several Java APIs for genetic algorithms. You can find links to some of these on the resources page. In this section, we'll look at one API called the *Java Genetic Algorithms Package (JGAP)*. Let's start with a few basic terms related to GAs. These terms are borrowed from genetics, although the entities in a GA can be any type of structure rather than DNA. The *chromosome* (or *genome*) represents the set of possible approaches to solving a problem, and a *gene* represents a unit within the chromosome (an *allele* is a particular expression of a gene, much like a class-instance relationship). A gene can be a `String`, number, tree, program, or any other type of structure. To use JGAP, you first need to select a genome that adequately represents your problem space. Then you define an appropriate fitness function for testing individuals within the population (also called a *genotype*). Finally, create a configuration object to describe characteristics of the process, and then let the critters start procreating.

We'll use an example from our truth-table code in the "High-Caliber Bits" section, where we made a 1-of-4 demultiplexer. In that section we built the truth table for a demultiplexer with two address inputs, one data input, and four outputs. This requires exactly 32 bits of truth table. You might think of trying a single fixed-length gene of 32 bits in our genetic simulation. As it turns out, this doesn't work very well for our application because the search space is the entire range of int values. We could design this better by using a 4-bit gene representing a group of output bits, and a chromosome length of 8. Because the 4 output bits work as a unit anyway, this turns out to be a much better choice for a gene. In numerous test runs with 100,000 generations each (and a population of 200), the 32-bit gene did not produce a single fit individual. But with a 4-bit gene, a winner evolved consistently in fewer than 20 generations.

The JGAP API has a Gene subclass called the IntegerGene. This is easy to convert into a Java Integer, so it will integrate well with our truth-table code. A JGAP fitness function has an evaluate method with a Chromosome parameter that returns a double value for the fitness quotient. A higher value means that an individual performs the task better. Here is our fitness function:

```
public class DemuxFitness extends org.jgap.FitnessFunction {
   private TruthTable tt;

   public DemuxFitness() {
      // this is our target, what we want to evolve to
      tt = new TruthTable(3,4);
      tt.store(4, 1);   // 100->0001
      tt.store(5, 2);   // 101->0010
      tt.store(6, 4);   // 110->0100
      tt.store(7, 8);   // 111->1000
   }

   public int correctBits(int data) {
      BitVector vecValue = new BitVector(new long[] {data}, 32);
      BitVector target = tt.getTruthMatrix().toBitVector();
      // we can find the number of correct bits using:
      //    count(not(xor(target,vecValue)))
      vecValue.xor(target);
      vecValue.not();
      return vecValue.cardinality();
   }

   public double evaluate(Chromosome chrom) {
      int valueTotal = 0;
      for (int i = 7; i>=0; i--) {
         IntegerGene gene = (IntegerGene) chrom.getGene(i);
         Integer value = (Integer) gene.getAllele();
```

```
            valueTotal += value;
            valueTotal <<= 4;
        }
        int correct = correctBits(valueTotal);
        // we return the square, to reward exact answers
        return correct * correct;
    }
}
```

We could just return the number of correct bits in an individual's chromosome. This is fine until the fitness value is near optimal, when there is not as much incentive for individuals to do better. Returning the square of the number of correct bits gives a greater reward to individuals that make small increases in fitness. Let's create a configuration object and then run the genetic algorithm:

```
Configuration config = new DefaultConfiguration();
// eight genes
Gene[] genes = new Gene[8];
for (int i = 0; i < 8; i++) {
    // each one a 4-bit integer (0-15 inclusive)
    genes[i] = new IntegerGene(0, 15);
}
Chromosome sample = new Chromosome(genes);
config.setSampleChromosome(sample);
DemuxFitness fitTest = new DemuxFitness();
config.setFitnessFunction(fitTest);
config.setPopulationSize(200);
Genotype population = Genotype.randomInitialGenotype(config);
for (int i=0; i<1000; i++) {
    population.evolve();
}
Chromosome fittest = population.getFittestChromosome();
```

The code creates a chromosome of eight genes, each of which can have a value from 0 to 15. It then puts this sample chromosome into the configuration object. We set the fitness function and the population size, create an initial random population, and run the simulation. At the end, we select the fittest chromosome. In this case, we already know the outcome, but if you needed the value of the winning allele, you could get it from the chromosome. If you want to use something besides a String, Integer, or bits for your genes, you can create your own Gene subclass.

Genetic algorithms are another great tool for the Java developer to know, especially for solving problems where solutions are testable and in dynamic environments where there may not be a single best solution that always applies. For an example that evolves neural networks, combining Joone (as in the previous section) and JGAP, see this book's companion website.

IA Is AI: Building Intelligent Agents Using Jade

JADE An *intelligent agent* is an autonomous software process, or one that is able to make decisions and take action without the involvement of a human being. This is something of a loose definition, but developers mostly use the term to specifically refer to agents that run within an agent framework. An intelligent agent is most useful when it is part of a cooperative *multi-agent system*. With these types of systems, you can break down a problem into much simpler parts and assign agents to each part of the task. Agents sometimes can move from one machine to another within a framework and are able to communicate with one another. Other types of agents stay on a single system. As *web services* become more ubiquitous and provide a greater diversity of data, you will see more agents using them as data sources and as communication channels. In many agent frameworks, the agents themselves act as miniature web services.

With a virtual machine capable of running on many different architectures, and a powerful security model, Java is a perfect fit for agent development. Think of this as the equivalent of many small non-graphical applets working on a distributed solution to a problem. There are many different Java APIs for agent development, and there is even a consortium called the Foundation for Intelligent Physical Agents (FIPA) that has created a set of standards for agent frameworks to follow. We'll be working with an API called Jade that is one of the more popular FIPA-compliant APIs. There are several completely unrelated Java projects called Jade, so make sure that you download the one that is the FIPA-based agent framework. (See the book's resources links online.)

In this section, we'll introduce Jade through a stock market example. Intelligent agents would work great for doing program trading in a stock market. *Program trading* involves automatic buying and selling based on events such as price movement, volume changes, or news reports. This lends itself well to a multi-agent system. Let's illustrate this idea by writing a simple agent that buys 100 shares of a stock when a specific set of events takes place. We'll use pseudocode that contacts a hypothetical web service to do this, and we'll ignore any privacy and security aspects for this example. (See the Jade documentation for examples of secure agents.) Here is the simplest agent possible:

```
public class WorthlessAgent extends jade.core.Agent {
   protected void setup() {
   }
}
```

Jade calls the setup method when an agent is first loaded. (It works much like the init method of an applet or the main method of a console application.) This is where you put initialization code for the agent and set up the agent's behaviors. *Behaviors* are things that the agent does in the course of its lifetime. You can think of these as being very similar to functors. In our case, we might want a behavior that periodically polls a quote server to get the latest price of the symbol. Another agent, a value-checking agent, might send a message to a purchasing agent when the price reaches some value. There are several Behaviour (the class name uses the British spelling) subclasses we can use. We will start a TickerBehaviour to check the value of the latest price quote. This type of behavior repeats at a specific interval. The name here has nothing to do with a stock ticker—it represents a clock, but the name is a nice coincidence! Here is the behavior that checks the price every 300 seconds:

```
public class CheckQuoteBehaviour extends TickerBehaviour {
   public CheckQuoteBehaviour(Agent a) {
      super(a, 300*1000);     // repeat interval in milliseconds
   }

   protected void onTick() {
      // get the current price from somewhere
      if (getCurPrice() < 5.0) {
         // send a buy message -- defined later
      }
   }

   public boolean done() {
      // stop after 1000 ticks
      if (getTickCount() > 1000) {
         return true;
      }
   }
}
```

A behavior stops when its done method returns true. As we have defined it above, the quote checker will stop after 1,000 ticks. We now plug this behavior into the quote server agent:

```
public class QuoteAgent extends jade.core.Agent {
   protected void setup() {
      addBehaviour(new CheckQuoteBehaviour(this));
   }
}
```

We've now completed the agent. You can load it into the agent server either through Jade's GUI or by writing code to do it. Next we'll send a buy message to the purchasing agent, replacing the onTick method that we defined earlier. When an agent is loaded into the system, it gets a unique name called an *Agent Identifier (AID)*. AIDs can be local identifiers or globally unique identifiers. We will assume here that we have a PurchasingAgent instance with a local AID of "buyer." (The Jade documentation explains how to assign AIDs to agents.) Here is the redefined onTick method:

```
// inside the QuoteAgent...
   protected void onTick() {
      // get the current price from somewhere
```

```
if (getCurPrice() < 5.0) {
    // send a message to the buyer
    jade.core.AID buyingAgent =
            new jade.core.AID("buyer", AID.ISLOCALNAME);
    // we are requesting that another agent do something
    ACLMessage msg = new ACLMessage(ACLMessage.REQUEST);
    // send a String message
    msg.setContent("buy 100 WHATEVER");
    msg.addReceiver(buyingAgent);
    send(msg);
    }
}
```

Here is the code for the PurchasingAgent to read and respond to the messages:

```
import jade.lang.acl.ACLMessage;
public class PurchasingAgent extends jade.core.Agent {
    protected void setup() {
        addBehaviour(
            new jade.core.behaviours.CyclicBehaviour(this) {
                public void action()
                {
                    ACLMessage msg = receive();
                    if (msg!=null) {
                        String data = msg.getContent();
                        // call some method to do the agent's work
                        Object result = tryToBuy(data);
                        // there is a special shortcut for responding
                        ACLMessage reply = msg.createReply();
                        reply.setPerformative(ACLMessage.INFORM);
                        reply.setContent(result);
                        send(reply);
                    }
                    block();
                }
            }
        );
    }
}
```

The CyclicBehaviour repeats an action indefinitely, or until the behavior's done method returns true. The block method will cause the behavior instance to block until a new message arrives. The *performative* is the type of message that is being sent to the recipient. There are other types of behaviors in Jade. The SequentialBehaviour class manages a group of child behaviors (this does not include thumb-sucking!) in a sequence. The ParallelBehaviour performs a group of behaviors in parallel. A more complex behavior is the FSMBehaviour, which works as a *finite state machine*. With this class, you define behaviors that represent different states of the system, and transitions between the different states are determined by the type of event that ended the previous behavior.

Jade has many other features that help to build distributed multi-agent systems. Agents can run inside J2EE servers, applets, and smaller devices such as cell phones and PDAs. Jade even has an ontology framework for agent semantics, so that agents can communicate about their tasks and share a common understanding. You'll want to take a look at the examples that are supplied with Jade to see some of its more advanced usage. Agent technologies will most likely play a big part in the future of the Semantic Web, and being able to work with existing agent frameworks will help Java developers to prepare for this.

Word Up: Navigating English with JWordNet

JWordNet

For many researchers, *computational linguistics* is a window into the operations of the human mind. By understanding what human beings mean when they use words in a particular sense, scientists may be able to learn more about how people think on a deeper level. But let's face it, people don't always make much sense, and understanding human language can be difficult even for other people. For aliens from Alpha Centauri (which some readers will swear is the author's true home!) or for computers, it's much more difficult. In the best of circumstances, it's possible for a computer program to get an idea of the syntax and structure of a sentence. Of course, getting the intended *meaning* is much harder. We would eventually like computers to take some kind of action based on what we say, and this requires a shared context as well as a model for cause and effect.

Never mind that we don't really have a way to measure true understanding. If we can at least get the computer to know which word senses the speaker or writer intended and their relations to other concepts within a knowledge base, we can build better natural language–understanding systems. It would be very helpful to have a tool we could use to look up meanings and word relations. At Princeton University's Cognitive Science Laboratory, researchers have created a lexical reference system for the English language. The system is called *WordNet* and has thousands of words organized into synonym sets. Each word sense is treated individually and is linked with other related words. Besides synonyms and antonyms, word relations come in a few other forms with exotic names such as *meronym, holonym, hypernym,* and *hyponym*. Despite having names that sound like diseases, these relations simply describe whole/part relationships and supertype/subtype classifications. These are very similar to aggregation (has-a) and inheritance (is-a) relationships in object-oriented programming. Table 5-2 describes the word relationship terms used in WordNet.

Table 5-2: Terms Defining Word Relations

Term	Definition
Meronym	A word that names a part of something larger. *Wheel* is a meronym of *bicycle*.
Holonym	A word that names a larger whole of which something is a part. *Bicycle* is a holonym of *wheel*.
Hypernym	A word that names a more general class of something. *Vehicle* is a hypernym of *bicycle*.
Hyponym	A word that names a more specific example of a word. *Bicycle* is a hyponym of *vehicle*.

There is an open-source Java interface to WordNet, called JWordNet, that you can integrate with Java applications. This API is useful in advanced text-processing applications. A program might be processing some text and encounter the word *wing*. This word could have several meanings. If the text had earlier included the word *feather*, you would use JWordNet to find the holonyms of *feather* and *wing*. The program would find that they are both parts of birds and that a bird is a type of animal. You could use this context to discover the most likely meaning of *wing* and perform further processing of the text using that knowledge.

Here is a "Hello Word" example of JWordNet code that looks up the word *wing* to find holonyms for each sense of the word:

```
configureJWordNet();    // see book's web site for configuration
Dictionary dictionary = Dictionary.getInstance();
IndexWord word = dictionary.lookupIndexWord(POS.NOUN, "wing");
System.out.println("Senses of the word 'wing':");
Synset[] senses = word.getSenses();
for (int i=0; i<senses.length; i++) {
  Synset sense = senses[i];
  System.out.println((i+1) + ". " + sense.getGloss());
  Pointer[] holo = sense.getPointers(PointerType.PART_HOLONYM);
  for (int j=0; j<holo.length; j++) {
    Synset synset = (Synset) (holo[j].getTarget());
    Word synsetWord = synset.getWord(0);
    // lemma belongs to a word, as synsets have multiple words
    System.out.print(" -part-of-> " + synsetWord.getLemma());
    // gloss belongs to the synset (it works like a definition)
    System.out.println(" = " + synset.getGloss());
  }
}
```

The code first looks up the word in the WordNet database, searching for nouns that match the word *wing*. This returns a Word object, from which you can obtain an array of Synset objects. A Synset (synonym set) represents a particular word sense and all of its synonyms. The program finds the related holonyms for each of the word senses of *wing*. It prints the gloss of each holonym. A *gloss* is a description that clarifies the word's meaning. The *lemma* is a heading or label for the gloss, for a particular word. The example code returned the following results:

```
Senses of the word 'wing':
1. a movable organ for flying (one of a pair)
  -part-of-> bird = warm-blooded egg-laying vertebrates...
  -part-of-> bat = nocturnal mouselike mammal...
  -part-of-> insect = small air-breathing arthropod
  -part-of-> angel = spiritual being attendant upon God
2. one of the horizontal airfoils... of an airplane
  -part-of-> airplane = an aircraft that has fixed a wing...
3. a stage area out of sight of the audience
4. a unit of military aircraft
5. the side of military or naval formation...
6. the wing of a fowl; "he preferred the drumsticks to the wings"
  -part-of-> bird = the flesh of a bird or fowl... used as food
7. surrounds the wheels of a vehicle...
  -part-of-> car = 4-wheeled motor vehicle...
8. an addition that extends a main building
  -part-of-> building = a structure that has a roof and walls...
```

I've used ellipsis markers to shorten some of the longer lines of the text. The JWordNet distribution that I used while writing this section did not yet support Java 5, but I hope that will be fixed by the time you read this! JWordNet supports file, memory, and database dictionaries. There is an RDF mapping of the WordNet terms, as mentioned in Chapter 4. JWordNet is a powerful tool when used with text-matching techniques from Chapter 2 and semantic analysis from Chapter 4. You can find a link to the RDF mapping and other information about WordNet and JWordNet on this book's website.

Chapter Summary

In this chapter, we've taken a look at a number of APIs for mathematical and scientific applications. In my opinion, this is one of the most powerful uses of Java, and I hope that open-source developers will continue to create exciting projects such as the ones explored here. In later chapters, we'll work with other libraries that can be used in scientific applications, as we work with graphics, multimedia, and project integration ideas.

6

GRAPHICS AND DATA VISUALIZATION

People have come to expect sophisticated graphics from their applications. Most users will look at a program's user interface first and, regardless of its capabilities, will not use a program that lacks an advanced graphical interface. We want to *see* our data. For analyzing data, we expect charting and graphing functionality, and for analyzing systems with complex relationships, we expect to see a graphical layout. In Java, we have the Swing and AWT classes, which are used to create windows, panels, buttons, fonts, and other graphical widgets. While it is possible to display data using only these classes, the application may seem dull. There are many libraries that can help you in your graphics programming, such as the charting and reporting APIs discussed here. This chapter also discusses other APIs for visualizing data and creating graphical applications in Java.

Gooey XML: Defining Java GUIs in XML

`SwiXML`

`JDOM XML`

Many applications have complex graphical user interfaces (GUIs) that involve many different components. The interface for these applications is usually defined in Java classes built upon AWT or Swing components. For example, a program may have a number of `JPanel` subclasses that define display widgets. One of the problems with this "subclassing" approach is that any changes to the layout or display properties require recompiling the code. Even something as simple as a color change requires rebuilding the application.

There is another reason why subclassing lots of panels and other GUI widgets may not be such a good idea. Some applications, such as applets or Java Web Start applications, must be first loaded across the network before the program can run. Of course, having many classes means a longer download time. Having many graphical panels also means additional classes will need to be loaded into memory, and this can lead to code bloat. One solution is to describe the GUI layout in an external file and interpret the definition file from a Java class. A few years ago, before any of the XML-defined user interfaces became popular, I was working on a Java project that involved many different complex graphical interface panels. The developers were coding the logic of the system, and because we were short on development time, I wrote a simple XML-based processor for defining the interfaces. The business analysts worked with the customer to finalize the layout, defining each panel in XML and testing its appearance before handing it over to the developers. Defining the GUI in XML helped because it was quick and easy to change, and it gave a good starting point for an interface that was close to what the customer wanted.

Defining Java user interfaces in XML is a lot easier now, because there are frameworks that are more complete than a simple home-brewed language. *SwiXML* (pronounced "swicks em el") is an open-source XML-based Swing layout engine. There are also other frameworks (such as Jelly and XUL), but SwiXML is the easiest to get started with. Let's define an interface in SwiXML and embed it within a Java program. Figure 6-1 shows a GUI with text fields for displaying information about a book.

Figure 6-1: A GUI to display book information

Let's define the XML for this layout:

```xml
<frame Size="400,400" Title="A Simple Frame" id="theFrame">
 <panel Border="EtchedBorder">
   <panel Constraints="BorderLayout.NORTH">
     <label Font="Times-BOLD-24" AlignmentX="0.5">Book Details</label>
   </panel>
   <hbox Constraints="BorderLayout.CENTER">
     <vbox Constraints="BorderLayout.WEST">
       <label Font="Times-BOLD-14" Foreground="black">Title</label>
       <label Font="Times-BOLD-14" Foreground="black">Author</label>
       <label Font="Times-BOLD-14" Foreground="black">Subject</label>
       <label Font="Times-BOLD-14" Foreground="black">Publisher</label>
     </vbox>
     <vbox Constraints="BorderLayout.EAST">
       <textfield id="title" Columns="30"/>
       <textfield id="author" Columns="30"/>
       <textfield id="subject" Columns="30"/>
       <textfield id="publisher" Columns="30"/>
     </vbox>
   </hbox>
   <panel Constraints="BorderLayout.SOUTH">
     <button id="btn1" Text="Press this" />
   </panel>
 </panel>
</frame>
```

This SwiXML code defines a 400x400 JFrame, with the title "A Simple Frame." The id attribute is used to assign generated Swing components to variables within the application. Each one will automatically be mapped to a public variable of the same name (if it exists). The example shows a nesting of several Swing containers. The hbox and vbox tags represent the horizontal and vertical layout containers from javax.swing.Box. The equivalent Swing code for this example can be found on the book's website at http://wickedcooljava.com.

The SwingEngine class from SwiXML reads the XML and generates the corresponding Swing components. To allow the engine to store references to these components in your application, you need to pass it a reference to a class that contains public variables of the appropriate name and type. Let's write the Java code to load the frame:

```java
import javax.swing.*;
import org.swixml.SwingEngine;

public class SwixMLTest {
    // these get populated by the SwiXML engine
    public JFrame theFrame;
    public JTextField title, author, subject, publisher;
    public JButton btn1;
```

```
   public SwixMLTest() {
      try {
         SwingEngine engine = new SwingEngine(this);
         // bookGUI.xml is the file we created earlier
         swen.render("bookGUI.xml");
         theFrame.setDefaultCloseOperation(JFrame.EXIT_ON_CLOSE);
         theFrame.setVisible(true);
      } catch (Exception e) {
         e.printStackTrace();
      }
   }
}
```

After the render method returns, the JFrame and other component variables (as defined in id attributes of the XML) are assigned their values. We can then use these objects as we would in an ordinary Swing application. Using XML documents to define the graphical elements of your application allows you to change many aspects of the presentation without having to recompile. Fonts, colors, borders, and other cosmetic changes are no longer tied to the Java source code. This has the benefit of increased maintainability and smaller compiled code. It also has potential uses in dynamically generated user interfaces.

To the Vector Goes the Spoils: Visualizing Data with SVG

BATIK *Scalable Vector Graphics (SVG)* is an XML-based two-dimensional vector graphics standard, created by the W3C. Unlike *raster* (bitmap) image standards such as BMP, JPEG, or GIF that work by defining the individual pixels of the image, *vector graphics* defines an image by drawing its constituent parts, such as lines, text, ellipses, and rectangles. Figure 6-2 shows a vector graphics image made from some drawing primitives.

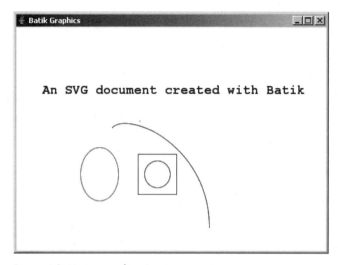

Figure 6-2: Vector graphics image

If you've done any work with Java 2D or AWT drawing, this should look familiar to you. You can use a `java.awt.Graphics2D` object to draw lines, ellipses, rectangles, and other shapes. This is usually done from the `paint` method of a display component. We could draw the same image with the following code:

```
// assume that we have a Graphics2D instance
// already defined somewhere (such as in a paint method)
Graphics2D graphics = ...
graphics.setColor(Color.BLACK);
graphics.drawRect(190,190,60,60);
graphics.setFont(Font.decode("Courier-bold-20"));
graphics.drawString("An SVG document created with Batik", 40, 100);
graphics.setColor(Color.BLUE);
CubicCurve2D curve =
  new CubicCurve2D.Double(150, 150, 175, 125, 300, 175, 300, 300);
graphics.draw(curve);
graphics.drawOval(200,200,40,40);
graphics.setColor(Color.RED);
graphics.drawOval(100,180,60,80);
```

We could also do the equivalent of this in SVG. Because SVG is an XML format, we can easily create and process it in Java. The structure of SVG is not extremely difficult to work with, as you can see from the SVG file below (some style attributes have been removed to keep the listing short—see this book's website for the full listing):

```
<svg xmlns="http://www.w3.org/2000/svg" version="1.0"
     contentStyleType="text/css" width="500" height="500">
 <g>
   <g>
     <rect x="190" y="190" width="60" height="60" />
     <text x="40" y="100" style="font-size:20; font-weight:bold;">
       An SVG document created with Batik
     </text>
   </g>
   <g style="fill:blue; font-size:20; font-weight:bold;">
     <path d="M150 150 C175 125 300 175 300 300" />
     <circle r="20" style="fill:none;" cx="220" cy="220" />
     <ellipse style="stroke:red;" rx="30" cx="130" ry="40" cy="220" />
   </g>
 </g>
</svg>
```

The most awkward part of this document is the `path` tag, which creates an arbitrary shape using special character codes to describe movement and drawing commands (for example, `M` moves to an absolute location, and `C` creates a cubic Bezier curve). One way to work with this format is to create the XML source in a DOM tree. To do this, you'd need to learn the SVG tags. For anyone who plans to directly manipulate SVG documents, I would suggest looking at the official documentation to become familiar with the standard. You might also consider creating SVG documents using an XSL-T stylesheet.

For most developers, it would be better to use a high-level API instead. Batik is an open-source SVG API from the Apache Group. Its SVGGraphics2D class is an implementation of Graphics2D (java.awt) that can write out the drawing canvas as an SVG file. You can use the AWT drawing methods shown earlier to create an image, by drawing onto an SVGGraphics2D instance. Once you have drawn the image, you can call methods to write out the SVG XML. The following code shows how to do this:

```
import org.w3c.dom.svg.SVGDocument;
import org.apache.batik.dom.svg.SVGDOMImplementation;
import org.apache.batik.svggen.SVGGraphics2D;
import org.w3c.dom.DOMImplementation;

DOMImplementation domImpl =
    SVGDOMImplementation.getDOMImplementation();
String namespace = SVGDOMImplementation.SVG_NAMESPACE_URI;
// create a document with the appropriate namespace
SVGDocument document =
    (SVGDocument) domImpl.createDocument(namespace, "svg", null);
// create an SVG Graphics2D instance using the document
SVGGraphics2D graphics = new SVGGraphics2D(document);
// now we insert the drawing code from above
graphics.setColor(Color.BLACK);
graphics.drawRect(190,190,60,60);

// create a writer that goes to an output file in UTF-8 format
FileOutputStream fileStream = new FileOutputStream("test.svg");
Writer out = new OutputStreamWriter(fileStream, "UTF-8");
// write the XML, using CSS style properties (true)
graphics.stream(out, true);
out.flush();
out.close();
```

You can see that we didn't need to know any of the SVG tags in order to create the file; we used only the Java 2D drawing primitives. Batik can also script SVG content using a JavaScript (ECMAScript) interpreter, convert SVG files to bitmap formats, convert fonts, and view SVG files. SVG images can be embedded in XSL-FO documents. The Apache FOP project is a Java API for working with XSL-FO documents and can create Adobe PDF documents from them. You'll find links to this project on the book's website. In the next section, we show how to display an SVG document using Batik.

Resources

- Eisenberg, J. David. *SVG Essentials.* O'Reilly, 2002.
- Batik API documentation (see http://wickedcooljava.com)

See SVG: Viewing SVG Content with Batik

 In the previous section, we created SVG content by using 2D drawing primitives on a Batik `Graphics2D` instance. We then sent the generated SVG output to a `Writer`. You can also use Batik as an SVG viewer for embedding in your Swing applications. The `JSVGCanvas` class is a Swing component that reads an SVG file and displays its contents. You can set the document with either a URI reference or a DOM `Document`. The following code displays an SVG image from a URI:

```
import org.apache.batik.swing.JSVGCanvas;
JSVGCanvas canvas = new JSVGCanvas();
String svgURI = "file:/projects/wcj6/test.svg";
canvas.setURI(svgURI);
canvas.setSize(500,500);
JFrame frame = new JFrame("Batik Graphics");
frame.add(canvas);
frame.pack();
frame.setVisible(true);
```

The URI could also be an HTTP URI, but in this case I've used a file. The Batik display classes support SVG documents with embedded ECMAscript scripting, interactive zoom, and many other features. The distribution comes with example SVG files and a sample application.

Body Art: Converting JGraphT into a JGraph View

JGraphT

JGraph

JGraph add-ons

In Chapter 5, we created a graph model of some organs and systems in the human body. To make the model, we used the JGraphT API, which is a model-only API and doesn't include any view capability. But it does have the advantage of a simple interface. Another API, *JGraph*, offers a complete Model-View-Controller graph framework for Swing. Unfortunately, its model API is more complex than JGraphT's. You can create your graph models much easier with the JGraphT API and use the `JGraphModelAdapter` class to convert them into JGraph models. Once you have a JGraph model, you can create a JGraph view for it. The following example creates a view from the JGraphT model that we created in Chapter 5:

```
import org._3pq.jgrapht.graph.ListenableDirectedGraph;
import org._3pq.jgrapht.ext.JGraphModelAdapter;
import org.jgraph.JGraph;
import org.jgraph.layout.CircleGraphLayout;
// use a JGraphT listenable graph
ListenableDirectedGraph graph = new ListenableDirectedGraph();
// create the view, then add data to the model
JGraphModelAdapter adapter = new JGraphModelAdapter(graph, null, null);
JGraph jgraph = new JGraph(adapter);
JScrollPane scroller = new JScrollPane(jgraph);
JFrame frame = new JFrame("The Body");
```

```
frame.setSize(600,600);
frame.add(scroller);
frame.setVisible(true);
// now add the data (the HumanOrgansGraph example from chapter 5)
HumanOrgansGraph hog = new HumanOrgansGraph(graph);
CircleGraphLayout layout = new CircleGraphLayout();
layout.run(jgraph, jgraph.getRoots(), new Object[]{});
// the layout cache maps the model cells to views
// we use this to reload the view after any model changes
jgraph.getGraphLayoutCache().reload();
jgraph.repaint();
```

In graph theory, the layout of the vertices is not considered to be important. In other words, two graphs are considered equivalent if they have the same edge connectivity. In order to display the items in JGraph, we'll need to physically arrange the vertices and edges in some way. The default conversion creates a layout with all the vertices in the same location—not very useful! The code above uses an add-ons API from JGraph to do a circular layout of the graph vertices. The result is shown in Figure 6-3.

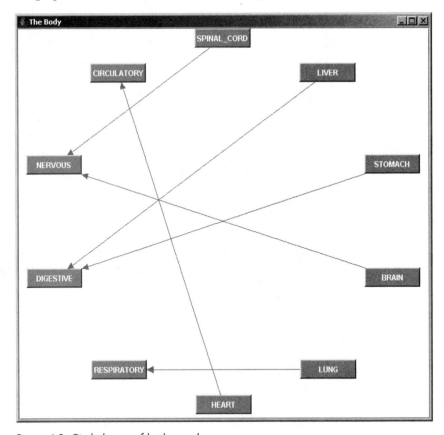

Figure 6-3: Circle layout of body graph

The edges also have their own view. By default, edges use the names of the source and target vertices as labels. This can be annoying, but JGraph does give you control over a graph's appearance. To remove labels from all the edges, run this code:

```
import org.jgraph.graph.GraphLayoutCache;
import org.jgraph.graph.CellView;
GraphLayoutCache cache = jgraph.getGraphLayoutCache();
CellView[] cells = cache.getCellViews();
for (CellView cell : cells) {
   if (cell instanceof EdgeView) {
      EdgeView ev = (EdgeView) cell;
      DefaultEdge eval = (DefaultEdge) ev.getCell();
      eval.setUserObject("");  // no label on the edge
   }
}
cache.reload();
jgraph.repaint();
```

We use the layout cache to obtain access to the view for our graph. An edge's view describes how to display the edge using properties such as line style and label. Each edge has a user object associated with it, which can be any Java object. The view uses the toString value of this object as a label. The above code removed the label by changing the user object to empty text. In the next section, we'll fix other problems with JGraph default views, by adding attribute maps.

Attri-Beauty: Using JGraph Attribute Maps

JGraph Graph connectivity represents only the interconnection of vertices, not the placement or arrangement of them in a graphical sense. We saw this in the previous section when we used JGraph's add-ons API to create a circular layout. We needed something besides the graph model to set the location of each vertex. In JGraph, every vertex has an attribute map associated with it. This map contains attributes for location, color, and other properties of the view. The CircleGraphLayout class from the previous section works by setting the location attribute inside each vertex's map.

You can work with the attributes of a vertex by obtaining its view object, which is an instance of the CellView class. The layout cache that we saw in the previous section, which maps the model cells to views, provides the access to this view object. First you retrieve the graph's layout cache using the getGraphLayoutCache method and use it to look up the view with the vertex as a key. You can then set values in the CellView's attribute map. There is a shortcut method for working with the vertex position and size. You can call the getBounds method to obtain the bounds of the view and set it directly. This example sets all the vertex locations to a random value:

```
GraphLayoutCache cache = jgraph.getGraphLayoutCache();
int width = 600;
```

```
int height = 600;
java.util.Random random = new java.util.Random();
// get the vertices, which are called roots
for (Object item : jgraph.getRoots()) {
    // each vertex is a GraphCell instance
    GraphCell cell = (GraphCell) item;
    // look up the corresponding CellView
    CellView view = cache.getMapping(cell, true);
    // getBounds is a shortcut to the vertex location and size
    Rectangle2D bounds = view.getBounds();
    double x = random.nextDouble() * width;
    double y = random.nextDouble() * height;
    bounds.setRect(x, y, bounds.getWidth(), bounds.getHeight());
}
cache.reload();
jgraph.repaint();
```

Other attributes of the view include arrow and line styles, icons, colors, fonts, resizeability, and text position. To work with these attributes, you will need to use the attribute map for the view. There is a GraphConstants class that contains the keys for these attributes. In this example, we change the background of each vertex to green:

```
GraphLayoutCache cache = jgraph.getGraphLayoutCache();
for (Object item : jgraph.getRoots()) {
    GraphCell cell = (GraphCell) item;
    CellView view = cache.getMapping(cell, true);
    AttributeMap map = view.getAttributes();
    map.applyValue(GraphConstants.BACKGROUND, java.awt.Color.GREEN);
}
cache.reload();
jgraph.repaint();
```

Using the attributes available in JGraph, you can completely customize the appearance of a graph. The API documentation contains many examples that show how to use these attributes.

Charting New Territory: Creating Charts with JFreeChart

JFreeChart

Creating charts is one of the most common types of data visualization. We showed in the section "To the Vector Goes the Spoils" that we can make vector images using the Batik API or by directly styling XML data into SVG. This requires a lot of work to create even a basic chart, because you'll have to draw each shape separately. The JFreeChart API is a solution to this problem. It uses Batik behind the scenes but has higher-level objects designed to make charting much easier. JFreeChart can produce pie, bar, line, area, scatter, time series, open/high/low/close, and other types of charts. The main chart class is JFreeChart (no surprise there), and the best way to get started with it is by using static factory methods of the ChartFactory class. You'll need a data set for the chart, and there are several types of these. For a pie chart, you can use DefaultKeyedValuesDataset (which is similar to a HashMap). This code snippet creates a pie chart and displays it in a ChartFrame (a JFrame subclass for displaying charts):

```
import org.jfree.data.general.DefaultKeyedValuesDataset;
import org.jfree.chart.ChartFactory;
import org.jfree.chart.ChartFrame;

DefaultKeyedValuesDataset dataset = new DefaultKeyedValuesDataset();
dataset.setValue("raining", 60);
dataset.setValue("snowing", 5);
dataset.setValue("sunny", 200);
dataset.setValue("cloudy", 100);
// Create a chart entitled "Weather", using the above dataset
JFreeChart pie =
  ChartFactory.createPieChart("Weather", dataset, true, true, false);
ChartFrame frame = new ChartFrame("My weather", pie);
frame.setSize(500,500);
frame.setVisible(true);
```

The createPieChart method has three boolean parameters. These control, respectively, whether to create a legend, tooltips, or URLs for the chart. The pie chart created by this code is shown in Figure 6-4. The ChartFrame has mouse-click handlers that let the user zoom into or out of the chart, change display characteristics, or save the chart as an image.

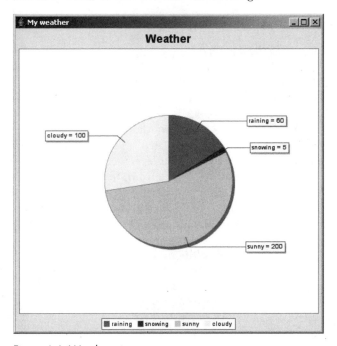

Figure 6-4: Weather pie

You can save any chart as an image, using the ChartUtilities class. For the pie chart, we could do the following to create a PNG image of the chart:

```
FileOutputStream fileOut = new FileOutputStream("pie.png");
ChartUtilities.writeChartAsPNG(fileOut, pie, 500, 500);
```

There are other types of datasets corresponding to different types of charts. You can also populate a dataset from a database connection rather than setting values programmatically as we did earlier. See the JFreeChart documentation for more information on the dataset implementations.

You can also use these methods to generate dynamic charts from a web-based application. One way to do this is with a servlet that calls the methods to create a chart and write its image to the servlet's output stream. But there is an even easier way to create dynamic charts. CEWolf is an open-source Java Server Page (JSP) tag library based on JFreeChart. If you are building a web-based application, you can use this tag library to generate charts very quickly. If you have a servlet engine such as Apache Tomcat installed, you can get started quickly by deploying the CEWolf example web application archive (WAR) file. It includes all the necessary libraries (JFreeChart classes and the tag library classes). As of this writing, the charts must currently get the data from a Java class external to the JSP. In the future, the CEWolf tags will be expanded to allow you to get data values from within the JSP. For links to CEWolf, see this book's website. JFreeChart and CEWolf are currently still in beta version, but they are already powerful tools for adding charts to your applications.

Reporting for Duty: Creating Reports in Java

Jasper
Reports

iReport

Most large applications have some type of reporting requirements. Of course, you could always create reports by dynamically drawing each part of the report based on some data values. This might be done with XML (such as in XSL-FO or SVG), AWT drawing primitives, or a report-generation utility. Commercial reporting packages make the task easier, but these are usually expensive. One of my principles in writing this book is to support open-source efforts where possible. By now you are probably wondering if there is an open-source tool that can help in creating reports. The answer is yes, and there are in fact several to choose from. In the previous section we created charts in Java. This same open-source group also created JFreeReport, a report-generation API. It is a powerful package, but currently you can only create the reports using its Java API or an XML description. A graphical report designer for this report engine, JFreeDesigner, is still under development and was not ready at the time of writing.

Because a graphical report designer is such a powerful tool for quickly and easily creating reports, in this section we are working with JasperReports. JasperReports is an open-source reporting tool for Java that has a visual report builder called iReport. It can use an XML or JDBC data source to populate the report. As a demonstration, we'll create the report shown in Figure 6-5 using a database connection.

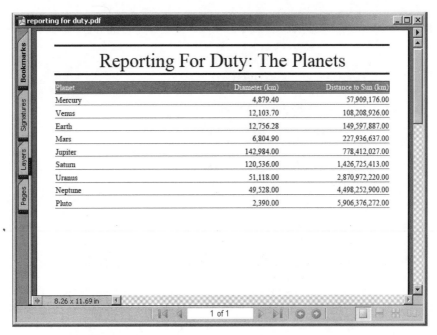

Figure 6-5: A simple report

The iReport application has a report wizard that can generate reports from a template, and it comes with some basic report templates (or you can create your own). The report wizard is started from the File menu, and it initially asks you to enter a SQL query. After selecting columns from the query result, you can then customize the report and run it using live data. The above report took less than two minutes to create using iReport!

Once you create a report, the layout is stored in a JasperReports XML file. You can run the report in iReport using a JDBC data source and save the output as a PDF, HTML, XLS, or CSV file. You can also integrate the report into your applications using the JasperReports API. The report engine can run from within a web and J2EE application or can use a Swing viewer for creating thick client applications. The JasperFillManager class is one of the first places to look in JasperReports. Much of the functionality of the API is exposed through static methods of this class. The following code shows how to load the report XML created earlier, fill it with data, and display it from a Swing application:

```
try {
    Connection conn = ....... // get a JDBC connection somehow
    // compile the report to a serialized report template object
    JasperReport report =
      JasperCompileManager.compileReport("report.jrxml");
    // populate the report with data from the database
    // the query will use field names from the report
    // there is an optional map (null here) for report parameters
    JasperPrint print =
      JasperFillManager.fillReport(report, null, conn);
```

```
      // create a viewer frame and display it
      JasperViewer viewer = new JasperViewer(print);
      viewer.setSize(400,400);
      viewer.setDefaultCloseOperation(JFrame.EXIT_ON_CLOSE);
      viewer.setVisible(true);
   } catch (Exception e) {    // several exceptions to catch
      e.printStackTrace();
   }
```

The iReport and JasperReports combination is a powerful one.
Although this is not yet at version 1.0 and there are still bugs, don't let
the version number fool you. You'll also want to keep an eye on the other
report engines, since there is a lot of active development work happening
there too. For links to these and other open-source reporting options, see
the book's companion website.

Periodic Patterns: Simple 2D Data Visualization

 Data visualization is about displaying patterns. It uses the human brain, our
own amazing neural network, to discover patterns and to understand relationships within the data. We can use computer graphics as a tool that makes
patterns stand out more clearly. Looking at a long list of numbers will probably
not reveal much about the data, but patterns in an image are more easily rec-
ognizable. In previous sections, we used charting and reporting to represent
data spatially. To make a chart, we needed to know ahead of time how the data
points were related. However, in some cases you may not know what to do
with the data. Imagine that you've found some data on a disk and want
to figure out what it is. After checking for common file types and running a
statistical analysis of the data, you might decide to look for spatial relationships. One simple type of data visualization is to display data points on a two-
dimensional grid, converting the data into pixels and arranging them in some
order. Figure 6-6 shows some mostly random data in a rectangular grid.

In Java, you can use a BufferedImage (java.awt.image) to create an image
from data in a byte[] buffer. For our purposes of data visualization, the most
useful types of buffered images are the binary and grayscale (see the JDK
documentation for the BufferedImage class). The size of the buffer array will
depend on the width and height of the image. The following class is a Swing
JPanel subclass that displays an image of binary data (packed as 8 pixels per
byte, or 1 bit per pixel).

```
public class BinaryPlotPanel extends JPanel {
  BufferedImage buffIm;
  private byte[] buffer;

  public BinaryPlotPanel(int x, int y) {
     // to make this a grayscale image (8 bits per pixel),
     // use TYPE_BINARY_GRAY instead
     buffIm = new BufferedImage(x, y, BufferedImage.TYPE_BYTE_BINARY);
     WritableRaster rasta = buffIm.getRaster();
```

```
      DataBufferByte buf = (DataBufferByte) rasta.getDataBuffer();
      buffer = buf.getData();
    }

  public byte[] getBuffer() {
    return buffer;
  }

  public Graphics2D getBufferGraphics() {
    return buffIm.createGraphics();
  }

  public int getImageHeight() { return buffIm.getHeight(); }

  public int getImageWidth() { return buffIm.getWidth(); }

  public void paint(Graphics g) {
    Graphics2D g = (Graphics2D) arg0;
    g.drawImage(buffIm, 0, 0, this);
  }
}
```

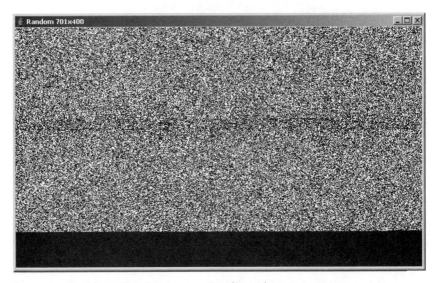

Figure 6-6: Pseudorandom data in a rectangular grid

The panel's constructor creates a buffered image, and the paint method displays the image whenever the component needs repainting. In the following code we create an instance of the BinaryPlotPanel class that we just created, add the panel to a JFrame, grab the data buffer, and populate it with some random bytes (plus some non-random data):

```
int x = 600;
int y = 400;
```

```
BinaryPlotPanel bpp = new BinaryPlotPanel(x, y);
byte[] data = bpp.getBuffer();
Random r = new Random();
// fill the buffer with random data
r.nextBytes(data);
Graphics2D graphics = bpp.getBufferGraphics();
graphics.setFont(Font.decode("Courier-48"));
graphics.setColor(Color.BLACK);
// draw on top of the existing data
graphics.drawString("Wicked Cool Java", 80, 200);
JFrame frame = new JFrame("Random " + x + "x" + y);
frame.setSize(x + 10, y + 30);
frame.add(jp);
frame.setVisible(true);
```

The data created is the same as that shown earlier in Figure 6-6, but it is shown below in Figure 6-7 using the correct width and height. Notice that data that should have been directly underneath was skewed by having the incorrect row size. The black region under the first image is an artifact of changing the row length without compensating by a shorter height.

Figure 6-7: Hidden data revealed

This type of data visualization can be useful in some applications. As you saw with the hidden text, even if spatial patterns exist within the data, they may not be noticeable under the wrong X and Y dimensions, so you may need to try many sizes to find the correct one. In the next section, we look at 2D transformations of images.

A Fine Transform: Using Affine Transformations in Java 2D

JAVA 1.2+ Java's *Abstract Window Toolkit (AWT)* provides a Graphics class with methods for drawing lines, ovals, rectangles, text, polygons, and other shapes. A Panel, Frame, or other AWT component draws itself using the Graphics instance passed to its paint method. The GUI environment automatically calls this method whenever the component needs redrawing. Sun added the Java 2D framework on top of the original AWT Graphics class, adding many new features to the Java core API. One important Java2D feature is known as the *affine transformation*. It works by transforming the coordinate system before any drawing is done on the Graphics object. To illustrate this, we'll skew the coordinates with a shearing transformation and draw some text and graphics to see how it looks with and without the transformation. First, let's draw some text, using the default coordinates, as shown in Figure 6-8. We'll do this in the paint method of a JFrame:

```java
import java.awt.Font;
import java.awt.Graphics;
import java.awt.Graphics2D;
import javax.swing.JFrame;

public class MyTransform extends JFrame {

    public MyTransform(String title) {
        super(title);
    }

    public void paint(Graphics g) {
        Graphics2D g2d = (Graphics2D) g;
        g2d.setFont(Font.decode("arial-bold-36"));
        g2d.drawString("Affinity", 100, 100);
        g2d.drawOval(100, 150, 35, 50);
        g2d.drawOval(135, 150, 35, 50);
    }

    public static void main(String[] args) {
        MyTransform aft = new MyTransform("Affinity");
        aft.setSize(300,300);
        aft.setDefaultCloseOperation(JFrame.EXIT_ON_CLOSE);
        aft.setVisible(true);
    }
}
```

In all affine transformations, the change affects the entire coordinate system and not just individual objects. We call the methods to apply the transforms before calling the drawing methods. Let's display the above text with a shearing transform, as shown in Figure 6-9. This is a transform where lines are shifted in a new direction but parallel lines still remain parallel. The call to the shear method happens before the drawing occurs. Here is code to perform the transform:

```java
public void paint(Graphics g) {
    Graphics2D g2d = (Graphics2D) g;
    g2d.shear(0.5,0.5);
    g2d.setFont(Font.decode("arial-bold-36"));
    g2d.drawString("Affinity", 100, 100);
    g2d.drawOval(100, 150, 35, 50);
    g2d.drawOval(135, 150, 35, 50);
}
```

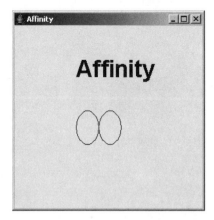

Figure 6-8: Text and graphics with no transform

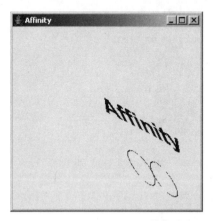

Figure 6-9: Text and graphics with shear transform

You can apply multiple affine transforms before performing drawing operations—for example, a shear combined with rotation, scaling, and translation. The order in which these operations are applied has a large effect on the combined result. The rotation and translation (moving the coordinate's origin) operations might be useful in a geographical display or in an image-editing program. The scaling (resizing) transform can be used to make your application zoomable, but this will require extra work to manage the zooming process. In the next section, we look at an API that makes building zoomable applications much easier.

Room to Zoom: Building Zoomable GUIs with Piccolo

PICCOLO   Piccolo is an open-source API for building 2D structured graphics. One of its most exciting features is the ability to create GUI widgets with interactive zooming capability. Dragging with the left mouse button pans the contents of the display widget. Dragging with the right mouse button zooms the display in and out. Other features include bounds management, object picking/selection, and animation.

Figure 6-10 shows some graphics drawn in a `PFrame` (a Piccolo frame class). The frame shows a closed line path made with randomly generated points. By default, the frame is zoomed out to display the entire contents.

Figure 6-10: Piccolo application at default zoom

The `PFrame` class is the starting point for creating a Piccolo application. Create your own class that extends `PFrame`. The `initialize` method of the `PFrame` is where you put the code to create the display elements. The following code example illustrates this:

```
import java.awt.Color;
import java.util.Random;
import edu.umd.cs.piccolo.nodes.PPath;
import edu.umd.cs.piccolox.PFrame;

public class PiccoloExample extends PFrame {

  public void initialize() {
```

```
        setTitle("Room To Zoom");
        Random random = new Random();
        PPath path = new PPath();
        path.moveTo(50, 50);
        for (int i = 0; i < 20; i++) {
            path.lineTo(random.nextInt(200), random.nextInt(200));
        }
        path.closePath();
        path.setPaint(Color.blue);
        getCanvas().getLayer().addChild(path);
    }

    public static void main(String[] args) {
        new PiccoloExample();
    }
}
```

Figure 6-11 shows a zoomed Piccolo application. The user can select the zoom amount dynamically, or it can be set in your code using Piccolo method calls. Because of the zooming feature, Piccolo is very useful for applications working with structured graphics content that is very large. Piccolo is not threadsafe, and you will need to use additional mechanisms for multithreaded applications.

Figure 6-11: Zoomed Piccolo application

Chapter Summary

In this chapter, we have looked at a few APIs and techniques that allow us to display our data in interesting ways. Using graphics effectively can make a big difference in the usability of your application and lead to greater user satisfaction. In the next chapter, we will explore multimedia and thread synchronization.

7

MULTIMEDIA AND SYNCHRONIZATION

Many applications work with audio, video, and other time-dependent processes. The difficulty in writing high-performance multimedia applications is that the response time must remain consistent during the program's execution. Audio and video processing are the most obvious of these, but the same characteristics can be found in many other types of applications. In a spacecraft system, for example, missing telemetry data can cause a catastrophic failure. In a video or audio system, the lack of predictable timing can lead to problems such as jitter, noise, frame loss, or other undesirable side effects. In this chapter, we will discuss some APIs related to sound and music, speech, and thread synchronization.

Fugue Fun: Making Music with JFugue

Adding music to your games, presentations, and business applications can make them much more interesting to the user. Some applications use *Musical Instrument Digital Interface (MIDI)* files for this purpose. MIDI is a standard for sharing music files in a way that preserves the music so that it can later be played on any MIDI-capable electronic musical instrument. This is different from music in MP3 and other audio file formats. Those formats preserve only the audio that was recorded using the original instruments. In a MIDI file, the music is stored as note-playing commands. Because all of the information is preserved, you can play the music back on different instruments or even modify the notes themselves. The MIDI standard also allows electronic musical instruments and computers to communicate with each other during a live performance. One common way of using MIDI is to have a computer program send sequences of notes to a bank of music synthesizers. A performer or composer can then have the resources of a complete orchestra on demand.

Java 1.3 introduced Java Sound to the core API, which added MIDI and sampled audio capability. However, its interface is awkward, because creating music requires knowing the correct MIDI commands to use. We can use a higher-level interface to make it easier to work with Java Sound. JFugue is an easy-to-use open-source API that uses String values to describe musical expressions that are then converted into MIDI commands and processed through the Java Sound interface. JFugue can play the music itself or save it as a MIDI file to be played later using another MIDI-capable program. To show how easy it is to play music with this API, let's see some code to play a simple song. If you've learned to play a musical instrument before, perhaps one of the first tunes that you learned was "Mary Had a Little Lamb." Here is some code that plays this song:

```
import org.jfugue.Pattern;
import org.jfugue.Player;

Pattern lamb = new Pattern();
lamb.add("eq dq cq dq eq eq eh");
lamb.add("dq dq dh eq gq gh");
lamb.add("eq dq cq dq eq eq eq eq");
lamb.add("dq dq eq dq cw");
Player jukebox = new Player();
jukebox.play(lamb);
```

The JFugue Pattern class represents a collection of MIDI commands—in this case, musical notes. The first part of each entry in the pattern is the note name (E or D, for example). The notes by default are in the fifth octave (the one with middle C), but you can use notes in other octaves by adding the octave number after the note name. The value "c7" would play a C two octaves above middle C. The second part of each note is the duration, where w is a whole note, h is a half note, and q is a quarter note. (The API documentation describes additional values for these duration codes.) An F in the sixth octave, with a half-note duration, would be "f6h". Another nice feature of the music String is its ability to create chords. For example, you can easily create a chord progression using the following:

```
Pattern progression = new Pattern();
progression.add("c5majw g5majw a5minw f5majw g5majw c5majw");
```

To make a chord, you use the name for the root note (for example, c5 and g5), followed by the chord name and the note length. The above code would play the chords C major, G major, A minor, F major, and C major as whole notes. See the documentation for a complete list of chord names recognized by the pattern parser. Once you have a Pattern object, you can also save the song as a MIDI file by giving the name of the new file:

```
jukebox.save(lamb, "/music/lamb.mid");
```

The JFugue API has a very small memory footprint and is useful for applications that need a quick and easy way to play music or to generate MIDI files. See this book's companion website, or go to www.jfugue.org for documentation and to obtain the libraries. In the next section, we'll discuss using JFugue as a simpler interface to the built-in MIDI API that is part of the Java core.

Fugue in Mid-D: Using JFugue with Java Sound MIDI

JFugue

JAVA 1.3+

In the previous section, we used the JFugue API to create and play music and to save it as a MIDI file. The open-source JFugue library is built on top of Java Sound, which is part of the core API in Java 1.3 and above. In the previous section, JFugue converted a Pattern into a series of low-level MIDI commands, usually consisting of a sequence of note-on and note-off events. The underlying Java Sound classes process these low-level events and send them to the sound card. You can access this sequence of low-level MIDI event data. The sound API can then perform advanced functions such as sending the data to a MIDI output device (for example, with an external music synthesizer connected). This music data is held in the Sequence class (from the javax.sound.midi package). After the JFugue parser is finished processing a Pattern, it creates a Sequence instance. You can access this data by using JFugue's Renderer class. The Renderer class is designed to be subclassed, so that you can process each MIDI event as it occurs and perform some action. In this case, we are using the Renderer only to create a MIDI sequence from the musical pattern.

```
import javax.sound.midi.Sequencer;
import javax.sound.midi.Sequence;

Player jukebox = new Player();
Pattern song = new Pattern("cq5 d5q e5q f5q g5q a5q b5q c6w");
```

```
jukebox.play(song);
Renderer renderer = new Renderer();
Sequence sequence = renderer.render(pattern);
```

Within a sequence, there are one or more tracks containing MIDI events (the MIDI command plus a timestamp). In the next bit of code, we get the first track and retrieve each MIDI event within it:

```
Track[] tracks = sequence.getTracks();
// sequence from the previous example
for (Track aTrack : tracks) {
    for (int i=0; i<aTrack.size(); i++) {
        MidiEvent event = aTrack.get(i);
        // now you could send the event to a device
    }
}
```

Without using the JFugue pattern String to load the MIDI commands, you'd have to learn the low-level MIDI protocol commands and explicitly add each event's bytes to the track. Populating a String with "cq5 d5q e5q f5q g5q a5q b5q c6w" is much easier than that! If you just want to access the data in an existing MIDI file, you can do this in a much easier way, using the following to obtain a Sequence object:

```
Sequence sequence = MidiSystem.getSequence(midiFile);
```

The MIDI source (the midiFile variable above) can be a File, InputStream, or URL instance, and you will need to catch InvalidMidiDataException and IOException. Once you have the Sequence object, you can use it to obtain the individual MIDI events as before or send it to a Sequencer to be played. You may be wondering what to do with the MidiEvent objects that we have now. In the next section, we'll see how to use the Java Sound API to send events to a MIDI device.

All MIDI-ed Out: Sending Events to a MIDI Output Device

JAVA 1.3+ Musicians often use MIDI to send musical commands from one device to another. A common scenario involves connecting a keyboard (the musical kind!) to a bank of synthesizers. The keyboard converts the player's key presses into MIDI events. A MIDI keyboard may not even be capable of producing sound; instead, it may only send note commands to the MIDI output port. A MIDI cable connects the output port to a synthesizer's MIDI input port, and the synthesizer then generates the sound.

Computers are often used as MIDI sequencers, to record and play back music. The musician plays a sequence on the keyboard, which is recorded via the computer's MIDI input port. Sequencer software can individually record many different tracks and later send them out simultaneously to the MIDI output port (to be played by a MIDI device such as a synthesizer). In Java, we can get the list of MIDI devices on the computer by calling the following code:

```
import javax.sound.midi.MidiSystem;
import javax.sound.midi.MidiDevice;

MidiDevice.Info[] devices = MidiSystem.getMidiDeviceInfo();
for (MidiDevice.Info deviceInfo : devices) {
   System.out.println(deviceInfo.getDescription());
}
```

Unfortunately, there is no way to get a handle on a particular device programmatically without searching through the MIDI devices using the descriptions. This is because each manufacturer's devices have different characteristics. The most common way of selecting a device is by letting the user select from a list that displays each one's description. When you find the Info instance (a public inner class of MidiDevice) for the device that you want to receive the events, you can obtain a handle on it by calling the static MidiSystem.getMidiDevice method. The MIDI events that we saw in the previous section each contain a MidiMessage, along with a timestamp that tells when to send the message. It is these messages that contain the note-on and note-off commands. This next code snippet shows how to send MIDI messages to a device:

```
// deviceInfo is a MidiDevice.Info instance obtained earlier
MidiDevice device = MidiSystem.getMidiDevice(deviceInfo);
device.open();
Receiver receiver = device.getReceiver();
MidiMessage msg;   // from a MidiEvent (see previous section)
long timeStamp;    // from a MidiEvent (see previous section)
receiver.send(msg, timeStamp);
receiver.close();
device.close();
```

We start with a MidiDevice.Info instance (deviceInfo) obtained from the earlier example where we looped through all the installed devices. We must first open the device to allow it to be used by the system, and then we can get a Receiver object. The Receiver accepts the MIDI messages and might represent either a synthesizer (such as on a sound card) or a MIDI output port. Once your program has finished using the device, you will need to close the Receiver and the MidiDevice.

Beeps and Bleeps: Synthesizing Sounds with JMusic

JAVA 1.3+

When I was in high school, my family purchased an electronic music synthesizer kit. After making a mess with the soldering iron, and burning some skin in the process, we had a (mostly) working synthesizer. It was an analog synthesizer, and we could use patch cables to connect oscillators, filters, mixers, and other audio components together to create sounds. The original idea was to use it to create music, but at the time I mostly just enjoyed using it to make unusual sounds—and, of course, to annoy my parents and siblings! Today, most music synthesizers are digital, and the commonly used ones have only a fixed set of sounds rather than allowing you to create new instruments by wiring components together. There are high-end units that still allow you to create new instruments, but it's also possible to create your own instrument *patches* without even spending any money on a music synthesizer. We can create our patches in software, using digital signal processing.

JMusic is an open-source API that is useful in generating music, synthesizing sounds, and analyzing musical data. One of its most powerful features is its sound synthesis capability. With JMusic, you can create your own instruments by chaining together audio synthesis components. You can then play music on the new instrument.

To create an instrument in JMusic, you connect sound processing units together. These units are instances of the AudioObject class in JMusic. Examples of AudioObject types include oscillators (to generate waveforms), filters, and mixers. You can easily create an instrument by subclassing the Instrument class. Your class must have a createChain method, which is automatically called when the instrument is first used. We will use this process to create a sawtooth wave, which would look like Figure 7-1 if seen through an oscilloscope. It shows the strength (amplitude) of the signal measured over time.

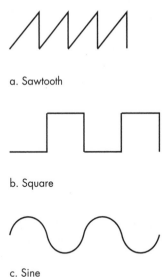

a. Sawtooth

b. Square

c. Sine

Figure 7-1: Sawtooth, square, and sine waveforms

Let's create an Instrument class now. We'll start with an oscillator, a device that creates a steady tone. The Oscillator class can create tones using one of several different waveforms, such as sine wave, square wave, or sawtooth. We override our Instrument's createChain method to create the chain of audio modules that produce the sound. Inside this method, we wire the sound modules together. For our first example, we'll create an oscillator and feed its output to a low-pass filter:

```
import jm.audio.Instrument;
import jm.audio.synth.Oscillator;
import jm.audio.synth.Filter;

public class FilteredSaw extends Instrument {
   public void createChain() {
      Oscillator saw = new Oscillator(this, Oscillator.SAWTOOTH_WAVE,
            44100, 2);
      Filter filter = new Filter(saw, 500.0, Filter.LOW_PASS);
   }
}
```

Our oscillator creates a sawtooth wave at 44,100 samples per second and with 2 channels (stereo). By default, the frequency will be determined by whichever note the instrument plays. The output of the oscillator is fed to a low-pass filter with a cutoff frequency of 500 Hertz.

Now we will need to send some music to our new instrument. In JMusic, a Score instance holds the musical data and contains Part instances that each represent a single instrumental part. A Part can contain one or more Phrases. Here is how you would play a short musical phrase using the instrument that we just created:

```
import jm.music.data.Note;
import jm.music.data.Part;
import jm.music.data.Score;
import jm.util.Play;
import jm.JMC;

// FilteredSaw is the instrument we created
Instrument inst = new FilteredSaw();
Score score = new Score();
Part part = new Part();
part.setTempo(180);
Phrase phrase = new Phrase();
phrase.addNote(new Note(JMC.C4, JMC.QUARTER_NOTE));
phrase.addNote(new Note(JMC.G4, JMC.QUARTER_NOTE));
phrase.addNote(new Note(JMC.E4, JMC.QUARTER_NOTE));
phrase.addNote(new Note(JMC.F4, JMC.QUARTER_NOTE));
phrase.addNote(new Note(JMC.G4, JMC.WHOLE_NOTE));
part.addPhrase(phrase);
score.add(part);
Play.audio(score, inst);
```

We create a Score and add a Part to it, set the tempo to 180 beats per minute, and add a short Phrase containing the desired notes. JMC is a class that contains many useful constants. Here we are using it for the note names and durations. There is much more that you can do with this API. See the JMusic documentation for more examples. In the next section, we will create a more complex instrument.

Hiss, Buzz, Hum: Using Noise and Complex Synthesis in JMusic

JMusic

JAVA 1.3+

In the previous section, we created a musical instrument by connecting a sawtooth wave oscillator to a low-pass filter. We then used it to play a short musical phrase. To make richer, more interesting sounds, we will need to use a number of different audio components and combine the sounds from them. A very common way of combining sound elements is to simply add the results as if the sounds were being played simultaneously. In this first example, we create a square wave oscillator and add it to the sawtooth from the previous section. This will give our instrument a richer sounding *timbre* (the combined characteristics of a sound that make it unique). To add the sounds together, we use the Add class, which takes an array of AudioObjects in its constructor:

```
import jm.audio.synth.Add;

public final class SquareFilteredSaw extends Instrument {
    public void createChain() {
        Oscillator saw = new Oscillator(this,
                Oscillator.SAWTOOTH_WAVE, 44100, 2);
        Filter filter1 = new Filter(saw, 500, Filter.LOW_PASS);
        Oscillator square = new Oscillator(this,
                Oscillator.SQUARE_WAVE, 44100, 2);
        Filter filter2 = new Filter(square, 4000, Filter.HIGH_PASS);
        Add adder = new Add(new AudioObject[] {filter1, filter2});
    }
}
```

This instrument uses two filtered oscillators and combines the sound from them. The sawtooth oscillator is filtered with a low-pass filter, which emphasizes the lower frequencies. This makes a difference in the sound because the sawtooth wave has many *harmonics*, or higher-frequency parts of the signal. We are filtering the square wave through a high-pass filter and emphasizing the higher harmonics of that signal. You can hear the sounds created by this and other instruments by going to the book's website at http://wickedcooljava.com.

Some sounds have *noise* associated with them. For example, a flute sounds a lot like a sine wave with a small amount of added noise for the breath sound. One common type of noise is called *white noise*, and it sounds like a hiss, as if you had tuned a radio or television between stations. In this next example, we will use two sine oscillators and a noise source to create a more complex sound. The first oscillator is tuned to the fundamental frequency of each note, to be determined when the note is played. This means that for the note A4, with a frequency of 440 Hz, the first oscillator will be at 440 Hz. The second oscillator is tuned to a multiple of five, which for A4 creates an overtone of 2200 Hz. Next, we send both of these tones through an Envelope, a wave-shaping object. You can use Envelope instances to change how the *amplitude* (volume) of a sound changes over time. Figure 7-2 shows how an envelope with volume levels of 0.2, 0.5, 0.7, 1.0, and 0.2 might look. Volume levels range from 0.0 (no sound) to 1.0 (full volume).

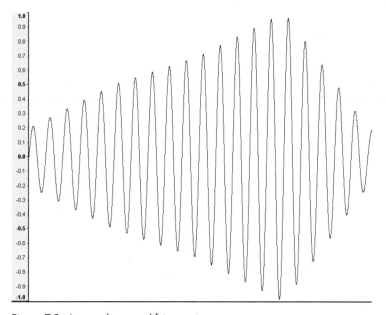

Figure 7-2: An envelope modifying a sine wave

Now let's put the audio chain together. We process the two oscillators and the noise generator using three separate envelopes, to give the sound some depth. We then combine the sounds using an Add object. The addition of the noise gives it a somewhat "breathy" quality. Here is the code:

```
import jm.audio.synth.Envelope;
import jm.audio.synth.Noise;

public class NoisySine extends Instrument {
  public void createChain() throws AOException {
    // this oscillator defaults to the fundamental frequency
    Oscillator sine = new Oscillator(this, Oscillator.SINE_WAVE);
    Envelope sineEnv1 = new Envelope(sine,
        new double[] {0.3, 0.5, 0.7, 0.9, 0.7, 0.5, 0.3});
    // this oscillator is at the 5th harmonic
    Oscillator sineHigh = new Oscillator(this, Oscillator.SINE_WAVE);
    sineHigh.setFrqRatio(5);
    Envelope sineEnv2 = new Envelope(sineHigh,
        new double[] {0.1, 0.2, 0.3, 1.0, 0.3, 0.2, 0.1});
```

```
// create a white noise component
Noise noise = new Noise(this);
Envelope env = new Envelope(noise,
    new double[] {0.01, 0.05, 0.1, 0.05, 0.01});
// add the three sound components together
Add adder = new Add(new AudioObject[] {sineEnv1, sineEnv2, env});
  }
}
```

Be careful that you have only one output stage of your sound chain, or you will get a runtime error. An example of this would be having two oscillators that do not join into a single line using a mixer. JMusic has many other signal-processing capabilities, such as stereo panning, creating delays, and modulating sounds. The JMusic documentation, to which you can find links on the book's website, has many more examples of music and sound synthesis.

Getting an Outside Line: Working with Low-Level Java Sound

JAVA 1.3+ For those of you who want to work with low-level signal processing (and individual sound samples), the Java Sound API provides the ability to do this. You can read and write data streams to and from audio ports, convert audio files between types, and process audio data in real time. In this section we will see how to obtain an audio line and use it to send or receive raw audio data. The details of real-time signal processing are beyond the scope of this book, and here we will be working only with the basics of getting an audio channel.

Java Sound's AudioSystem class provides access to sampled audio resources, including mixers, input/output ports, microphones, speakers, audio streams, and audio files. The first thing to remember about the audio lines is their naming convention, which is a bit counterintuitive. An input line such as a microphone is a TargetDataLine, and an output line such as a speaker is a SourceDataLine. These are named for the fact that an output line acts as a source to its mixer (the mixer takes it as input).

We will first work with a SourceDataLine, using the default mixer and output line, which is usually the speaker port. There are several types of formats for audio data samples, and we must first select one to use for the output. The most common is called *Pulse Code Modulation (PCM)*, which uses values for each sample that are in a linear proportion to the amplitude of the signal at that moment. We also must choose the *sampling rate*, or how fast the samples are taken, along with how many bits are in each sample and whether the samples are signed or unsigned values. We create an AudioFormat instance to represent the desired sampling characteristics and use that to get a line from the AudioSystem with those characteristics. In this example, we obtain an output line with 44,100 samples per second, 16 bits per sample, 2 channels (stereo), signed, and in little-endian byte order:

```
import javax.sound.sampled.AudioFormat;
import javax.sound.sampled.AudioSystem;
```

```
import javax.sound.sampled.LineUnavailableException;
import javax.sound.sampled.SourceDataLine;
try {
    AudioFormat format = new AudioFormat(44100, 16, 2, true, false);
    SourceDataLine line = AudioSystem.getSourceDataLine(format);
    line.open();
    line.start();

    // now you may write data to the line

    // insert code here to generate audio data
    line.drain();    // send out any data still in the buffer
    // when you are done, drain and close the line

    line.close();    // close the line
} catch (LineUnavailableException e) {
    e.printStackTrace();
}
```

Using the getSourceDataLine method in this fashion returns the default output line of the default mixer, and with the audio data in the specified format. You must open the line before it can be used, which assigns any required system resources to it. You also need to start the line, so that the line will begin sending sample data to the output device. Now we have a line that is ready for use. To send data to it, you fill the line's buffer with data in the proper format (see the documentation for data format details). To complete this example, let's write some random data to the line. This will generate white noise, as discussed in the previous section. Here is the code to fill the buffer with random data:

```
// now you may write data to the line

int size = line.getBufferSize();
byte[] data = new byte[size];
java.util.Random random = new java.util.Random();
for (int i=0;i<10;i++) {
    random.nextBytes(data);
    line.write(data, 0, size);
}
line.drain();    // send out any data still in the buffer
// when you are done, drain and close the line
```

As you may have guessed, this is the same middle section of code from the previous example. We first get the size of the line's internal buffer and create a byte array of that size. On my test run, the buffer size was 88,400 bytes, representing a half-second of data for 2 stereo channels at 16 bits. You can use your own buffer size, as long as it is an integral number of samples. The code above runs for 10 complete buffer lengths, which is 5 seconds of wonderful noise. Each time through the loop, we refill the buffer with data from a Random object. The write method takes a byte array, starting location, and size. This method blocks until the buffer is ready to accept the incoming data. To make more interesting sounds, you will need to fill the buffer with more appropriate sample data. That is where things get much more complicated, and you will need a good understanding of digital signal–processing theory. On the book's website, there are links to Java Sound documentation and other digital audio and signal-processing resources to get you started. In the next section, we continue the low-level discussion of Java Sound, this time processing audio data from an input line.

Yes, Dear, I'm Listening: Reading Audio from an Input Line

JAVA 1.3+ In the previous section we worked with an audio output, creating a Source-DataLine and sending some random data through it to the speaker. The Java Sound API also allows you to capture audio data from an input line such as a microphone. In this section, we will record audio into a data buffer, where it can be processed or saved to a file. There may be many input ports on the computer depending on the hardware configuration. To be sure we are using the correct device, we can let the user select from a list of installed mixers and select the appropriate line from the mixer (similar to what we did in the MIDI section earlier in this chapter). See the book's website for links to example code for doing this. However, for many applications we can get away with using the default audio input device. This will usually be the microphone or line in.

The process of obtaining an input line is very similar to working with output lines as we did in the previous section. You can select the default TargetDataLine from the AudioSystem, based on the desired format. Here we are using 22.1 kHz, at 8 bits per sample, and 2 channels (stereo). The internal buffer is not guaranteed to be a particular size, and it may be better to use your own value to maintain loop timing under different platforms and JVM versions. This code reads five full buffers worth of data from the default audio input device (2.5 seconds on my test run):

```
AudioFormat format = new AudioFormat(22100, 8, 2, true, false);
TargetDataLine input = AudioSystem.getTargetDataLine(format);
input.open();
int size = input.getBufferSize();
byte[] data = new byte[size];
input.start();
// loop through 5 buffer lengths
for (int i=0;i<5;i++) {
    input.read(data, 0, size);
    // process the input data buffer
    // (save it, transform and replay it, analyze it)
}
input.drain();
input.close();
```

You can perform all sorts of interesting operations on the audio data. The simplest is to store the data in a file for later processing or playback. Other interesting operations might include reverb effects, distortion, filtering, and analysis. Once you have the data in memory, you will need to know something about how the raw data translates to individual sound samples. This will depend on the number of channels, the encoding, and other aspects of the AudioFormat being used. See the Java core documentation for more information on the data formats.

Talk to Me! Using Java Speech to Make Programs Talk

FreeTTS

Adding speech capabilities to your applications can not only make them more interesting but can also make them more accessible to the vision-impaired. The *Java Speech API (JSAPI)* is a standard extension to Java, with features for speech synthesis as well as speech recognition. As with most other standard extensions to Java, you can plug in different implementations, and a number of speech engines are available. We will be using FreeTTS, an open-source speech engine. To use FreeTTS, you must first set up the JSAPI environment according to the documentation. This involves agreeing to Sun's JSAPI license terms, making sure the libraries are in the classpath, and placing a speech.properties file in your home directory. Once you've done this, it is very easy to make your Java applications talk. Here is an example that speaks a short text message:

```
import java.util.Locale;
import javax.speech.AudioException;
import javax.speech.Central;
import javax.speech.EngineException;
import javax.speech.EngineStateError;
import javax.speech.synthesis.JSMLException;
import javax.speech.synthesis.Synthesizer;
import javax.speech.synthesis.SynthesizerModeDesc;

try {
    // create a synthesizer for US English,
    // using the general-purpose configuration ("general").
    // See the JSAPI documentation for more information
    // on the mode descriptions.
    SynthesizerModeDesc modeDesc =
    new SynthesizerModeDesc(null, "general", Locale.US, null, null));
    Synthesizer talker = Central.createSynthesizer(modeDesc);
    // Allocate resources and start the synthesizer
    talker.allocate();
    talker.resume();
    talker.speak("Java is Wicked Cool, tell all your friends!", null);
    // Wait until speaking is finished
    talker.waitEngineState(Synthesizer.QUEUE_EMPTY);
    // Clean up synthesizer resources
    talker.deallocate();
```

```
} catch (IllegalArgumentException e) {
  e.printStackTrace();
} catch (EngineException e) {
  e.printStackTrace();
} catch (AudioException e) {
  e.printStackTrace();
} catch (EngineStateError e) {
  e.printStackTrace();
} catch (InterruptedException e) {
  e.printStackTrace();
} catch (JSMLException e) {
  e.printStackTrace();
}
```

There are other advanced features of the API, but it's not that difficult to get your application talking. The current FreeTTS voices sound robotic, as you might expect from previous experiences with speech synthesis. This is improving, and some of the other implementations have more realistic-sounding voices. FreeTTS does not yet support speech recognition, but some of the other speech engines do. The others are not free or open source as of this writing. For links to FreeTTS and other speech engines, and Sun's JSAPI documentation, see this book's companion website.

Reduce, Reuse, Recycle: GC and the Javolution Real-Time APIs

Javolution

JAVA 5+

Object creation and garbage collection are a very costly part of most Java programs. The idea behind real-time systems is to have a deterministic (predictable) execution time for certain operations. For example, in video or audio applications you would not want any unexpected delays to interfere with playback and recording. In Java, this is made more difficult because of the garbage-collection thread, which might run at any time. There are some third-party Java virtual machines that do provide real-time guarantees. However, that isn't much consolation for the developers who are not using one of them! An open-source API called Javolution can help to make your Java programs run more predictably, without replacing the virtual machine. Its main feature is providing classes (the equivalents of String and some other basic classes) that perform deterministically. These classes reuse their own contents without being recycled by the garbage-collector thread. In the standard Java Collection classes there are sometimes unpredictable delays because of array reallocations and rehashing. The Javolution equivalents have delays that are predictable within a very small variation.

Why might we not want to use Java's built-in String or Collection classes in a real-time program? The first answer is related to the performance of Java's own text-manipulation routines. The insert, delete, and concatenate operations of java.lang.StringBuffer and String have an $O(n)$ performance, whereas the Javolution Text and TextBuilder classes have $O(Log\ n)$. The Text class stores the text in a binary tree. This makes a big difference in applications with a large amount of text manipulation and that also have real-time requirements. Another reason to consider using Javolution is its object pool implementation. You can often avoid garbage-collection delays by using a pool of objects, reusing each instance after you have finished with it. The Javolution classes are designed to work well as pooled objects. A third reason is because the classes have XML serialization features built into them. You can even make your own real-time–compliant classes, by extending the RealtimeObject class. The Javolution documentation shows how to do this.

Let's look at a short example of some Javolution code. The PoolContext class associates an object pool with the current thread, and objects are retrieved from the thread's stack memory instead of being constructed in the heap. If you avoid constructing objects using the new operator and do not reference factory-created objects outside of the context, then the objects will never be garbage-collected. In the following example, we create a PoolContext and enter the context by calling its static enter method. Until you exit the context, any instances of RealtimeObject that you obtain from a factory will belong to the context's pool (for recycling) and will not be garbage-collected. The code is placed in a try/finally block to ensure that the exit method will always run (this is a try/finally without a catch clause, which some of you may not have seen before):

```
import javolution.realtime.PoolContext;

PoolContext.enter();
try {
    // perform operations on RealTimeObject instances
    // we are using our own subclass of RealTimeObject: RTData
    // the RTData class will be created later
    RTData[] telemetry = new RTData[200];
    for (int i=0; i<200; i++) {
        // assume that readData is some method that collects data
        RTData data = RTData.valueOf(System.currentTimeMillis(),
                        readData(), 0.07);
        telemetry[i] = data;
    }
} finally {
    PoolContext.exit();
}
```

Our hypothetical RTData class stores telemetry data, along with an acquisition time and an uncertainty value. The class is real-time compliant and compatible with the PoolContext because it is a subclass of RealTimeObject. Notice that it has no public constructor. All instances of the class must come from a Factory. The Factory class is an inner class of RealTimeObject and knows how to use recycled objects where possible. If the instances are not preallocated, you will incur an initial overhead because of construction. However, subsequent requests for an object instance will be much faster and within a narrow range of time. The Javolution documentation has timing information that shows how this works in practice. Here is the definition of our RTData class:

```
import javolution.realtime.RealtimeObject.Factory;

public class RTData extends RealtimeObject {
    private long acquireDate;
    private double telemetry;
    private double uncertaincy;

    private static final Factory<RTData> FACTORY =
        new Factory<RTData>() {
        protected RTData create() {
            return new RTData();
        }
    };

    // this constructor is private, and cannot be accessed
    // outside this class, forcing the use of the factory
    private RTData() {}

    public static RTData valueOf(long acqDate,
                                 double tele, double uncert) {
        RTData data = FACTORY.object();
        data.acquireDate = acqDate;
        data.telemetry = tele;
        data.uncertaincy = uncert;
      return data;
    }

    public long getAcquireDate() {
      return acquireDate;
    }

    public double getTelemetry() {
      return telemetry;
    }

    public double getUncertaincy() {
      return uncertaincy;
    }
}
```

Notice how we used its valueOf method in the earlier example, which uses the class's factory to get the instance. If we simply called new each time, the garbage collector would eventually run once the object goes out of scope. The PoolContext manages this process of recycling objects without running the garbage collector. Make sure that you don't reference any of the objects outside of the pool context, unless you first call the object's export method. For more information on creating real-time–compliant objects (such as the RTData class in this example) that you can use within a pool context, see the Javolution documentation.

Hurry Up and Wait: Synchronizing Threads Using CyclicBarrier

JAVA 5+

Remember in primary school at the end of each day, when you waited along with the other students for the school bell to ring? Some classrooms may have finished their day's work earlier than others, but everyone still had to wait for the bell before they could leave. The schools did this to make sure that the students left simultaneously at the proper time (and not a moment earlier!). There are similar situations in an application, where you have a number of threads that depend on each other's results and must all reach some milestone before continuing. In this section, we'll show you a technique (new to Java 5) for synchronizing such groups of threads.

Java 5 added a number of new concurrency utilities to the core API. One of these new classes is the CyclicBarrier, in the java.util.concurrent package. This class works as an invisible barrier that each member of some group of threads must reach before any of them can continue. Imagine that we are back in school again and that this time the bell doesn't ring at 3:00 P.M. but instead rings after every classroom has submitted its day's work to the principal's office. No one can leave until then. Using a CyclicBarrier, the room threads would each call the barrier's await method. The method blocks until a specific number of other threads call the method. Let's first create a Room class to simulate the students submitting work to the principal:

```java
import java.util.concurrent.CyclicBarrier;
public class Room extends Thread {
    CyclicBarrier barrier;
    public Room(CyclicBarrier cb) {
        barrier = cb;
    }
    public void run() {
        try {
            submitWork();    // pretend we do something useful first
            barrier.await();
        } catch (InterruptedException e) {
            e.printStackTrace();
        } catch (BrokenBarrierException e) {
            e.printStackTrace();
        }
    }
}
```

This Thread subclass uses a barrier passed in at construction time. In the run method, we perform our required work and then call the barrier's await method, which blocks until the others have called await also. We must catch two exceptions that might be thrown here. The JavaDoc for `CyclicBarrier` explains these exceptions in more detail.

Applications using the `CyclicBarrier` will most likely need to run some code immediately after the last thread enters the barrier. There is a constructor for this purpose that accepts a `Runnable` to be executed by the last thread that calls `await`. We can create a barrier for 100 threads by using the following:

```
Runnable finishAction = new Runnable() {
   public void run() {
      System.out.println("Ringgggg! School is dismissed!");
   }
};
CyclicBarrier barrier = new CyclicBarrier(100, finishAction);
```

After the barrier is crossed, you can reset it by calling the reset method, and it is ready for another round of `await` calls. A barrier is most applicable when each thread contributes something to a final result and the threads must then use the composite value. One example of such usage in the context of the school scenario is for each classroom to submit votes for the student council, and then each classroom prepares a report using the elected students' names before leaving for the day. This obviously cannot happen until the other rooms have cast their ballots. A more real-world example where the barrier might help is in a simulation with many interrelated components. In Chapter 5, we worked with one such system when we built a digital component with input and output values. We were able to avoid complex synchronization issues there because the wires performed the task of moving output values of a previous stage to the inputs of the next stage. But the `CyclicBarrier` could also have been used in that scenario, and we could then have assigned each component to its own thread. In the next chapter we'll discuss a distributed hardware and software system called the *Cell Matrix*. This system is made of many coordinated digital components and would be a good candidate for synchronization using the `CyclicBarrier`.

Chapter Summary

In this chapter, we looked at several techniques for working with time-dependent processes. Managing garbage collection and thread synchronization is important in real-time systems, and Java 5 added many new features such as the `CyclicBarrier` to the threading system. We also explored speech, music, and sound APIs. Using sound effectively can make your applications much more engaging and can also be useful in providing accessibility to the visually impaired. In the next chapter, we will discuss miscellaneous open-source projects and provide ideas for integrating code from the rest of the book.

8

FUN, INTEGRATION, AND PROJECT IDEAS

In this chapter, we take a look at miscellaneous open-source projects and discuss ideas for creating your own projects and integrating code from earlier sections. Some are just for fun, and others are more useful but don't really fit anywhere else. A few of them are long-term projects that I think would be nice to have as open source. On the book's website at http://wickedcooljava.com, there is a public forum for discussing these and other project ideas, where readers can collaborate on creating open-source projects. I hope that if you start on a project described here, you will make it open source so we can all benefit from it! Check the website forum for more ideas and to keep track of the latest developments.

Think Outside the Blocks: Using Java to Control a LEGO Robot

`LEJOS` LEGO bricks are well-known items among parents and children in many millions of homes around the world. Children have loved using these building blocks ever since 1934 when they were first created in Denmark.

The LEGO Group, which now produces many other toys besides the classic bricks, makes a robotics construction set called Mindstorms. The Mindstorms kit has bricks of various shapes and sizes, but this is not the reason for the product's popularity. The main attraction is a small handheld computer, called the RCX. This computer has three motor controller ports and three sensor ports, and the kit provides a small collection of sensors and motors to use with it.

The RCX computer includes a Windows application to help you write robot-control programs graphically. The interface for this programming environment is fine for teaching kids to write simple robot-control programs but is not sophisticated enough for real development work. The RCX firmware provided by LEGO works specifically with the graphical programming environment. However, you can download open-source replacement firmware called LEJOS that runs a small subset of Java. This allows you to write robotics programs in Java. The TinyVM in LEJOS isn't technically Java because it is not a complete implementation of the core classes. However, it does run a subset of Java executable bytecodes, and you write the source code in Java. You compile the source code using the LEJOS compiler and then download the classes to the RCX.

The Motor class provides access to the motor controllers, using three static variables (A, B, and C) to represent the three motor connectors on the RCX. The following bit of code moves the A motor forward, moves the B motor forward and then reverses the A motor:

```
import josx.platform.rcx.Motor;
// set the motor power levels
Motor.A.setPower(5);
Motor.B.setPower(5);
// move motor A forward
Motor.A.forward();
// sleep for 500 ms
Thread.sleep(500);
// move the motors
Motor.B.forward();
Motor.A.backward();
// sleep for 500 ms
Thread.sleep(500);
// stop the motors
Motor.A.stop();
Motor.B.stop();
```

Of course, the behavior of this program will depend on what the motors are driving. They could each be connected to a different wheel, track, hand, arm, or other mechanical device. This means that every robot design will have a different program customized for it.

You can also work with the three sensor connectors on the RCX. The sensors are accessed using the Sensor class and its static variables S1, S2, and S3. The sensors could be light, sound, touch, temperature, or some other type. For each combination of physical layout of the robot and locations and types of sensor, the program will perform a different function. The `Sensor` documentation describes how to create and register a `SensorListener` that will be informed of any changes in the sensor values as they occur.

Once you finish writing a program, you must compile it using the LEJOS compiler. You then download the class files to the RCX using the infrared communications tower that comes with the Mindstorms set. Turn on the RCX (with robot attached, of course), and your robot is ready to roam.

Aye, Robot: Controlling the Mouse with the AWT Robot Class

JAVA 1.3+

The Java core (1.3 and above) includes a class called `java.awt.Robot`. This class does not represent a physical robot as in the previous section. Instead, it lets you control the mouse and keyboard as if the user had directly operated them. In fact, the mouse actions can even interact with external programs and the user environment (desktop, menus, and so on). You might use this to run an automated testing process, for example, or to simulate user actions in a demonstration or help program. The methods work using absolute screen coordinates rather than window coordinates. Let's assume that you want to move to a specific position on the screen, click the mouse button, and then type some text. Using the `Robot` class, you could write a Java program to interact with another application such as a text editor. To illustrate this, you can open up a text editor so that it is in the top-left corner of the screen and run the following code (you may need to adjust the coordinates for your system and your text editor of choice):

```java
java.awt.Robot robot = new java.awt.Robot();
robot.mouseMove(20,90);
robot.mousePress(InputEvent.BUTTON1_MASK);
robot.mouseRelease(InputEvent.BUTTON1_MASK);
robot.keyPress(KeyEvent.VK_B);
robot.keyRelease(KeyEvent.VK_B);
robot.keyPress(KeyEvent.VK_O);
robot.keyRelease(KeyEvent.VK_O);
robot.keyPress(KeyEvent.VK_T);
robot.keyRelease(KeyEvent.VK_T);
```

If the text entry region of a text editor is onscreen at (20, 90), then this robot will click the text region, select it, and press the keys to spell the word *bot*. For this to work, the console window or development environment from which you run the Java program must not be on top of the other application. On some platforms, you will need additional security privileges to be able to control the mouse and keyboard devices.

Click and Pick: Picking Dates Using JCalendar

JCalendar

Many applications have data entry screens with date fields in which the user must enter a month, day, and year. Although it may be less work for the programmer to just let users manually enter these dates as text, it's not as friendly to the user as having a pop-up window with a date-picking calendar. Also, by using a date picker, the values will never be entered incorrectly and data validation is much easier. JCalendar is an open-source component for picking dates from a calendar. Adding the JCalendar class to any Swing container displays the calendar and allows the user to move backward and forward in time (figuratively speaking!) to select a date. For most applications, however, you will want to use the JDateChooser class. This class has an editable field with year, month, and day values and a calendar image that pops up a JCalendar for choosing the date. This is closer to the functionality that most applications will need. It is very simple to use, as the following code illustrates:

```
import com.toedter.calendar.JDateChooser;
import java.util.Date;
// add the chooser to a panel or frame
JDateChooser chooser = new JDateChooser();
myFrame.add(chooser);
// some time later....
// when you are ready to read the data, call the getDate method
Date dateValue = chooser.getDate();
```

The date field initially looks like a normal text field. When you click the small calendar icon to the right of the text, a calendar pops up that lets you select the date to place in the field. You can use the JCalendar and JDateChooser classes anywhere that you need to enter dates in your Swing applications, instead of simply using a text field.

Post Haste: Using HttpClient to Post Forms to HTTP Servers

JAKARTA
COMMONS

Java developers commonly write applications that connect to a website to retrieve a resource from a URL. The data might be HTML, XML (as in Chapter 3), a standard text file, an image, or any other type of content. Perhaps the data will be incorporated into a Swing GUI or placed into a dynamically generated web page. In other cases the program further processes the data in some other way. Long ago, the core Java API provided a convenient way to make simple web requests and read the data as a stream. The java.net.URL class can make a request and read data from the HTTP response, as if the URL had been entered into the address window of a web browser (this is called an HTTP GET method). However, the core API doesn't include convenient support for POST methods, automatic cookie handling, or adding form fields to the request.

The Jakarta Commons project comes to the rescue with a class called HttpClient, in the org.apache.commons.httpclient package. To send a GET request to a web server and read the document and any cookies returned along with it, use the following code:

```
import org.apache.commons.httpclient.HttpClient;
import org.apache.commons.httpclient.HttpException;
```

```
import org.apache.commons.httpclient.HttpStatus;
import org.apache.commons.httpclient.methods.GetMethod;

HttpClient client = new HttpClient();
// an example only... replace this with your site
GetMethod method = new GetMethod("http://wickedcooljava.com");
try {
    // get the response code, hopefully "successful" (SC_OK, or 200)
    int response = client.executeMethod(method);
    if (response == HttpStatus.SC_OK) {
        String result = method.getResponseBodyAsString();
        // this is the document returned by the response
        System.out.println(result);
        Cookie[] cookies = client.getState().getCookies();
        System.out.println(Arrays.toString(cookies));
    } else {
        System.err.println("Response code: " + method.getStatusLine());
    }
} catch (IOException e) {
    e.printStackTrace();
} finally {
    method.releaseConnection();
}
```

The cookie handling is automatic and is accessed through the HttpState object. The cookies will be held in the state and handled in the same way as a browser would. To send data using a POST method with form data, you would use the following:

```
import org.apache.commons.httpclient.methods.PostMethod;
String results = "";
HttpClient client = new HttpClient();
PostMethod method =
    new PostMethod("http://search.dmoz.org/cgi-bin/search");
method.addParameter("search", "coffee");
try {
    int respcode = client.executeMethod(method);
    if (respcode == HttpStatus.SC_OK) {
        results = method.getResponseBodyAsString();
    } else {
        System.err.println("Failure: " + method.getStatusLine());
    }
} catch (HttpException e) {
    e.printStackTrace();
} catch (IOException e) {
    e.printStackTrace();
} finally {
    method.releaseConnection();
```

```
            }

            System.out.println("--- Results obtained ---");
            System.out.println(results);
```

The HttpClient class could be used to write your own custom browser or for testing web applications. It is especially useful for retrieving data from websites using a POST-based form interface. You can also use it for connecting to web services.

She Sells C Cells: Simulating a Cell Matrix in Java

Perhaps you've heard the old programmer's joke: "How many programmers does it take to change a light bulb?" Of course, by now everyone should know that it's a hardware problem and not to bother the programmers with it! Joking aside, as programmers we typically think of the hardware as being separate from the software. This is especially true with Java, where our programs are cross-platform and can run in a wide variety of systems. We don't normally write anything differently for a Unix system than for a Windows system, or for a Pentium versus a PowerPC. But there are also advantages to writing code tailored to a particular type of hardware—higher performance and access to special features of the hardware. It would be nice to have a blend of software and hardware—the high performance of custom hardware but with the flexibility and mutability of software.

There is a type of computer hardware called the Cell Matrix that works very differently than most computer systems do. The Cell Matrix belongs in a category somewhere between software and hardware. It consists of interconnected digital components, each with a truth table (as discussed in Chapter 5) that controls the output function of the cell. This is useful because the cells can perform any Boolean function depending on how the table is configured. However, these cells are also capable of programming their neighbors' truth tables—this is what makes it somewhat like software. A cell looks like Figure 8-1 and has C and D inputs and outputs on each side. The D (data) signals work as in a normal digital component, except that the function of the cell is determined by the internal truth table of the cell. The normal operation of a cell is in D mode, where the circuit operates using the function defined by the truth table. Cells can also operate in C (code) mode, where the cell's truth table is programmed by one of its neighbors. A cell goes into C mode when one of its neighbors has an active C signal output. Once this happens, the bits in the cell's truth table are set to values coming from the neighbor's D output. Once the truth table is loaded, and the neighbor's C output returns to the inactive state (0), the cell begins operating according to the new truth table. Figure 8-1 shows a Cell Matrix operating in C and D modes.

Cell Matrices are a new way of thinking about computer systems and about programming. Not only can you easily change the way a circuit operates by changing its truth tables, but you can also create matrices that dynamically repair or reconfigure themselves (using C mode). Systems with this type of design have many potential applications in intelligent adaptive systems.

Because the exact configuration of each cell determines how the system behaves as a whole, it's very important to experiment with different models to understand how they work. This is especially true when the circuit is self-modifying via C mode operation. We can simulate a Cell Matrix in Java, using the metacomponent system from Chapter 5 as a baseline (and a functor that simulates a single cell in a Cell Matrix). To complete the simulator, we can use JGraph for the display, showing the state of the system and how it changes over time.

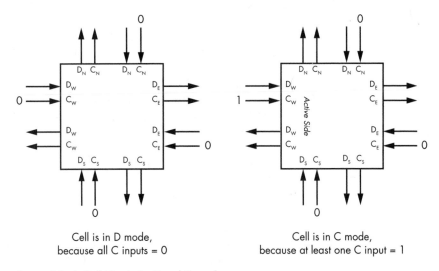

Figure 8-1: A Cell Matrix in C and D modes

The book's website has a complete implementation of a Java-based Cell Matrix simulator and examples of matrix configurations for performing some larger-scale logic functions. Once you have designed and tested your circuits in a simulator, you can try them on a real hardware implementation. Hardware is available for purchase from the Cell Matrix Corporation, the company that holds the patent on the Cell Matrix. For more information on the Cell Matrix, see the official website at www.cellmatrix.com.

Nature's May Tricks: Evolving Cell Matrices

Spring is usually seen as a period of growth and rebirth, but in reality it is also testing time. In the natural world, it is during spring when the next generation is conceived and born. The creatures that are successful in this process will continue to propagate their genetic material for yet another generation. In the previous section we discussed the Cell Matrix, a type of system that has characteristics of both hardware and software. The configuration of a matrix is the set of all its truth tables and the current state of each C and D wire in the system. Creating configurations for self-modifying systems such as these involves a painstaking design and testing process. We still don't have much experience in creating these types of systems, and our efforts to date are far from ideal. However, nature seems to create these types of systems quite well.

It does this through an iterative design process. It tries all types of new things, a countless number of variations on some theme, and then puts them through the rigorous testing process of life and death. The ones that survive the testing are used in creating new design variations. You may refer to this process by its better-known name: evolution.

Most likely, the successful self-modifying systems of the future will not be explicitly designed in a laboratory by humans but through an evolutionary process. The JGAP API, discussed in the section "It's Alive! Using JGAP for Genetic Algorithms" in Chapter 5, can be used to create evolved systems of any type (including a Cell Matrix). One useful application would be an environment where the user can manage the evolution of Cell Matrix configurations. This type of application would allow the user to start with existing matrix designs, create scenarios for fitness tests, start new tests, and manage the testing process. To make the application even more useful, the evolutionary process could be distributed across many machines for greater performance. Once a newly evolved design is ready, the user could then export the configuration for use in a software simulator or in real hardware.

A Real Worker Ant: Running Applications with Apache Ant

Usually we don't like bugs anywhere near our Java code, but Ant is one bug that you will like. Apache Ant is an open-source Java build tool. Developers often use it for managing multiple build, test, and deployment operations when working on large projects. Ant uses an XML file to describe the available targets that you can run. A target consists of one or more tasks. There are tasks available that can do many different things: compile or execute Java code, create JAR files, run external programs, work with change-control systems (such as CVS and SourceSafe), copy files, and much more. In some ways it is similar to the make tool available on some systems. Like make, Ant can also manage dependencies between targets.

If you are distributing an application that requires a complex process to run, such as a complex classpath, you can set up an Ant target to run it. First you will need to install the Ant classes in your system and make sure that the ant command is in your system path so that the operating system can find it. Once this is done, you must create the XML file (build.xml) to describe the target. Here is a sample Ant file with a target that runs a Java program:

```xml
<project name="sample" default="run" basedir=".">
  <target name="run" description="Run the program" >
    <java classname="org.example.MainProgram">
      <classpath>
        <pathelement location="lib/someapi.jar" />
        <pathelement path="classes" />
      </classpath>
    </java>
  </target>
</project>
```

The java task executes the class provided in the `classname` attribute (substitute the name of your own class for `org.example.MainProgram`). The classpath for the program will include all the path elements described in the `pathelement` tags. These can be either JAR files or locations of directories containing class files. Once you have created the Ant project file, you can easily run the Java program by typing the following in the same directory as the XML file:

```
ant
```

The Ant program will look for an XML file called `build.xml` and execute the default target in the file (`run`, in our example).

Playing a Shell Game: Using BeanShell

BeanShell

JAVA 1.3+

As Java developers, we often need to experiment with new ideas before integrating them into an application. Now, I'm usually all in favor of the strongly typed nature of Java, but there are times when I want to be just a bit lazy so that I can test something! What I really need at those times is a scripted environment that is pure Java, yet where I can work with loosely typed variables and not have to write and compile classes. For this purpose, the *BeanShell* environment, an embeddable interpreter and scripting environment for Java, works quite well.

BeanShell works in two ways that can be helpful. First of all, you can use it as a shell scripting language—either directly from a command prompt in interactive mode or by loading a script from a file. Interactive mode is particularly great for experimenting with GUI components. In the following simple example, BeanShell starts from a command prompt. All you need is to have the BeanShell JAR file in the classpath, and then you can start the `bsh.Interpreter` class. You can interactively enter Java code from the interpreter and see the effects immediately. This code will display a JFrame with a button:

```
C:\projects\beanshell> java bsh.Interpreter
bsh% frame = new JFrame("From Bean Shell");
bsh% pane = frame.getContentPane();
bsh% panel = new JPanel();
bsh% panel.add(new JButton("Don't push me"));
bsh% pane.add(panel);
bsh% frame.setSize(200, 200);
bsh% frame.setVisible(true);
```

If you want to read the script from a file, you can pass the filename as a parameter to the interpreter:

```
C:\projects\beanshell> java bsh.Interpreter coolbeans.txt
```

For those of you who would prefer to use a simple editor for writing your BeanShell scripts, use the `bsh.Console` class instead of `bsh.Interpreter`. This puts you in a desktop that is vaguely reminiscent of the early Unix windowing environments and starts you in an open shell. There is a basic text editor, accessible from a right-click on the console, which has an option where you can also run the script.

Interactive mode is great for debugging. Let's say that you have some code that doesn't work and you're not quite sure what's wrong. You can enter the code into BeanShell (or paste it in), print the value of variables, and even change their values before using them in a method. This can save a lot of time in debugging, and it sure beats sprinkling your code with lots of `System.out.println` statements.

The second way to use BeanShell is to embed it within an application. You can use this feature to add scripting capabilities to an application. In this next example, the class starts an `Interpreter` instance and uses the eval method to evaluate a BeanShell script containing Java code. It then loads a script from a file, using the source method. Notice that you can share variables between the application and the script by using the set and get methods of the interpreter.

```java
import bsh.Interpreter;
import java.util.Date;

public class InterpreterTest
{
    public static void main(String[] args)
    {
        Interpreter shell = new Interpreter();
        shell.set("varName", "my data");
        shell.eval("date = new java.util.Date();");
        shell.eval("System.out.println(date);");
        shell.eval("System.out.println(varName);");
        shell.source("test.bsh");
        Date myCopy = (Date) shell.get("date");
    }
}
```

Some things about BeanShell make it slightly different (easier and more suitable for scripting) than typical Java code. You do not need to declare a variable before you use it, and the types are dynamically assigned. The example above clearly shows this, in the use of the date variable. And here is the feature that gives BeanShell its name: if you want to work with properties of a JavaBean, simply use the name of the property. This works for both setting and getting properties. These automatically get translated into the appropriate method calls for property accessors and mutators, as in the following BeanShell code:

```java
frame.visible = true;
System.out.println(frame.visible);
```

By now, I'll bet you already think BeanShell is wicked cool, and you don't even need to "shell" out any cash—it's free! We could have used BeanShell for most of the examples in this book without writing a Java class or compiling the code.

Testing, Testing, Testing: Creating JUnit Tests

Thorough testing is one of the most important things that you can do as a developer. In a well-organized development project, there are several types of testing. There is the obvious functional testing that tests how well the application does the tasks that it is supposed to perform (based on system requirements, of course). Performance testing is another common type of testing, where we measure the application's response time and ability to handle higher user loads. Unit testing is yet another type of testing, one that is often underutilized. This involves writing tests for individual classes and methods, to ensure that each part of the system works on its own. Once you know that each part works by itself, you can try to integrate them into a complete system. Integration testing will then be able to show whether the components work properly when combined. Integration testing should focus on the combined whole, and we can be sure about this only if we already know that each part works properly on its own.

JUnit is a unit-testing framework for Java. It can be used for running individual tests or automated test suites against the classes in your application. The ideal is to have a matching test class for every class in the application. To write a test class, start by subclassing TestCase. One useful naming convention is to use the name of the class being tested, followed by the word Test. For example, if we are testing a class called Component, the test class would be called ComponentTest. Next, create methods in the test class that check the functionality of the application's classes. The names of these methods should begin with test, and the name should describe the functionality that is being tested.

```
import junit.framework.TestCase;
public class ComponentTest extends TestCase {
    public void testProcess() {
        // initialize the objects used in the test
        // use the objects, and obtain the result
        String result = .......
        String expected = "abcdef";
        // check if the result is the correct output value
        Assert.assertTrue(result.equals(expected));
    }
    // you can create other methods to test other functionality

    // create a test suite
    public static Test suite() {

    }
}
```

The `testProcess` method initializes the objects we are testing, runs the desired code, and then compares the expected output against the actual output. The `assertTrue` method signals to the test-management system that the `boolean` expression parameter must evaluate to `true` or the test is marked as a failure. JUnit comes with a GUI class called `TestRunner`, which graphically shows the results of running a suite of tests and displays each one as passing or failing. To create a suite, add the following method to the `ComponentTest` class:

```
public static Test suite() {
    return new TestSuite(ComponentTest.class);
}
```

JUnit uses *reflection* to find the names of the unit tests. Any methods in your test class that start with `test` will be included in the results. To see the results, run the following:

```
java junit.swingui.TestRunner
```

Enter the name of your test class when the GUI starts, and then press the Run button. The results of all the tests will display in the GUI once they are completed.

Peering into the Future: Using JXTA for Peer-to-Peer Applications

 An increasing number of applications are being built using peer-to-peer frameworks. Peer applications are different from client/server systems, because in peer systems each network node is both a client and a server. Peer-to-peer systems became well known a few years ago because of the controversy over public music file-sharing systems. But there is much more that you can do with a peer-to-peer environment besides sharing files. JXTA (which is shorthand for *juxtapose*) is a standard language- and network-independent network protocol as well as an API. A peer provides a service that is advertised to other peers. Peers can discover the services of other peers, communicate with them, and collaborate on tasks. Peers come in all shapes and sizes: everything from micro-connected devices such as Java phones to desktop computers and mainframes. There are many types of applications that would benefit from JXTA: gaming, distributed collaboration, file sharing, information sharing, and web services, to name a few. The best place to get more information on JXTA is at the official website: www.jxta.org. There are example applications, tutorials, demos, and documentation at the JXTA site.

Grid Is Good: Using the Globus Toolkit and Grid Computing

A *grid* is a type of distributed system where resources such as memory or processing power are shared among a large number of computers and appear to be a single system. Grids can combine the resources from thousands of machines into a single virtual supercomputer. The SETI@home project is one example of grid computing. This project was launched in 1999 to help researchers analyze radio signals from space, in search of evidence of extra-terrestrial life. SETI@home takes advantage of underutilized processing power on many thousands of machines to process large amounts of data in a distributed manner. Many other grids are in operation around the world, with applications in physics, bioinformatics, weather, and numerous other areas. You can create your own grid applications in Java, using the open-source Globus toolkit API. It has facilities for data and resource management, security, communications, and resource discovery. Using the Globus toolkit, you can create large-scale applications that pool resources from many different machines into a single service. The toolkit is being used in commercial grids by IBM, Oracle, Sun, and other companies; it is also heavily utilized in scientific and research applications at universities and government agencies in the United States and the European Union. For more information on Globus and grid computing, you can visit www.globus.org or this book's website.

Jabberwocky: Adding Chat to Your Application with Jabber

Many types of applications are collaborative, and the users of such applications would benefit from the addition of an instant messaging (IM) capability. A new protocol called *Extensible Messaging and Presence Protocol (XMPP)* allows applications to stream XML elements across a network, and it was created especially for working with instant-messaging applications. Jabber is a set of protocols based on XMPP, as well as an API for working with them. You can use the Jabber API to add messaging functionality to your programs. There are several ways to use Jabber for instant messaging. The easiest is to use Jabber directly "out of the box"—you can use the Jabber client program to connect with multiple chat servers. You can run your own Jabber servers or use a public one. Jabber can also connect to other IM systems such as Yahoo, MSN, or AOL. The most interesting feature of the Jabber API is the ability to embed IM client and server functions into your own application. For instance, you might build a collaborative editing application and include a chat feature so that the users could discuss work issues (or to gossip and make lunch plans!). The Jabber API has many other advanced features, such as connecting through a firewall, encrypting messages, and interfacing with email systems. Visit the official Jabber website at www.jabber.org.

Some Assembly Required: Writing JVM Assembly Language

JASMIN

BCEL

The *Java Virtual Machine (JVM)* is one of the most amazing things about Java, and it took the software industry by storm when it was released back in 1995. The JVM is important because it allows developers to write code once and run it on multiple target platforms without recompiling. In other languages, source code is compiled into an executable for a single platform. This is still true with Java, but the target platform is the JVM. The ability to run on different platforms comes from the many implementations of the JVM for different machines and operating systems. You have probably heard of bytecode and are aware that it is the machine language for Java. However, most people are not aware that there is also an assembly language for the JVM. You can see the assembly code for a class by running the javap program that comes with the compiler, using the -c option, as shown by this sample run using the Date class:

```
C:\projects> javap -c java.util.Date

Compiled from "Date.java"
public class java.util.Date extends java.lang.Object implements
java.io.Serializable,java.lang.Cloneable,java.lang.Comparable{
public java.util.Date();
  Code:
   0:    aload_0
   1:    invokestatic    #393; //Method java/lang/System.currentTimeMillis:()J
   4:    invokespecial   #399; //Method "<init>":(J)V
   7:    return

public java.util.Date(long);
  Code:
   0:    aload_0
   1:    invokespecial   #383; //Method java/lang/Object."<init>":()V
   4:    aload_0
   5:    lload_1
   6:    putfield        #372; //Field fastTime:J
   9:    return
```

The -c option shows the disassembled code from the class file. Of course, to most Java developers this code doesn't make much sense! The commands shown above, such as aload_0 and putfield, are known as *opcodes*. You will need to learn the Java assembly language to be able to understand what this code does or to write classes using assembly code. For some applications, you may want to tightly optimize a section of code for speed, and you may have considered writing some code in C/C++ and using the *Java Native Interface (JNI)* to hook it into your Java application. This will probably give you a speed boost, at the cost of platform independence and maintainability. Instead, you can try writing the class in Java assembly code and hand-optimizing that section. For some operations, this will give you a large increase in performance without sacrificing the platform independence of the JVM. The Java compiler usually does a great job of compiling source code into machine language, but an experienced assembly programmer would probably still win the competition for code optimization.

If you choose to write a class in assembly code, there are a couple of options. Jasmin is an assembler that converts assembly language source files into machine language for the JVM (class files). The *Byte Code Engineering Library (BCEL)* is another open-source project that allows you to programmatically read and write class files and Jasmin assembly code. You can use it to write compilers, optimizers, transformers, and interpreters for Java and other languages. It can even modify existing class file structures. Both of these tools have an extensive learning curve and will require you to learn the Jasmin assembly language and the internals of the JVM. You will find links to these projects on the book's website.

Writing JVM assembly language code should be a last resort. Most of the time, only a few small sections of code are the performance bottlenecks slowing down an application the most. A profiling tool can help to locate these problem areas. On the book's website you will find links to profiling tools that can help you in this process. Optimization is certainly not a bad idea, but keep in mind that according to Donald Knuth, a renowned computer scientist at Stanford University, "premature optimization is the root of all evil." You should wait until you are sure that the area in question really is a bottleneck before doing any optimization.

Bytecode Critters: Combining Genetic Programming with BCEL

In the previous section, we discussed the use of alternative tools to generate bytecodes, rather than compiling Java source code to make class files. One of these tools is BCEL, an API for manipulating the structure of class files. With BCEL you can create classes dynamically by calling methods to add each line of JVM assembly code to the class. The hardest part of creating a class in this manner is knowing which opcodes to use to perform the desired task. You may be able to use a genetic algorithm API such as JGAP (discussed in Chapter 5) to dynamically create classes for some types of applications. The most useful cases are when you have a class with existing methods, and you need a slight variation from these methods but don't know what it is ahead of time. If it is something easily testable (perhaps with a JUnit test), then you could write a fitness function for it and create classes with random variations using slightly different bytecodes. You might even consider writing a graphical environment for managing the evolution process, as mentioned in "Nature's May Tricks: Evolving Cell Matrices."

Coffee Substitutes: Compiling Other Languages to Bytecode

In the previous two sections, we discussed alternative ways to create bytecode besides simply writing Java source. In the most extreme cases, we can write programs at a very low level by working directly in JVM assembly language (Jasmin). We can also write programs to generate bytecode using BCEL, as mentioned in the previous section. A third option is to compile into bytecodes from a high-level language other than Java. There are now many alternative compilers that can convert other languages into bytecode. Examples of languages that can be compiled into bytecode include Basic, Scheme, Lisp, Logo, Prolog, Ada, COBOL, and many others (the book's website has links to many of these compilers). This can be useful for working with special-purpose languages or for reusing legacy code written in another language within a JVM.

If you don't see an existing compiler for your desired language and are looking for an ambitious project to work on, you could write your own! This would require a combination of JavaCC, parsing techniques from Chapter 3, and BCEL. You'll also need an extensive knowledge of your language's grammar and the details of JVM machine code.

LojViz: Grammar Visualizer for Lojban

In Chapter 4, in the section "Simply Logical: Lojban, RDF, and the Jorne Project," we discussed the constructed spoken and written language called Lojban. Here we are speaking of a human language, not a programming language! Because the language is syntactically unambiguous, and because of its logical nature, sentences in Lojban can be easily diagrammed and represented graphically. An application that parses Lojban text might display it as a graphical view, something like that shown in Figure 8-2.

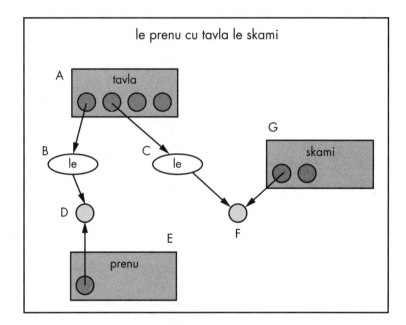

Figure 8-2: A diagrammed Lojban sentence

This type of display would be useful for text in other languages, too, but you'd need to disambiguate the words and sentences for most natural languages. The user might select the intended meaning from a list of possible meanings for a word, or the system would use some type of heuristics to determine the intended meaning of each word based on context. A sophisticated version of this might determine word context using a rule-based intelligent agent or a neural network and have the user select from a list when the process does not lead to a clear selection for the most likely meaning.

Pitch Patch: Synthesizer Patch Editor

In Chapter 7, in the section "Beeps and Bleeps: Synthesizing Sounds with JMusic," we created musical instruments by wiring together sound-processing components with the JMusic API. To create and use our custom digital instruments, we needed to write Java code that connected the output of each unit to the input of another. This is quite tedious for more complex sounds, and it would be nice to be able to wire these components together using a graphical interface. Such an application would allow the user to drag audio components onto the work area and connect them together into a working musical instrument. The application would generate the appropriate Java source code and allow you to save the new instrument, compile it, and then play music using it.

Words with Wires: WordNet Explorer

In the Chapter 5 section "Word Up: Navigating English with JWordNet," we looked at a lexical reference system for English and worked with an API that can obtain the related words for any word sense. Words may be related by inheritance or by encapsulation; in linguistic terms, these are hypernym/hyponym and meronym/holonym relationships. WordNet contains many thousands of these relationships, and JWordNet allows you to follow the links between words. You could use this API to create an application for graphically exploring semantic relationships. The user could type in a word and select the desired word sense from a list. A graphical display of related words would then appear, with different-colored links to indicate the type of relationship. Clicking a word expands the relationships for that word. This type of application would be helpful for learning English or could be used like a thesaurus. You could combine it with SUMO and the other Semantic Web ontologies described in Chapter 4 to add semantic concept exploration as well.

News on Tap: Automated Newsfeed Generator

In the Chapter 4 section "Guess What? Publishing RSS Newsfeeds with Informa," we discussed an API called Informa. Informa allows you to create RSS feeds, by adding individual news items to a feed, and to generate an XML file of the desired RSS flavor. The hard part about creating a feed programmatically is writing the text summary. A completely automated newsfeed generator would be extremely useful, especially if the text summary was also written by the automated process. Currently, most of this work is done manually.

There are two difficult tasks here. The first problem is in correctly identifying the subject of the text in a document. You could use some combination of heuristics, such as keywords in the title and text, along with a weighted list of topics usually covered in the site. Since words often have multiple meanings, the program would use context to find the right word senses (and perhaps use JWordNet to find related words). It would also need to decide which of the keywords were most important in determining the subject matter and generating a sensible and appropriate name for it. The second problem, creating summary text, is much more difficult. Summarizing the document means understanding its content at a deeper level and generating meaningful text that clearly describes the main ideas. Here are some technologies and projects described in earlier chapters that might help in this endeavor:

- Neural networks
- Intelligent agents
- WordNet, SUMO, and other ontologies
- Jena and RDQL
- Regular expressions
- Grammar specifications

If you are feeling very ambitious and would like to attempt this project, prepare to be working on it for quite some time.

Robot School: Neural Net Robotics

In an earlier section, "Think outside the Blocks: Using Java to Control a Lego Robot," we used a Java API (LEJOS) to control a Lego Mindstorms robot. If you are building a robot to perform complex tasks based on some combination of sensor inputs, you might want to use a neural network in your robot design. We saw the Joone API in Chapter 5, and with some modifications this could be applied to a LEJOS-based program running on an RCX controller. As an example, suppose that your robot must look for some pattern of light fluctuations before it can move. If you take this approach, the most important step is in training the neural network to recognize the pattern. This will be tricky, since the training will be offline (that is, not running within the robot's brain). The sensors used by the robot will not be available during the training process. You will need to collect the pattern of numeric values expected from the sensors ahead of time. The training program in Joone will need this information. Once the neural network is ready, you can embed it into your robot's programming. Be aware that if anything about the robot hardware changes, such as using different sensors, your network's training might no longer be valid.

Annotation Innovation: Java 5.0 Annotation Management Tool

Java has the ability to describe classes using metadata within your source code. This metadata, known as an *annotation*, is defined in the class along with your source code but is mostly ignored by the compiler and usually processed with some other tool. The compiler will include this data in the compiled class files but in an area outside the generated code. If you have written JavaDoc with a @Deprecated tag (to mark a method as being deprecated for documentation purposes) or have seen JavaDoc generated using it, then you have used annotations. Another annotation from Javadoc is @Author.

These are examples of standard annotations from the Java core. In Java 5, you can create your own annotation types using @interface (instead of interface) and use them within your classes to mark up the code with metadata. You can write your own tools to process this custom metadata using the new annotation-related methods of java.lang.Class in Java 5. See the documentation for details on how to create custom annotation classes and read annotations from your code using reflection.

One interesting project would be to create an annotation-management tool. This type of application would read metadata from classes and allow the user to manage the metadata and display it in unusual ways. This could even be integrated into a source code editor to allow the developer to work with annotations in application-specific ways. A more advanced version of this could use annotations related to concepts in standard Semantic Web ontologies such as SUMO (discussed in the Chapter 4, in the section "Who's a What? Using RDF Hierarchies in Jena"). Using a development tool based on semantic annotations, the developer would tag sections of code to relate them to real-world entities. If other projects used the same semantic annotations, then developers could share code for domain-specific applications much easier. Next-generation search engines would be able to quickly locate code that performs specific tasks.

The Winds of Change: Using CVS and Source Code Control

Whoosh! That sounds like the winds of change, or perhaps it is the sound of developers fighting over some code changes. Some of the more popular open-source projects have many developers working on the same sections of code. How do they keep chaos from taking over? There is a very high likelihood that developers will be stepping over each other's code unless there is some system in place to keep track of the changes. All of the open-source communities use some form of source control to manage changes to their files. The *configuration management (CM)* tools of choice in most open-source projects are CVS and Subversion. These work in similar ways: the programmer checks out copies of source code from a server, makes some changes on a development machine, and commits the changes back to the server. All of the changes are kept in archives, and it is possible to revert to an earlier version if something goes wrong.

CM tools are not just for use with open-source projects. Whether you are working on an open project or a commercial package, source code control is extremely important. Even with only a single developer on the team, the ability to revert to an earlier version is very powerful. As developers, we know that we can easily introduce new bugs into an application. Many of the source code control systems have a "diff" function, where you can see the differences between two versions of a file. When a new version of your application is broken after some changes, you can locate the lines of code that are different and take corrective action (such as reverting). Many different packages are available, and it's much better to use some type of CM than none at all.

Forging Ahead: Using SourceForge for Your Projects

If you are starting an open-source project, you will need several things in place to ensure its success. First, you'll want a place to host the project's website, documentation, and source code repository. Second, it helps to have a forum to discuss issues with other developers on the team. Finally, you'll need a bug-tracking system to manage software defects. You can find all these free of charge at a site called SourceForge. SourceForge hosts many of the popular open-source projects, including some of the ones we've seen in earlier chapters. The added visibility of being listed in the open-source directory will bring a few extra visitors to your site, and the directory is also a great place to locate developers who are interested in helping with the project. It has a section called the Java Foundry, where you can host Java projects. Regardless of which programming language you use, this site is a valuable place to start in creating a new open-source project. You can find more information at http://sourceforge.net.

Chapter Summary

Wicked Cool Java is designed to share information about interesting Java APIs and tools that are available via open source. This chapter discussed some interesting open-source projects and presented ideas for other projects that have not yet been created. The purpose of this chapter is to encourage readers and other Java developers to work together in creating exciting new open-source projects. On the book's website, http://wickedcooljava.com, you can join a forum for discussing the ideas in this book with other readers, and you can obtain updated information and links to any projects discussed in the book.

GLOSSARY

A

abstract class
A class that cannot be directly instantiated, except via a subclass that overrides abstract methods

abstract method
An unimplemented method of an abstract class

abstract syntax tree (AST)
A hierarchical representation of parsed text, showing the relationships between tokens

abstract window toolkit (AWT)
The graphical user interface provided by the Java core API; see also *Swing*

affine transformation
A transformation of the coordinates in a two-dimensional coordinate system

Agent Identifier (AID)
A unique identifier for an intelligent agent, used for sending messages between agents

aggregated content
Data that is managed by an aggregator, consisting of changed content from various sources

aggregator
An application that collects data from multiple newsfeeds and presents them to the user

allele
A particular instance or expression of a gene

alphanumeric
Consisting of letters and/or numbers

amplitude
The level of strength (volume) of an electrical or audio signal

annotation
Metadata held within a Java class

anonymous class
A class that has no name, often used for event handler implementations

Application Programming Interface (API)
A library of methods and classes

arity
The number of parameters of a method, procedure, function, or predicate

ArrayList
A class that represents a resizable array

assertion
A check that the state of the application is as expected at some point in the code, used to enforce the assumptions of a programmer

AssertionError
An error that occurs when an assertion fails

attribute map
In JGraph, a mapping of the edges and vertices in the graph to the corresponding display characteristics

attributes
Text variables attached to an XML element as name/value pairs

autoboxing
In Java 5, the automatic conversion between an intrinsic type (such as int) and its wrapper class (such as Integer)

B

backreference

A reference to a previously occurring subpattern in a regular expression; see also *group*

Base64

A compact way of encoding binary data, using 8 bits of text to represent 6 bits of data, and using a base of 64 characters; defined as part of the MIME standard

big-endian

An ordering of bytes within an integer's internal representation where the most significant bits occur first; see also *little-endian*

BigInteger

A class in the Java core that represents an integer of arbitrary precision

BinaryCodec

A class that performs binary-to-text conversion, from the Apache Commons project

BitMatrix

A class that represents a two-dimensional matrix of bits, from the Colt API

BitVector

A class that represents a one-dimensional matrix of bits, from the Colt API

blog

A web log; a type of interactive public journal or log that is viewable online. Also, the act of maintaining such a journal.

Boolean function

A function that operates only on Boolean values

Byte Code Engineering Library (BCEL)

An open-source library for directly manipulating bytecode

bytecode

The low-level platform-independent machine code of the JVM

C

capturing group

See *group*

casting

Converting from one type to another compatible type; for object references, there must be an inheritance relationship

Cell Matrix

A parallel computer architecture in which computing elements (cells) are programmed by their neighbors

channel

RSS metadata about some content that is periodically updated, usually a website; the main entity in a newsfeed

character class

A category or class of characters used in a regular expression, such as *whitespace* or *alphanumeric*

chromosome

The set of all possible genes; also called the genome; in GAs, the chromosome is the set of all possible approaches to solving a problem; see also *gene*

ClassCastException

An exception that occurs when an object reference is cast to an incompatible type

closure

See *function pointer*

codec

Coder/decoder, a function that converts from one format to another, usually from binary data to a text representation

Collection

An interface representing a bag or collection of objects, which any class can implement to act as a collection

comma-separated values (CSV)

A file format for storing tabular data, where data items in a column are delimited by commas, and each row is on a separate line

compiler

A program that converts source code into executable code

compose

To combine functions by sending the result of one as input to the other

composite function

A function created by composing two or more functions

computational linguistics

The study of language from the perspective of computing

configuration management (CM)

The process of managing changes to documents (or code)

connectionist system

A parallel computer system where the computing elements are highly interconnected

ContentHandler

In SAX, the event handler interface that processes an XML document's data

crawler

A program that collects data by following links from websites; sometimes called a *spider*

cryptography

The science of encrypting and decrypting data

cubic Bezier curve

In two-dimensional graphics, a type of parametric curve described by a cubic Bezier function

CyclicBarrier

In Java 5, a synchronization class that works as an invisible barrier that each member of some group of threads must reach before any of them can continue

D

decimal

A base-10 representation of a number, and the system used by most people for describing numbers

deep

A type of tree traversal that processes nodes at a deeper level; a deep String representation of an array includes the contents of any embedded arrays

delimiter

A separator character in a list of items; often a comma, semicolon, period, tab, or space

demultiplexer

A Boolean function that sends a single data bit to one of n outputs, depending on a set of address bits; also called a decoder

deterministic

Able to be predicted, as in a program that has a small variance in its time performance

digital signal processing (DSP)

The processing of a signal using digital means

directed graph

A graph where each edge has a direction associated with it (a source and a destination vertex)

Document Object Model (DOM)

An API for processing XML data as a tree representation

DOM4J

An easy-to-use Java API for processing XML, with functionality similar to DOM

Dublin Core (DC)

A standard set of RDF metadata elements to use for describing content

durian

A sweet fruit native to Southeast Asia, covered with sharp spikes, that has a strong and distinctive smell that some consider unpleasant and others consider fragrant

E

edge

A connection between two vertices in a graph

element

A node in an XML document

encapsulation

The characteristic of OOP that refers to the hiding of implementation details in a class

end tag

The closing tag of an XML element

enum

An enumerated type in Java 5

enumerated type

A type that allows the use of only a specific set of values or instances

envelope

The shaping of an audio or electrical waveform; commonly consists of attack, decay, sustain, and release periods

escaping

Using special-purpose characters within text that are not interpreted as part of the text itself; for example, the \ character within a Java `String`

extended ASCII

An 8-bit character set consisting of the standard ASCII characters plus some additional non-Latin characters

Extensible Messaging and Presence Protocol (XMPP)

A standard XML-based protocol for sending instant messaging data

F

finite state machine (FSM)

A type of behavior model for computer systems, using actions to model transitions from one state to another

fitness function

In genetic algorithms, a function used to determine the programs that will "breed" to create the next generation of programs

format String

A String that describes an output format pattern for use in printing, used by Java's MessageFormat and Formatter classes; note that there are two different types of output format in Java 5

fortnight

An old English time unit of 14 days

function pointer

A reference to a function that can be passed as a value and invoked elsewhere; also called a *closure* or a *functor*

functional programming

A programming style based on the use of function pointers

functor

See *function pointer*

furlong

An old English length unit of one-eighth of a mile, or 220 yards

fuzzy search

A type of search that uses similarity rather than exact comparison

G

garbage collector

In Java, a thread that finds objects with no more references to them and makes their memory space available for new objects

gene

A unit within a chromosome; in genetic algorithms, a gene can be any type of value (e.g., class, integer, or character)

generic

A type restriction where the type is not known until object construction; generics are new to Java 5

genetic algorithm (GA)

An algorithm where solutions are chosen by trying many different approaches and selecting variations on the ones that perform the best according to some criteria

genotype

An individual's genetic makeup; in a GA, the program code that represents a particular solution to the problem

GET

A command for retrieving content from an HTTP server, with no data sent in the body of the request; see also *POST*

gismu

A predicate root word in Lojban

gloss

A description that clarifies a word's meaning

grammar

The syntax, or structure, of a document

grammar description language

A language that describes a grammar, often used to create parsers

graph

An abstraction showing relationships between things, where related vertices (nodes) are connected by edges (links)

graph theory

The study of graphs and graph algorithms

graphical user interface (GUI)

A user interface based on windows, buttons, icons, and other graphical components

grid computing

A parallel distributed system that allows computing resources to be shared seamlessly

group

In a regular expression, subexpressions within parentheses that can be captured separately from the rest of the matching text

H

harmonics

Higher-frequency components of a signal

HashMap

A lookup object in the Java core that maps keys to values

heap memory

An area of unused memory from which new objects are allocated

hexadecimal

A base-16 representation of a number, where the digits are 0–9 and A–F

Hibernate

An open-source project for mapping objects to relational databases that also provides persistence and query services

holonym

A word that names a larger whole of which something is a part; for example, *bicycle* is a holonym of *wheel*

hypernym

A word that names a more general class of something; for example, *vehicle* is a hypernym of *bicycle*

HyperText Markup Language (HTML)

The markup language used in creating web pages

HyperText Transfer Protocol (HTTP)

The protocol used in web requests, for transferring any type of content (HTML, images, audio, and other content)

hyponym

A word that names a more specific example of something; for example, *bicycle* is a hyponym of *vehicle*

I

identity transform

An XSL-T transform where the output is the same as the input (no change)

inference

Logically obtaining conclusions based on facts that are known to be true

Informa

An open-source API for reading and writing RSS files

inheritance

The characteristic of OOP that allows classes to inherit behavior from a parent class

inner class

A class contained within another class that has access to the member variables of its enclosing class

intelligent agent

An autonomous software process able to make decisions and take action without the involvement of a human being

interning

The process where all Strings with a particular value are internalized within a pool

Iterables

An interface in Java 5 that allows classes to be used with the enhanced for loop

Iterator

An interface that allows any Collection class to be iterated

J

Jasmin

An assembly language for the JVM

Java 2 Enterprise Edition (J2EE)
A set of enterprise server APIs, usually implemented within a vendor's enterprise server

Java Database Connectivity (JDBC)
An API, part of the Java core libraries, for working with relational databases

Java Development Kit (JDK)
The Java compiler, core libraries, and related development tools

Java Native Interface (JNI)
An interface for calling native code (such as C/C++ or native assembly language) from Java

Java Runtime Environment (JRE)
The environment in which Java programs run

Java Server Page (JSP)
A technology for creating servlets by using a simplified syntax consisting of HTML mixed with Java code sections; JSPs run within a servlet engine and are translated into servlets before execution

Java Sound
An API in the Java core, for working with MIDI and sampled sound

Java Speech API (JSAPI)
An extension API for working with speech synthesis and recognition in Java

Java Virtual Machine (JVM)
The virtual machine that runs Java's cross-platform machine code, known as bytecode; see *Java Runtime Environment (JRE)*

JavaCC
A Java-based compiler for generating parsers for arbitrary grammars, using a grammar description language

JavaDoc
A documentation-generation tool for Java, part of the JDK, that uses specially formatted comments to create HTML documentation

JavaScript
A lightweight interpreted scripting language, used mostly with client-side HTML, with a syntax similar to Java (however, JavaScript is not Java!)

Jena
An open-source API for working with RDF graphs

L

layout cache
In JGraph, a lookup object that maps the model's cells to their views

lemma
> A heading or label for the gloss of a word

lexical analysis
> The separation of text into individual tokens; see also *token*

lexing
> See *lexical analysis*

linked list
> A list structure where each data item is contained in a node that has a link to the next node; a linked list is traversed by following links

List
> An interface implemented by ordered collections in Java

little-endian
> An ordering of bytes within an integer's internal representation, where the most significant bits occur last; see also *big-endian*

logical connective
> Connects one logical statement with another according to a Boolean function; examples include AND and OR

Lojban
> A constructed human language (spoken and written) based on predicate logic that has a non-ambiguous syntax and a machine-parseable grammar

M

Matcher
> A Java class that performs regular expression pattern matching

meronym
> A word that names a part of something larger; for example, *wheel* is a meronym of *bicycle*

MessageFormat
> A Java class that formats text for display or input; see also *format String*

meta tag
> A tag placed in the head section of an HTML document, used to attach metadata

metadata
> Data used to describe other data

metalanguage
> A language for describing other languages

microsecond
> A time unit representing one-millionth of a second

millisecond
A time unit representing one-thousandth of a second

Moore's Law
A well-known observation, made by Gordon Moore in 1965, that the number of transistors in a computer and its processing speed increase exponentially over time

multi-agent system
A system of cooperating intelligent agents

Multipurpose Internet Mail Extensions (MIME)
A standard for including binary content within a text-only medium such as email; also commonly used to indicate the type of data being sent across a connection (such as text/html or image/jpeg)

Musical Instrument Digital Interface (MIDI)
A standard protocol for transferring musical data from one device to another; also, a format for storing musical commands within a file for later playback

N

N3
Notation 3, a shorthand format for representing RDF triples

namespace
A way of avoiding name conflicts by qualifying elements and attributes (using a URI and a prefix) within an XML document

nanosecond
A time unit representing one-billionth of a second

nanoTime
In Java 5, a method of the System class that returns a nanosecond-resolution timer

neural network
A group of simple processing cells that are highly connected and work together to form a larger computing system, having connectivity modeled after the brain's neurons and synapses

neuron
An individual processing unit within a neural network

newsfeed
Information about recent changes in web content and periodically retrieved by an automatic process; used by aggregators to create custom news channels

node
A part within a larger connected structure; examples of nodes include graph vertices, list items, and XML elements

noise
A disturbance within an audio or electronic signal, exhibiting various levels of randomness; noise sounds like a hiss to the human ear

notation 3
See *N3*

O

object-oriented programming (OOP)
A programming practice that makes use of inheritance, polymorphism, and encapsulation

object pool
A pool of instances from which objects can be obtained, to avoid garbage collection and object construction delays

object URI
A URI that refers to the "object" of an RDF triple

ontology
A collection of terms and the hierarchy of relationships between them

opcode
A command in an assembly language program

origin
The center of a two-dimensional coordinate system

oscillator
An audio component that generates a tone

overloaded methods
Methods with the same name that have different parameters; see also *signature*

override
To redefine a method inherited from a parent class

OWL Web Ontology Language
A language for defining RDF ontologies; see also *ontology*

P

parser
A program that recognizes a grammar

parser generator
A program that generates a parser from a grammar description language (such as JavaCC)

parsing
The process of recognizing a grammar and extracting or processing the content

patch

A configuration created by wiring audio components together to generate a specific sound

pattern

Text that describes which Strings will match a regular expression

peer-to-peer system

A type of network architecture where each node is both a server and a client

performative

A message sent to an intelligent agent that describes a desired outcome expected from the agent's action

platform independence

The ability of a program to run on multiple platforms without modification

polymorphism

The characteristic of OOP that refers to a class behaving differently depending on how its methods are overridden in a subclass

polynomial

A mathematical expression made up of sums of variable terms containing different exponents; examples include $5x^2 + 8$ and $12x^3 + 10x + 1$

port

A location in a graph where edges can be attached

Portable Document Format (PDF)

A document format from Adobe, commonly used for printable documents on the Web

POST

A command for retrieving content from an HTTP server, with data submitted in the body of the request, usually used with web forms; see also *GET*

predicate

A function that returns a true or false value; a statement of truth or falsehood

prefix

In XML, a value placed before a name to associate it with a namespace; see also *namespace*

printf

A method of the Formatter class that does output formatting using a format string, based on a similar function in the C language; see also *format String*

procedural language

A language based on procedure calls, without OOP capabilities; examples include C, Fortran, and Pascal

production rules

Rules in a grammar description language that describe how to build a syntax tree out of tokens

program trading

Automatic buying and selling of securities based on events such as price movement, volume changes, or news reports

property

In Jena, another name for the predicate (verb) of an RDF triple

property (of an object)

See *state*

Pulse Code Modulation (PCM)

A way of digitally encoding an analog sound, based on periodic sampling of the signal

Q

qualified name

An XML name that includes a namespace prefix

R

raster graphics

A type of graphics where images are drawn using individual pixels

RDF Data Query Language (RDQL)

A language for querying RDF documents; see also *Resource Description Framework (RDF)*

RDF Site Summary (RSS)

A standard for creating summaries of website changes for use in aggregated content; see also *aggregated content* and *syndication*

real-time system

A system that requires deterministic time performance, often to avoid video and audio distortions

recursive

Functions or methods that call themselves directly or indirectly

reference

A handle on an object that provides access to it; usually held in a reference variable

reflection

The ability to get metadata about the methods and fields of a class in Java and invoke methods dynamically

regular expression

A type of pattern used for determining whether a string matches

relative expression

An XPath expression that is evaluated relative to a particular node

relative URL

A partial URL, interpreted as being relative to the document in which it occurs

resource

In Jena, something that can be used as either a subject or object in an RDF triple

Resource Description Framework (RDF)

A way of representing information on the World Wide Web as a semantic network; the basic foundation of the Semantic Web

ring

In algebra and number theory, a type of structure that behaves similarly to integers

rotation

In two-dimensional graphics, rotating the axes of the origin by a number of degrees

Runnable

An interface used in multithreaded programming; anything that implements the interface can be used as a Thread's action

S

sampling rate

The rate at which sound is recorded; a higher rate indicates better-quality sound

sawtooth wave

A waveform that looks similar to a ramp or a saw blade; the signal slowly rises on each cycle and then drops suddenly; a sawtooth wave has many harmonics

scalable vector graphics (SVG)

An XML-based format for creating vector graphics

scaling

A transformation of the two-dimensional coordinate system where the coordinate values are multiplied by a constant factor

Scanner

A Java class that performs text scanning

scanning

See *lexical analysis*

schema

A description of the requirements for an XML document's grammar beyond well-formedness; used to check whether a document has valid content (specific tags, attributes and data types); see also *well-formed*

screen scraping

Reading an HTML document to extract data from it

semantic network

A graph where the vertices and edges represent concepts

Semantic Web

A next-generation web, based on semantic networks; see also *N3* and *Resource Description Framework (RDF)*

shallow

A type of tree traversal that processes nodes at only a single level; a shallow `String` representation of an array does not include the contents of any embedded arrays

signature

The combination of a method's name and parameter types that determines the uniqueness of a method

Simple API for XML (SAX)

A low-level XML API that reads data using an event handler; see also `ContentHandler`

sine wave

A waveform based on the sine function; a sine wave contains only a single frequency and has no harmonics

spider

See *crawler*

split

To separate text into a list using a delimiter; see also *delimiter*

square wave

A waveform where the signal rises and falls very sharply and has many harmonics

start tag

The opening tag of an XML or HTML element

state

The properties or fields of an object

static

Belonging to a class rather than to an instance of the class

`StringBuffer`

A text object that can be modified; often used instead of a `String` (which is immutable)

subject URI

A URI that refers to the "subject" of an RDF triple

subpattern

See *group*

subsequence

See *group*

Suggested Upper Merged Ontology (SUMO)

An RDF ontology of high-level concepts, created by the IEEE; see also *ontology* and *Resource Description Framework (RDF)*

sumti

A slot within a Lojban gismu; similar to a noun or a predicate's parameter

Swing

The more advanced graphical user interface provided by the Java core that builds upon AWT

SwiXML

An XML format for dynamically creating Swing GUIs

synapse

An input to a neuron; see also *neuron*

synchronization

Techniques for safely allowing threads to cooperate; see also *Thread*

syndication

Subscribing to an RSS feed; see also *aggregator* and *RDF Site Summary (RSS)*

synonym set (Synset)

In WordNet, a particular sense of a word

syntax

The structure of a language; see also *grammar, parser,* and *parsing*

synthesizer

A sound generator

T

tag

An XML or HTML element in serialized form, consisting of a start tag and an end tag

terminal

A production rule that is not dependent on other rules; equivalent to a token

Thread

A Java class that represents a lightweight process

Tiger

Sun's code name for Java 1.5, also known as Java 5

timbre

The quality of a sound that makes it unique, and composed primarily of the different harmonics of the signal

token

An indivisible component of a grammar

translation

In two-dimensional graphics, moving the origin to a different location than the center (0,0)

tree

A graph without cycles, usually with one node marked as a root (top level)

triple

A tuple with three elements; in RDF, the triple contains subject, verb, and object URIs

truth table

A mapping of inputs to outputs used to completely describe a Boolean function

tuple

An ordered set of values (numeric or other types)

Type Vocabulary

Part of the Dublin Core that refers to the type of content; example types include dataset, interactive resource, and software

U

Unicode

The 16-bit character set used in Java and XML and that contains characters to handle text from all the world's writing systems

Uniform Resource Identifier (URI)

A unique sequence of characters that identifies a resource; URLs (as used in web addresses) are a subset of the more general term URI

unit testing

Software testing of parts of the system in isolation to ensure that each component works properly on its own

Universal Business Language (UBL)

An XML-based format for business documents such as invoices and purchase orders

UTF-8

Unicode Transformation Format, a character encoding for Unicode that uses a variable-length representation; for documents using only Latin characters, UTF-8 is the same as ASCII; other characters require 2 to 4 bytes of storage

V

values method

In Java 5, a method of an enum that returns all of its instances

vararg

Variable arguments; in Java 5, a technique that allows methods to accept a variable number of parameters

vector graphics

Graphics produced using a description of the constituent drawing components; for example, lines, circles, text, and curves

vertex

A node in a graph; see also *edge* and *graph*

Visitor pattern

A design pattern for letting visiting objects tour an object with many subcomponents

vocabulary

A collection of terms that can be used in an RDF document; see also *ontology* and *Resource Description Framework (RDF)*

W

W3C

The World Wide Web Consortium, a standards body focused on developing standards for the World Wide Web; W3C standards include HTML, HTTP, XML, and XML Schema

Web Application Archive (WAR)

An archive file (a JAR/Zip file with a .war extension) that contains an entire web application; a standard WAR file can be deployed on any J2EE application server

WebRowSet

A JDBC RowSet that is able to convert its data into an XML format

web service

Application-to-application service that uses HTTP for its transport and XML for its data representation

weight

In neural networks, a multiplier value assigned to a particular synapse

well-formed

Following the rules of XML syntax; an XML document is said to be well-formed if it has correct syntax

white noise

A type of noise that is mostly random and contains frequencies ranging across the entire sound spectrum

whitespace

Characters such as carriage return, line feed, tab, and space

Wikipedia

An online encyclopedia edited according to a collaborative process, where anyone can make changes

WordNet

An English dictionary in a database format, with each word sense linked to other related words; see also *holonym, hypernym, hyponym,* and *meronym*

X

XHTML

HTML that is also well formed according to the XML standard

XLS (Excel)

The file format of the Microsoft Excel spreadsheet application

XML

The Extensible Markup Language, a markup language for creating documents with hierarchical data structures of any type

XMLFilter

An interface that is a combination of ContentHandler and XMLReader and that works as both a parser and an event handler; used in making SAX filters

XMLReader

A SAX parser, used to read XML data

XPath

An expression language used by XSL-T to access or refer to parts of an XML document (W3C definition)

XSL

Extensible Stylesheet Language, a family of recommendations for defining XML document transformation and presentation (W3C definition)

XSL-FO

XSL Formatting Objects, an XML vocabulary for specifying formatting semantics (W3C definition)

XSL-T

XSL Transformations, a language for transforming XML (W3C definition)

INDEX

await method, 169–170
AWT (Abstract Window Toolkit), 149

B

backreferences, 27
backslashes (\) in regular expressions, 22–23
base concepts in Lojban, 92
Base64 encoding, 38–39
Batik API, 138–139
BCEL (Byte Code Engineering Library), 184–185
BeanShell environment, 179–181
behaviors in intelligent agents, 127
BigDecimal class, 112
BigInteger class, 39–40, 112
binary data, encoding and decoding, 37–40
BinaryCodec class, 39–40
BinaryFunctor functor, 102, 105
BinaryPlotPanel class, 146–147
BitMatrix class, 108–109
BitSet class, 106
BitVector class, 40, 106–108
block method, 129
blog entries, 93
brains, artificial neural networks, 122–124
BufferedImage class, 146
build tools, 178–179
build.xml file, 178, 179
Byte Code Engineering Library (BCEL), 184–185
bytecodes
    compiling other languages to, 185–186
    for JVM, 2

C

canAddItem method, 98
case-insensitive matches, 28
casting, 7–8
Cell Matrix, simulating, 176–178
CellView class, 141
CEWolf library, 144

chaining
    audio components, 158
    in DOM4J, 61
    function, 105
ChannelBuilder class, 93–94
channels in RSS, 93–94
characters in regular expressions, 22–23
characters method
    in IgnoringFilter, 54
    in LineItemReportHandler, 49
    in SAXException, 47
    in SellerFilter, 63
ChartFactory class, 142
ChartFrame class, 143
charts, 142–144
ChartUtilities class, 144
chat applications, 183
CheckQuoteBehavior class, 128
ChoiceFormat class, 41
chords in MIDI, 155
chromosomes, 124–126
CircleGraphLayout class, 141
ClassCastException class, 8
classes, anonymous, 16–18
Cleaner class, 98
close method, 52
CM (configuration management) tools, 189
codecs, 39
Collection class
    delays in, 166
    for loops for, 2–4
Colt API, 106–108
comma-separated value (CSV) files, 24
comments for assertions, 12
comparisons, 18–20
compiling languages to bytecode, 185–186
Complex class, 113
Component interface, 115–116, 121
ComponentTest class, 181–182
compose method, 104–105
composite functors, 104–105
computational linguistics, 130–132
ComputerConfig class, 110

IntegerGene class, 125
intelligent agents, 127–130
@interface tag, 189
interning, 19
Interpreter class, 179
interpreters, BeanShell, 179–181
InterpreterTest class, 180
InvalidMidiDataException class, 156
invisible tags, 61–63
IOException class, 156
iReport report builder, 144–146
Iterables class, 104

J

Jabber API, 183
Jade, intelligent agents using,
        127–130
Jakarta Commons Lang project, 35
Jasmin assembly code, 184–185
JasperFillManager class, 145
JasperReports, 144–146
Java Genetic Algorithms Package
        (JGAP), 124–126
Java Native Interface (JNI), 184
Java Sound API, 154–156, 162–164
Java Speech API (JSAPI), 165
java.util.concurrent package, 169
java.util.regex package, 22
Java Virtual Machine (JVM)
        assembly language for, 183–185
        bytecode for, 2
JavaCC parser, 64–68
javap program, 184
javax.sql.rowset package, 45
Javolution API, 166–169
JCalendar class, 173–174
JDateChooser class, 174
JDBC family, 45
Jena API
        RDF graphs in, 82
        RDF hierarchies in, 86–87
        RDQL queries in, 89–91
JFreeChart API, 142–144
JFreeReport API, 144
JFugue API, 154–156
JGAP (Java Genetic Algorithms
        Package), 124–126

JGAP API, 178
JGraph API
        attribute maps, 141–142
        converting to, 139–141
JGraphModelAdapter class, 139
JGraphT API
        converting from, 139–141
        generic processing unit connec-
                tions, 119–122
        node connections with, 117–119
JMC class, 160
JMusic API, 157–162
JNI (Java Native Interface), 184
Joone API, 122–124
Jorne project, 92
JPanel classes, 134
JSAPI (Java Speech API), 165
JScience API
        algebraic functions in, 113–114
        quantities in, 109–111
JSVGCanvas class, 139
JUnit class, 181–182
JVM (Java Virtual Machine)
        assembly language for, 183–185
        bytecode for, 2
JWordNet interface, 130–132, 187
JXTA protocol, 182

K

keywords in Semantic Web, 80
Knuth, Donald, 185

L

labeled directed graphs, 117
LargeInteger class, 113
LEGO robot, 171–173
        Mindstorms kit, 172
lexical analysis in parsing, 64
LineItemReportHandler class, 49–50
lineOfText production rule, 66, 71
linguistics, computational, 130–132
link tags, 88, 94
linked lists, 17
LinkedNode class, 16–17
Linker class, 16–17
logical languages, 91–92
LogParser class, 65, 70–71

values method, 7
vararg methods, 10–12
variables in BeanShell, 179–180
vector graphics, 136–138
vertices, graph, 117–119, 140
visualization. *See* graphics and data visualization
visualizer for Lojban, 186
vocabularies, RDF, 83–86

W

WAR (web application archive) files, 144
waveforms, sound, 158
web application archive (WAR) files, 144
web services, 127
WebRowSet class, 45
WebRowSetImpl class, 45
weight in neural networks, 122
well-formed XML documents, 44
white noise, 160
whitespace in regular expressions, 22
Wikipedia encyclopedia, 74–76
Wittgenstein, Ludwig, 114
WordNet, 130–132, 187
write method, 164

X

XML (Extensible Markup Language), 43
  basics, 44–45
  converting grammars into, 68–73
  DOM4J for, 56–57
  GUIs in, 133–136
  invisible tags in, 61–63
  parsers for, 46, 64–68
  SAX, 44
    for ContentHandler, 50–56
    tag relationships in, 46–50
  WebRowSet for, 45
  XPath for data extraction, 58–61
XMLFilter interface, 53
XMLFilterImpl class, 53, 62
XMLReader class, 53–55

XMPP (Extensible Messaging and Presence Protocol), 183
XPath, 58–61
XSL-FO documents, 138

Z

zoomable GUIs, 151–152

Electronic Frontier Foundation
Defending Freedom in the Digital World

Free Speech. Privacy. Innovation. Fair Use. Reverse Engineering. If you care about these rights in the digital world, then you should join the Electronic Frontier Foundation (EFF). EFF was founded in 1990 to protect the rights of users and developers of technology. EFF is the first to identify threats to basic rights online and to advocate on behalf of free expression in the digital age.

> ## The Electronic Frontier Foundation Defends Your Rights!
> ## Become a Member Today!
> ## http://www.eff.org/support/

Current EFF projects include:

Protecting your fundamental right to vote. Widely publicized security flaws in computerized voting machines show that, though filled with potential, this technology is far from perfect. EFF is defending the open discussion of e-voting problems and is coordinating a national litigation strategy addressing issues arising from use of poorly developed and tested computerized voting machines.

Ensuring that you are not traceable through your things. Libraries, schools, the government and private sector businesses are adopting radio frequency identification tags, or RFIDs – a technology capable of pinpointing the physical location of whatever item the tags are embedded in. While this may seem like a convenient way to track items, it's also a convenient way to do something less benign: track people and their activities through their belongings. EFF is working to ensure that embrace of this technology does not erode your right to privacy.

Stopping the FBI from creating surveillance backdoors on the Internet. EFF is part of a coalition opposing the FBI's expansion of the Communications Assistance for Law Enforcement Act (CALEA), which would require that the wiretap capabilities built into the phone system be extended to the Internet, forcing ISPs to build backdoors for law enforcement.

Providing you with a means by which you can contact key decision-makers on cyber-liberties issues. EFF maintains an action center that provides alerts on technology, civil liberties issues and pending legislation to more than 50,000 subscribers. EFF also generates a weekly online newsletter, EFFector, and a blog that provides up-to-the minute information and commentary.

Defending your right to listen to and copy digital music and movies. The entertainment industry has been overzealous in trying to protect its copyrights, often decimating fair use rights in the process. EFF is standing up to the movie and music industries on several fronts.

> **Check out all of the things we're working on at http://www.eff.org and join today or make a donation to support the fight to defend freedom online.**

ELECTRONIC FRONTIER FOUNDATION · 454 SHOTWELL STREET · SAN FRANCISCO, CA 94110 · 415.436.9333

HACKING
The Art of Exploitation

by JON ERICKSON

A comprehensive introduction to the techniques of exploitation and creative problem-solving methods commonly referred to as "hacking," *Hacking: The Art of Exploitation* is for both technical and non-technical people who are interested in computer security. It shows how hackers exploit programs and write exploits, instead of just how to run other people's exploits. Unlike many so-called hacking books, this book explains the technical aspects of hacking, including stack based overflows, heap based overflows, string exploits, return-into-libc, shellcode, and cryptographic attacks on 802.11b.

NOVEMBER 2003, 264 PP., $39.95 ($59.95 CAN)
ISBN 1-59327-007-0

HOW LINUX WORKS
What Every Superuser Should Know

by BRIAN WARD

How Linux Works describes the inside of the Linux system for systems administrators, whether you maintain an extensive network in the office or one Linux box at home. After a guided tour of filesystems, the boot sequence, system management basics, and networking, author Brian Ward delves into topics such as development tools, custom kernels, and buying hardware. With a mixture of background theory and real-world examples, this book shows both *how* to administer Linux, and *why* each particular technique works, so that you will know how to make Linux work for you.

MAY 2004, 368 PP., $37.95 ($55.95 CAN)
ISBN 1-59327-035-6

SILENCE ON THE WIRE
A Field Guide to Passive Reconnaissance and Indirect Attacks

by MICHAL ZALEWSKI

Author Michal Zalewski has long been known and respected in the hacking and security communities for his intelligence, curiosity, and creativity, and this book is truly unlike anything else out there. In *Silence on the Wire*, Zalewski shares his expertise and experience to explain how computers and networks work, how information is processed and delivered, and what security threats lurk in the shadows. No humdrum technical white paper or how-to manual for protecting one's network, this book is a fascinating narrative that explores a variety of unique, uncommon, and often quite elegant security challenges that defy classification and eschew the traditional attacker-victim model.

APRIL 2005, 312 PP., $39.95 ($53.95 CAN)
ISBN 1-59327-046-1

THE LINUX COOKBOOK, 2ND EDITION
Tips and Techniques for Everyday Use

by MICHAEL STUTZ

Linux is cool, but it's not always well documented. There are tons of inconsistent HOWTO files, out of date FAQs, and programs scattered everywhere. Whenever you want to do anything with Linux, you usually have to read every piece of documentation out there and basically reverse-engineer a solution. Many Linux books for non-geeks are organized by major system, with a chapter on installation, one for video, one for sound, one for networking, and so on. But what if you want to write a book? Or record an album? If you can't dig around on the Web to find someone else doing the same thing, you are out of luck. Unless, that is, you have *The Linux Cookbook.*

AUGUST 2004, 824 PP., $39.95 ($55.95 CAN)
ISBN 1-59327-031-3

THE DEBIAN SYSTEM
Concepts and Techniques

by MARTIN F. KRAFFT

The Debian System introduces the concepts and techniques of the Debian operating system, explaining their usage and pitfalls and illustrating the thinking behind each of the approaches. The book's goal is to give you enough insight into the workings of the Debian project and operating system that you will understand the solutions that have evolved as part of the Debian system over the past decade. While targeted at the well-versed UNIX/Linux administrator, the book can also serve as an excellent resource alongside a standard Linux reference to quickly orient you to Debian's unique philosophy and structure. Co-published with Open Source Press, an independent publisher based in Munich that specializes in the field of free and open source software.

SEPTEMBER 2005, 608 PP. W/DVD, $44.95 ($60.95 CAN)
ISBN 1-59327-069-0

PHONE:
800.420.7240 OR
415.863.9900
MONDAY THROUGH FRIDAY,
9 A.M. TO 5 P.M. (PST)

FAX:
415.863.9950
24 HOURS A DAY,
7 DAYS A WEEK

EMAIL:
SALES@NOSTARCH.COM

WEB:
HTTP://WWW.NOSTARCH.COM

MAIL:
NO STARCH PRESS
555 DE HARO ST, SUITE 250
SAN FRANCISCO, CA 94107
USA

COLOPHON

Wicked Cool Java was laid out in Adobe FrameMaker. The font families used are New Baskerville for body text, Futura for headings and tables, and Dogma for titles.
    The book was printed and bound at Malloy Incorporated in Ann Arbor, Michigan. The paper is Glatfelter Thor 60# Antique, which is made from 50 percent recycled materials, including 30 percent postconsumer content. The book uses a RepKover binding, which allows it to lay flat when open.

UPDATES

Visit **http://www.nostarch.com/wcj.htm** for updates, errata, and other information.